D1351192

# The ELUSIVE BUTTERFLY of HAPPINESS

An Inspiring Autobiography

Anthea DeVito

BALBOA.PRESS
A DIVISION OF HAY HOUSE

Balboa Press books may be ordered through booksellers or by contacting:

Balboa Press
A Division of Hay House
1663 Liberty Drive
Bloomington, IN 47403
www.balboapress.com.au
AU TFN: 1 800 844 925 (Toll Free inside Australia)
AU Local: (02) 8310 7086 (+61 2 8310 7086 from outside Australia)



Print information available on the last page.

ISBN: 978-1-9822-9538-7 (sc)
ISBN: 978-1-9822-9539-4 (e)

Balboa Press rev. date: 11/08/2022

*To my son, Steven, and my granddaughters, Eloise and Bella, all of whom I love to the moon and back.*

# Contents

# Preface

In these pages, I trace the history of "the family" in my time on earth and how that has changed, looking at different events, as well as societal attitudes happening in the world and my country to change the family unit to what it is today. I look not only at *the* family but also at my family as I tell the story of my life.

I have called this book *The Elusive Butterfly of Happiness* because I have found happiness to be elusive like the butterflies. It comes and goes and, like a butterfly, is something you can't catch. And like a butterfly, it is beautiful when you find it. Butterflies and sunflowers have always made me feel happy—hence, the title of my life story.

Essential to happiness, it would seem, is a sense of meaning and belonging. I have always had a strong belief that I was meant to be—an indestructible self-belief instilled in me by my father. I never felt loved by my mother and asked him from time to time as a young adult, "Dad, was I an accident? "Didn't you and Mum want me? Am I adopted?"

He would always answer, "My darling daughter, you were a gift to your mother on her twenty-first birthday."

After some years, I grew up believing I was an unwanted gift.

This book is about my search for happiness and meaning in my adult life, my life's purpose. I have endured an amazing number of traumas and tragedies and ill health. The truth of my life is unbelievable, like a fiction novel, and this book is like Pandora's box with the unbelievable number of traumas constantly appearing. I think there are many who will be shocked, and some will find this book fascinating and/or inspirational. It is a story of survival against absolutely all odds.

It is also a fascinating historical account, in that I document some of the history of the world's significant events in my time, trying to understand what influences there were on my world and family. I take a look at how all that was going on in a wider context impacted my life and the society I was living in at any given point in time. I have included lots of events from the 1950s and some from the 1960s to recreate that era in your mind as you read.

This makes an interesting read, allowing the reader to see how the world has changed and, thus, changed the society within it. It wasn't just the family unit that changed. The whole world has changed. But perhaps that's life. It is always evolving. Day by day, nothing changes. But looking back, it's all so different.

This book looks at the last sixty years and how the world has changed. From the 1980s on, I look at the growth in technology, which will appeal to my younger audience or anyone really.

This is my story, about me—about the difficult life I have had and my attempt to make sense of it all. Why did all this trauma happen to me? Why did it turn out that way? Do the things that happen in childhood lay down a pathway for adult life for what we will attract in to our life? This was Freud's belief and the belief of many psychiatrists and psychologists today. We are all unique individuals, and there are so many factors that come into play, which will determine who we grow up to be.

There are genetics and personality, environment, and circumstances at different ages in our growth, as well as influences on us by the significant people in our lives. All of these things and more will go to shape who we turn out to be, as well as what we do and don't attract into our lives as adults. So, this story takes a good long look at my childhood, to try and understand and make sense of why the entire traumas in my adult life happen to me.

Besides the trauma, I have led a very interesting and fascinating life with my formative years spent in Penang (Malaya) and spending my early adult life in different parts of Australia. Despite suffering an almost total amnesia after the birth of my son, I continued my career sometime later and enjoyed many high points as a nurse. Nurses and doctors or anyone with an interest in medicine will enjoy reading about nursing in the 1970s and my entire career.

I also trained in another career in beauty therapy and did this simultaneously with nursing. I have always been the eternal optimist and look at how I managed to cope with this entire trauma without turning to drugs or alcohol, though I would fully understand if anybody did.

When I look at how I have always managed "to keep on keeping on," I realise that music has been my medicine. Throughout this book, I talk about the music of the time as each stage of my life goes through. So, it contains some kind of historical account of music starting with the fifties.

I've included just the music I tuned into or the music that was changing or impacting on the world. I have also found movies a wonderful distraction. I believe what we see in movies impacts our being and our inner world, as well as our outer world. For this reason, I do give details of a range of movies I either saw or I believe influenced the world.

Every parent has a story to tell of the difficulties or experiences they had as a child and what their parents experienced, as well as the circumstances and experiences they endured to bring you into the world and to bring you up. So, in effect, with understanding and true empathy, you can forgive your parents for whatever short falls or failings you may perceive they had.

I believe forgiveness is a magical and powerful tool, which will free people from emotional pain and speed the pathway to true happiness. I believe I was born a victim of victims and am just grateful I was given life.

The other tool I have found is gratitude—to count one's blessings is essential to being able to overcome grief and trauma. It is impossible to feel unhappy when you experience real gratitude, or humour for that matter.

In my search for the elusive butterfly of happiness, I discovered its central core is about connection—connection to life, to people, to places, to nature, to your community, to the world. And on the list goes on—connection.

There is also purpose. It seems having a sense of purpose, feeling useful is also integral to this thing called happiness. There were other factors as well, like feeling good in your own skin and with yourself.

This book is the story of my childhood and adult life and of my search for love, happiness, and a sense of purpose. I believe you, my readers, will find my life story intriguing and fascinating. As hard as it is to believe that it is true, it is a true story!

I hope you get something out of it for yourself and that you find it inspirational. For me, I have had this overwhelming compulsion to tell my story, whether it sells or not or whether it becomes a blockbuster movie has been irrelevant to me in the writing of it.

My son, granddaughters, and God-daughter are all very keen to see this story told. So here goes. Let's get started. Like me, once you start, you may not be able to stop, so read on. The story starts in 2014, when I started writing this book, and then goes to the 1950s, when I was born.

To begin, I try to recreate that era, the '50s, with a lot of detail about that time. I hope that does interest you. If not, just move on to the next section. I have written each chapter with subsections and subheadings for ease of reading. I think many people will enjoy reading this book.

# Acknowledgements

I wish to thank my son, Steven, for doing all the backups and for recovering the first forty thousand words when I lost them, as well as for his constant encouragement. I want to thank Richard Johnson for his support, particularly financial, in getting this book published.

I could not possibly include all of those who have taken interest in my book in the writing stage and given encouragement. But some would be my granddaughter, Eloise; Martin Board; and many from the Meals on Wheels staff, as well as my Auntie Mescal and one of my housemates, James Roa, as well as my friend Suzanne Banning. I am also appreciative of my cat Lucy sitting on my lap while I wrote the last seventy-five thousand words.

I need to acknowledge the team of people who reviewed the book prior to publication. You know who you are. Thank you.

I need to sincerely thank all of the staff at Balboa Press for their untiring dedication and hard work in getting this book published. A really great publishing house indeed.

Lastly, I need to acknowledge and thank the producers of Scrivener software for writing a book, which has enabled me to write this book.

I also acknowledge my sister Charlie for never believing anything about my life, which spurred me on to write my life story and have it published.

# CHAPTER 1

# Childhood: From Toowoomba (Australia) to Penang (Malaysia)

## Beginnings of this book

It is a hot, humid evening, Saturday January 25, 2014. And here I am sitting in front of my laptop in the writing and painting nook, a corner of my dining room in my apartment at Coorparoo.

"Now where is that?" I hear many of you asking.

Don't worry; I have lived in so many different houses and locations in my life that I, too, have to sometimes stop and think about where I am, putting my life in perspective. Memories of Penang, part of Malaysia from my childhood still rattles around in my brain.

Coorparoo is a suburb of Brisbane, which is the capital of Queensland, a state of Australia. And it's a place in the world where I feel I really belong.

I am thinking of all the different houses and towns I have lived in and am consumed with this compulsion to tell my life story. I have such vivid memories of the first eight years of my life, especially time spent in Southeast Asia and prolific memories of my childhood and teenage years.

I ask myself, Does the world you live in as a child, as well as what is happening in the world, shape how you end up as an adult? What about the effects significant people in your life have on you at different stages of development?

At this point, Steven and Eloise come bursting through

the front door with hot takeaway from McDonald's, exploding my quiet time spent in reflection. They are both so excited, and Eloise is obviously happy for the opportunity to see me. We have all been busy since Christmas.

"It's so great, Mum, to see you finally writing your life story," Steven declares loudly.

Eloise follows with, "Aw, how exciting, Grandma. Can't wait to read it."

Steven interrupts, "C'mon, Mum. We bought some for you. C'mon, join us."

Though I am not really into McDonald's, I accept that, like technology, takeaway (especially McDonald's) is part of this modern world in 2014. And if I want to connect with my son and granddaughter, I would be crazy not to accept their invitation. Like today's instant world, they have the table set in an instant, all with hot food.

Eloise wants to know all about my proposed book. She is fifteen; tall for her age; slim; and, with long blonde hair, extremely attractive. She's going into grade ten this year and an avid book reader. As we eat, I decide I don't mind McDonald's after all. Perhaps it is just the generation I was brought up in. There really wasn't any takeaway when I was a child.

Eloise is really grilling me about my book. "C'mon, Grandma. Tell me, how are you gonna write it?" She's more interested in my project than her phone.

Now that speaks heaps. She and her sister, Bella, a year younger, are always checking their mobile phones constantly when they visit. But so do all kids their age today.

Steven chips in. "Yeah, Mum, tell us. We want to know!"

As I try to eat my chicken fillet burger, and during the scurry for everybody to get their share of French fries, I talk about the book and satisfy their curiosity and excitement. I start explaining how I'll be looking at some history and how the world has changed by giving an example. I mention how the face of Australian society has changed and how we became a multicultural nation.

Eloise replied, "And you're starting to write it on the eve of Australia Day."

I think for a moment with amazement and reply, "Wow I didn't realise that, but it's probably Australia Day and thinking about what it means to be Australian that got me started. I mean I often feel more Southeast Asian than Australian after growing up in Penang."

Eloise asks if I'm going to include anything about her great-grandpa, my father, in the book, because she knows she takes after me and her father's mother's father's side of the family. This starts another conversation about family, where I explain that I am going to trace the history of the family unit and how societal attitudes have changed towards the family unit. Steven is not interested in this discussion and has quickly cleaned up after the meal as fast as he produced it.

He gets a word in, talking quickly and with genuine excitement. "Well, Mum, I am just so happy you finally started writing your life story. I'm heading off to my room to watch some shows. You can join me, Eloise, when you and Mum finish talking."

Eloise and I talk for about another half hour, and I am so fired up to write the story of my life I can't wait to start. She leaves me to join her father and watch shows he has downloaded from the internet. I sit thinking deeply about how the world has changed—how I didn't even have television, and the internet came when I was in my late forties. Then there was my determination to learn computers and the internet.

I think of how much that family support I've just received means and just how much my own immediate family never gave me that in my lifetime. I think about what Eloise and I talked about. I think of the fact that her family today is the same as her great-grandfather's was yesterday in the '30s and '40s when he was growing up and how he, my father, suffered personally, as a family unit like that wasn't accepted in those days.

With all of this discussion and my family driving me to write this story, I simply have to start somewhere tonight. I retire to the lounge to read some of the library books I got out as research for this book as a Brisbane storm passes over. I love storms, so I open the balcony sliding door and can smell the fresh smell of rain in the air coming inside. In no time, I'm startled by Steven emerging to get a drink from the kitchen.

"Haven't you started writing yet?" he blurts out.

I'm surprised two hours has gone by, and I quickly retort, "Don't worry! I will tonight, later, promise."

I could be forgiven for being startled by my son. He is a tall man at six foot three, six inches taller than me, and of very solid build. He is the spitting image of his father, reminding me of his father every day. Besides, I have really only recently adjusted to him living with me again.

Steven is thirty-four and has lived with me on and off since a tragic fire in 2006 almost took his life and everything he owned. His partner died in the fire. So, he has lived with me for the last sixteen months, and he himself is no stranger to trauma. He was with me through many traumas in my adult life and is very keen for me to tell this story.

I am currently sixty years of age and have been ill with

complex post-traumatic stress disorder (PTSD) for the last three and a half years, following a strange event, a trigger in a workplace. (Complex relates to several traumas.)

This followed my very successful career in two professions, having worked nearly all my life. I ask myself, right now, where did it all begin? Answers come to me, and I am so relieved to start finally writing at last.

## My beginnings

I was a gift to my mother, Janet, on her twenty-first birthday from her husband Charles Daley, so the story goes, as told to me by my father when I asked him, "Dad, was I an accident?" My Dad was twenty-one too at the time of my conception.

I made my debut on July 22, 1953, twenty-one days after my father's twenty-second birthday. My mum was still twenty-one and they had a twenty-one-month-old son at the time, my brother, Jack Charles. As the story continues, I was twenty-one days *late*, due on my father's birthday, July 1.

The numbers twenty-one and twenty-two keep reappearing and surfacing everywhere throughout my life. Two-one are currently the last two digits of my home telephone number and the first two of my post office box number and appear in my bank account numbers and scores of other areas in my life. I married a man whose birthday was 21 August, and our son was due on his birthday.

There was a new prince born to Kate and Wills on July 22, 2013, Prince George. So, it is a very special date.

Strangely enough, I am not into numerology; however, I do believe—given all that—that I was meant to be, even if I was an unwanted gift.

I mean what do you do with your unwanted gifts? Never give them back, heaven forbid! Do you recycle them, re-gift them, or perhaps give them to charity? Unwanted mail you can return to sender. If you order something and change your mind, you can cancel it and perhaps even get a refund.

Some people just stash unwanted gifts away in a cupboard somewhere, but I guess you can't do that with human life. I might have been a return to sender, but I was meant to be. And I have managed to stay in this world despite everything that has happened to me, enjoying as much as I can while I have been here.

So, let's get on with this story, and no better place to begin but my debut into this world, my very real beginnings.

## My debut into the world

So, it came to pass that, on July 22, 1953, in the early hours of a cold Wednesday winter morning (3:15 a.m.), in the Hospes Perpetual General Hospital, I was born, following a normal pregnancy and birth. I was named Anthea Louise Daley. Anthea was after an ex-girlfriend of Dad's, which didn't get me off to a good start. And Louise was after my paternal grandmother, who Mum absolutely hated.

This was July, and over in Britain, the world had just experienced the coronation of a new queen, Queen Elizabeth II, on June 2, 1953. The world was experiencing a breakthrough to combat the terrible scourge of polio, which affected mainly the young, condemning them to a life of paralysis. Dr Jonas Salk had discovered a vaccine that could immunise entire populations.

One really needs to go back even farther than my birth

in 1953 and look at who my parents were and what brought them together and how they created me. My mother was born Lucille Janet Johnson, known as Janet, and raised at the bottom of the Toowoomba range (a few kilometres down the range from Toowoomba) in Grantham on a big farm in what is known as the Lockyer Valley. Her father was Joseph Johnson a farmer and a councillor. She was one of three, the eldest.

Her mother died when she was eleven, and Mum had to look after the other two, Henry and Mabel. Mum was highly intelligent, but in the '50s, women didn't pursue careers or work after they got married. They became good wives and homemakers. Both Mum and Dad were adolescents throughout the Second World War, which ended 1945, and rationing continued till 1948 in Australia and 1951 in the United Kingdom.

Dad was from out west Queensland from Charleville and from a family structure that, in those times, was frowned upon and shamed but in today's times is perfectly acceptable and quite common. His mother had had four children to three different fathers, with one set of twins.

She was married to Mr Daley at the time she had Dad, but Dad's father was Jack Bryant, a watchmaker out at Charleville. Dad had an older sister, Vera, and two younger siblings, Mescal and Michael, who were twins. By the time Dad met Mum, his mother and family were living in Ipswich, about halfway between Toowoomba and Brisbane.

Dad was bullied at school and received lots of bashings in the schoolyard because of his being seen as "illegitimate". This meant he was born out of wedlock. This is a term not even used in today's world. His father refused to acknowledge him. All of this cruelty served to make him very strong, with an indestructible self-belief.

It did not make him evil due to his high level of intellect. He was determined to make it in life—to build an empire, have lots of children to one mother, and build a fortune. He had a strong drive to be successful and, as such, had joined the air force at a time following the war when the military was viewed as extremely important.

Dad had met Mum in the cake shop she was working in at Grantham in 1949. She was eighteen; he was nineteen. There was a strong mutual attraction, and they married the following year, 1950, after a romantic courtship. They married in a Catholic church two days before Christmas on December 23, 1950. Mum had to convert to Catholicism to marry Dad, and that was a bone in their marriage in the first fifteen years. I think religion was something that had given Dad great strength throughout his difficult childhood years.

Their first child, a son, Jack Charles was born the following year, 1950, on October 20 and was christened not long after into the Catholic Church. They were very proud and happy parents. Jack had Mum's features, dark hair, and olive skin. The first two children, my brother and I, were the only two of the five children Mum and Dad had who were given any religious upbringing, and this died out in our early teens.

On October 23 the following year, 1951, Mum's twenty-first birthday, Mum fell pregnant with me. All I know is that she found it very difficult with a young baby and being pregnant. From the age of eleven, she had looked after her younger siblings after her mother died.

This—combined with the fact she was highly intelligent and desired to make something of her life and was destined to be a mother and housewife because that's what women did in the '50s—made it hard to accept a second child on the way.

So, what else was happening in the world in 1953? The radio was the only form of media entertainment in the home (in Australia) and *Blue Hills* was a favourite serial I know my mother listened to. There were lots of other serials on the radio. Queen Elizabeth was crowned, as earlier mentioned, after the death of the British king, George VI, who died of cancer on February 6, 1952.

Sir Edmund Hilary, a New Zealand beekeeper, was the first to climb and reach the peak of Mt Everest. The Holden car had been around for a few years in 1953 in Australia (with the FJ in 1957), and cars did not have blinkers or seat belts! Not all homes had a telephone, which was seen as a luxury; there were telephone boxes everywhere. Even when making a local call, an operator connected you.

There were no great big shopping centres, and every few streets had their own corner store. Shopping was "going into town," which was the central hub of wherever you lived. There was no self-service. An attendant took your order and served you at the counter.

Everything was home delivered, with the milkman coming every morning, and you put the money out every night. The baker came Monday to Friday to your house, as did the butcher. Not everybody had a refrigerator; they might have an ice chest. People took Bex or Vincent's, a powder in an envelope, to feel good if they didn't feel well.

A good majority of people smoked cigarettes, and that was seen as being really cool. My mother smoked, but my father didn't. The music scene in the United States of America was really changing in the early '50s with the birth of rock and roll mid '50s and the birth of folk music. The 1950s formed a decade of transition between old and new worlds.

## Life in Darwin, Northern Australia

I think I was about nine months old when my father was transferred to Darwin Air Base. In Darwin, capital of the Northern Territory, the very north of Australia, it was very hot and humid. Here, we found a completely different way of life, with lots of thunderstorms and cyclone warnings. My parents moved there and had accommodation provided by the air force, which I am told had a hot water system and a toilet upstairs.

There were lots of modern wooden houses on stilts, built very simply and inexpensively and not so old compared to Brisbane or Toowoomba, both of which have a longer history of settlement in Australia. Darwin had a lot of suburbs sprawling out over the land beside the sea and built beside Darwin Harbour, which was bombed by the Japanese in the Second World War. This meant that a military presence was important and still is today, being the closest tip of Australia to Asia.

Mum did not have the family support or friendships of Toowoomba and had never lived out of that region, the Darling Downs. The weather in Darwin was shockingly hot, but she did have an electric stove and loved cooking. She would cook Dad his favourite sponge cake, which had originally attracted him to her.

There were no fast-food outlets or frozen dinners in Australia in the early '50s. There were milk bars with jukeboxes to play music, and coffee shops were really starting to take off after having taken off in the United Kingdom and United States of America. Milk bars were the place where young people met. Or young women would wait there while their partners were at the pub, a strictly male preserve in that time.

Australia was behind America in almost all things. It happened in America first and then came to Australia. The idea of "takeaway" or "fast food" was beginning to happen in the States.[1] The first McDonald's outlet opened in Illinois in America at Des Plaines in 1955. A hamburger was fifteen cents, and French fries were ten cents.

It was the early '60s before it would become a chain of stores throughout America and the late '60s before it came to Australia. The first Pizza Hut opened in Kansas in 1958 in America. Colonel Sanders sold his first Kentucky Fried Chicken franchise in 1952 in the States.

The idea of frozen food was also beginning to happen with Birds Eye producing the first frozen peas in 1952. It was followed the same year by Mrs Paul's fish sticks, which were to become fish fingers. And then came Eggo frozen waffles in 1953 and then the first TV dinner, Swanson's TV dinners, in 1954.

I got the feeling from a young age that Mum was tired of cooking the evening meal after all she had taken over at the age of eleven, when her mother died. The idea of takeaway or frozen dinners hadn't really taken off in Australia yet, so Mum cooked all the meals. She peeled the vegetables nightly. I can remember climbing around her legs while she did this wanting her to pick me up.

There was pressure on the '50s housewife to have the meal on the table when her husband got home and to be there for her husband. Mum needed someone to be there for her after looking after two little toddlers all day, and all her family and friends were in Grantham and Toowoomba. Dad tried his best I know. He would pick me up and cuddle me and call me "his little princess" and play with me blowing bubbles on my tummy. I felt loved by him, and he was so very proud of his first little boy and girl.

Mum would lose herself in books. She went to the library regularly, as she loved reading and dreamed of owning J. R. R. Tolkien's *The Fellowship of the Ring*, the first in his three-volume series *The Lord of the Rings*, published July 1954. The first print run of this book sold out within a month. *The Two Towers*" was published in November 1954.

By the time *The Two Towers* was released, *The Fellowship of the Ring* was on its fourth reprint. It was the talk of the literary world all over the world. Tolkien was to go on and release a third *The Return of the King*, published in October 1955. Dad was saving all his pennies, trying to build lots of pounds in the bank, and he held the purse strings.

Meanwhile, at home, Mum read my brother and me stories from a very young age. There was the *Noddy* series by Enid Blyton, which was being read to children all over the world. The series began in 1950 with *Hurrah for little Noddy. Noddy and His Car* came out in 1951 after the war, when the car industry was about to really take off. Petrol was as cheap as chips.

Enid Blyton had *The Famous Five* series and *The Secret Seven* series, which was always about children from happy families and their adventures. In peacetime 1950s, the nuclear family was the quintessence of domestic bliss; father was the breadwinner, mother the homemaker.

Mum loved the radio, which played her favourite serial, *Blue Hills*. There were lots of serials on the radio, and people would tune in at the same time every day to hear the latest update. She would sing along to her favourite songs, Perry Como's "Don't Let the Stars Get in Your Eyes" (1953) and other of his songs. The radio was full of the songs of Doris Day throughout the entire '50s. The song I remember Mum singing to me was "Que Sera, Sera," which she sang to us right up till the time I left home at seventeen and is a classic in today's time.

Doris Day made many movies throughout the '50s. In 1953, she made *By the Light of the Silvery Moon*, which Dad took Mum to see at the local cinema in Darwin in 1955. Mum would sing the song by the same name often throughout my life. Mum loved music, and through her love of music from as early as I can remember, I grew up to also have a love for music. Throughout my life, it has been my medicine.

I remember Mum also singing the songs from the great musical that was Rodgers and Hammerstein's first musical production; *South Pacific* played in Majestic Theatre, Broadway, New York, from 1949 to 1954. Songs from this musical were all over the radio. Her favourite song from the musical was "I'm Gonna Wash That Man Right out of My Hair." Sean Connery had his first acting part in this production when it opened in London. He was in the chorus.

A lot of movies were made in America in Hollywood and took some time to reach Australia. Other famous movies being shown in Australia in the early '50s, which Dad took Mum to see, were *The African Queen*, which starred Katherine Hepburn and Humphrey Bogart, who won an Oscar for his performance of Charlie Allnute. Another was the film version of *A Streetcar Named Desire*, which was also really big and starred Marlon Brando and Vivien Leigh. Leigh won an Oscar for her performance as Blanche Dubois. Both films were made in 1951.

Also, on the radio in the early '50s (and musicians my mother listened to) were Louis Armstrong, Duke Ellington, Harry Belafonte, Frankie Laine, Guy Mitchell, Patti Page, and Chet Baker. There was lots of jazz. My mum was not into country music, but there was a lot of country as well, which Dad did like. Some of the country singers of the day included Patsy Cline, Slim Dusty, Johnny Cash, and Jim Reeves. But the music scene was really changing, and so was the world—really changing.

For me, in July 1954, living in Darwin, I turned one and went straight from the breast to a cup. I never had a bottle, and my mother wouldn't allow a dummy. I tried to suck my thumb, but my parents definitely wouldn't allow that. Freud would not have agreed with this!

I was already walking at nine months of age. I was climbing up on everything and out of the cot all the time hardly sleeping at all, nearly driving my mother and father crazy. Dad built a special cot for me to keep me in. It was a double bed with wire mesh over the top, which I couldn't stand upright in. I nearly went stark raving mad. I would scream out, so Mum locked me in the duck pen with the ducks and gave me the hose to play with.

I actually loved this. The ducks were my first real friends, and so grew a lifelong love of ducks. To this day, I have collected duck ornaments of all different types. I won't eat duck either and have never been able to. When you walk in my door into the lounge room, you see a great big '30s painting of ducks flying over. The painting of ducks is three metres by 1 metre, which shows what impression our early days have on us.

Behind me in the dining room is a contemporary painting, medium size of ducks in flight, and over in the kitchen on the windowsill are all my duck ornaments made from different mediums. I become intensely aware as I write this story of the powerful influence our childhood years have on us all, and I become more fired up to tell this story.

My long hours spent in the duck pen as a toddler also brought a great love of water in all its forms, and to this day, the sound of water soothes me. As I write this story, I listen to a water feature in the dining room. I have loved being on or by the water or in it all my life. I also learnt that water was very powerful stuff because whoever had the water had all the power in that duck pen.

These two experiences of being in that custom-made cot and locked in the duck pen made me claustrophobic as a young child. I could not and cannot stand being locked in anywhere or in a confined space. It has been that way since I was about two. I have trouble travelling in an aircraft or being in a lift. When my mother went out, she would put me on a harness, as I had this habit of running off. It was the level of intellect; I was deeply inquisitive. In those days, it was OK to put a child on a harness, though not a lot of people did it.

There were lots of thunderstorms, and Mum was clearly frightened. I felt this as she would pick me up and hold me tight and hold my brother's hand. I came to love thunderstorms, as it was the one time, she always picked me up and cuddled me; and it was about water, as it always rained. I just wanted to go out and stand in it. Mum put the fear of God into me. "You don't go out in a thunderstorm." And it has lasted all my life.

At some time, when I'm not sure, Dad was transferred to where I'm not sure. But the family moved back to Toowoomba, to the same house in Railway Parade that Mum and Dad were buying. I think this was mid to late 1955.

## Life back in Toowoomba

Auntie Mabel visited with her hair pulled back in a French roll. We would also go and visit Grandpa, Mum's dad, as well as Uncle Henry, her brother, down the bottom of the mountain from Toowoomba at Grantham. They were truly country folk. These were very happy times. And somehow, I knew my mother was a lot happier. Though my mother was happier, and so was I, the world was really changing. My world was not long off changing.

So back in Toowoomba sometime around mid-1955, and I had a whole big backyard enclosed to run around in. My mother always put shoes on me, partly due to my ankles buckling out from my walking too early and partly because my father kept beehives. There was lots of clover in the backyard, and the bees loved the clover. So did the butterflies.

My mother was always trying to find a four-leaf clover among the clover for my brother, not that I really knew what it was all about. I now slept in a bed in the same room as my bigger brother, who had his own bed just the same as mine. My brother and I played together a lot.

My Auntie Mabel came to visit again, and I just loved being in her company. I never forgot her. She was a tall, slim lady with light brown hair she wore up so beautifully done. She would pick me up and hug me and cuddle me.

Now, moving on, there were the rest of 1955 and 1956 for me in Toowoomba.

My brother and I were very close; however, he was Mum's favourite, and I was Dad's favourite at that time before more children came along. One day we were playing in our room with blocks, and Jack got very angry with me. He got up to run out of the room, and I got up to run after him, and he slammed the door on me. The end of my left ring finger (my wedding finger) got trapped in the door hinge section and was severed.

I screamed and screamed so loudly that the doctor who lived next door came in to see what was wrong. He gave me pain relief from his doctor's bag and put the piece back and bound it up firmly. After a week they took the dressing down, and the tip of my finger had reattached. I understand the doctor did dressings every few days on it. I have suffered with neuropathic pain in my finger all my life and simply learnt to live with it.

Mum cooked a lot and had an old mix master to help cook cakes and biscuits. She loved her wood stove, and Dad loved her cooking. She continued to listen to the radio and read lots of books and got on well with the neighbours, especially the Turnbulls at the back of us behind our sandpit.

I really liked Mrs Turnbull too and would listen to all the stories Mum would tell her about me when she came over for morning tea. Mum wanted a Kenwood Chef, a food processor, as Mrs Turnbull had one. They were released in America in 1950 and had only just come to Australia.

Dad was terribly strict with the money. He really wanted to get somewhere in life and saved every penny he could. Dad held the purse strings, and he wouldn't buy her one. In 1955, the idea of frozen food was taking off in Australia, and Mrs Turnbull had all the latest and was investing in a freezer. I do remember it was very cold in this thing she called her freezer with white smoke coming out, and I thought they were both crazy.

The only things that were static to me was Mum loved her music, and Dad came home every night, picking me up and hugging me. I so much wanted Mum to love me, but I knew my brother and Auntie Mabel loved me, and I loved them.

About this time, another family member came to visit, my dad's half-sister Auntie Mescal. She brought with her a birthday present for me—a beautiful lifelike ceramic doll with eyes that open and shut and real eyelashes. For some reason, she was named Peggy, and Auntie Mescal then set about making her lots of clothes and would bring them often when she visited. I came to love this doll and Auntie Mescal. I would have so much fun when she visited.

Somehow, I sensed I was like her, with blonde hair and fair skin, and she felt like real family to me. Peggy had lifelike blonde hair, which I would brush, and she had fair skin. It was very common for young girls to have ceramic dolls that looked like this in this era.

Through the early fifties, there was this transition after the war, where the world was gearing up for a different place—a place where it was OK to enjoy yourself and have fun. By 1955, a decade after the war, this new world started really exploding all over the place.

Preparations began in 1951. Fender produced the first solid body electric guitar, the Telecaster. Gibson launched a solid body guitar in 1952 designed and named for Les Paul, a legendary 1940's guitarist. Rock and roll music was born. Elvis Presley had started singing tunes with backing bands, and it was a really different sort of music with him dancing his own style to the music.

He put out "I'll Never Stand in Your Way" in 1954 and was really starting to become a worldwide phenomenon by late 1955. He said, "Some people tap their feet, some people snap their fingers, and some people sway back and forth. I just sort of do them all together I guess." This became a new way of dancing "rock and roll."

In England, Buddy Holly was becoming as big as Elvis. Little Richard claimed he was the creator of rock and roll. Bill Haley and the Comets also put out some of this new music. The Everly Brothers, Phil and Don, were making great music of the times as well, with acoustic guitars and great harmonies.

It was OK to let go, to not worry so much; this was the message being sent out all over the place in 1955. On July 17, 1955, the happiest place on earth opened; in Disneyland, named after its creator, there were Main Street U.S.A. and Adventure Land, as well as Frontierland and Fantasyland and Tomorrowland. Walt Disney was quoted as saying on opening day, "Disneyland will never be completed. It will continue to grow as long as there is imagination left in the world."

The Miss World pageant had begun in 1951, and it was putting women up there and out there in swimsuits. The competition was first televised on the BBC in 1959.

The first issue of *Playboy* was published in 1953, in the United States of America.[2] It cost fifty cents and sold 54,175 copies. It was undated because Hugh Hefner didn't know whether there would be a second issue, He also didn't put his name on it in case it was a failure. By 1955, millions of more copies had been sold. Skirt lengths were getting shorter, and gone were the days where women fully covered up.

The movies being made at the time showed women showing a lot of flesh, and they were many about romance, sex, and having fun—and not always within the sanctity of the earlier "marriage."

Lots more movies were being made in Hollywood and in Europe with Sophia Loren and Bridget Bardot. They were showing almost everybody smoking cigarettes, pipes, or cigars, and drinking alcohol to relax was the norm.

Marriages of actors and actresses in Hollywood were breaking up and being publicised in newspapers everywhere, while they went on to have more marriages. It was in the era of the fault divorce, where someone had to be at fault for it to be granted. It wasn't so easy in those days.

There was this actress in America named Marilyn Monroe who made a lot of movies. In 1955 the most famous photograph of all time was shot. It was shot while filming Billy Wilder's *The Seven Year Itch*, with Marilyn Monroe standing on the ventilation grating in a white pleated dress with her dress blowing right up and her holding her dress at her crotch. After this came her movie *Bus Stop*.

She was in the process of divorcing her second husband, Joe DiMaggio. The next year, 1956, she married Arthur Miller and was photographed all around the world and shown in newspapers heading off on her honeymoon in a Ford Thunderbird to Connecticut. She had just finished filming her next movie. *The Prince and the Showgirl.* Other earlier movies were *Monkey Business*, *We're Not Married*, and *How to Marry a Millionaire.* She was highly sexed and had the appearance that went with it.

Clearly, by the mid '50s, there was a beginning of a shift in attitude towards sex and marriage. Marilyn Monroe, known as "the blonde bombshell," and Elvis Presley went on to become pop icons of timeless adoration.

There was also another, an actor who was known as "the teen rebel," James Dean. His movies *Rebel without a Cause* and *East of Eden*, both released in 1955, touched everybody the world over. On September 30 that year, he was killed in his car, the Spyder, which he'd had custom made into a Batmobile. He had a need for speed, and had he not died, he probably would have also reached timeless adoration.

There were other well-known actresses like Janet

Collins, who in 1956 attended the premiere of *The King and* I on September 12. It was a busy year for her. She made three films—*The Opposite Sex, Sea Wife and Biscuit,* and *Island in the Sun*—and divorced her first husband, Maxwell Reed, after extraordinary rumours he had tried to sell her to an Arabian sheikh.

Bridgette Bardot was also appearing in movies in 1956, including *And God Created Woman*, which was filmed with Roger Vadim in St. Tropez. The film was described by the Catholic League of Decency as "an open violation of conventional morality."

Now I'm not saying I agree with this or that there was anything wrong with any of the movies or music. I'm simply trying to show how the world was changing in the '50s and that they were transition years to a whole new world.

My parents were living in this changing world at the time, as a newly married couple of five years with two young children. I was one of those children, two years of age in 1955 and three in 1956, in a changing world, with my parents trying to cope with that changing world and continually changing the geographic location of our world.

Mum had a very sheltered upbringing on a farm during the war years. And my father, with his parents' history, went to the other extreme from his parents. He was very strict and didn't accept the new world or the new music and was totally immersed in Catholicism, much to my mother's distaste. Mum was more radical. I mean she even smoked cigarettes. Mum loved music but not country and western like Dad liked.

It was obvious they loved each other dearly. Mum had all these beautiful ball gown-like dresses, and Dad would take her out to dances—old time dances, ballroom dancing.

Auntie Mabel would come and look after us, my brother and me. Oh, how we just loved Auntie Mabel looking after us.

Dad would sometimes take Mum out to dinner. She was very attractive, and Dad was very proud. She really was his princess, and he took his marriage vows seriously. He had planned to stay by her forever, no matter what, after the experience he'd had with his own mother and father.

Dad, being terribly strict, kept a strap behind the kitchen door, which my brother and I were threatened with if ever we stepped out of line. I know my brother did receive some beatings with it. The only time I remember being beaten with this strap was when I had scribbled on the centre lounge room table, as I wanted to draw, and they did not provide me with anything to draw on. I went running up the road after Dad saw me, and he chased me and brought me back into the garage and beat the living daylights out of me.

I clearly remember him carrying me up the back steps of the house at Railway Parade, with Mum saying "Oh, Charles! She's dead."

I had collapsed. He laid me on my bed, and there I lay for hours with my eyes shut and my brother crawling around me on the bed.

Jack kept saying, "Nay, Nay." That's what he called me, as he couldn't say my name. This was late 1956, and I was two and a bit.

This experience caused an "artist's block," which was not undone until therapy some forty years later. From then on, I always drew in the correct places. In colouring, I never went outside the lines, and I could never draw outside the square or "the box" so to speak. I wanted to draw and use pencils so badly throughout my whole childhood and felt frustrated when asked to draw anything. I had an "artist's block" from the whole experience and this prevented me from being able to draw.

Auntie Mabel was good on the sewing machine and would make me these beautiful little girl dresses, which I loved parading around in. At these times, I felt noticed by my mother and that she was happy with me.

Mum and Auntie Mabel went shopping together in the Toowoomba town centre, and these were also times I really enjoyed. Toowoomba was well known for its beautiful gardens, and they would have lunch in the botanical gardens. My brother Jack and I could run around as much as we liked.

In those days, women sewed a lot of their own clothes, and they would look at patterns and materials. I managed to collect a whole lot of scraps of material and wool from Auntie Mabel and Mum's sewing and clumping it all together, I made my very own pretend cat. I apparently, as the story goes, would spend a lot of time pulling this bundle around the yard behind me and playing with it, pretending it was my cat. The doctor next door had a cat, as did the Turnbulls, and I very much wanted my own cat.

I was totally oblivious to what was going on in the world outside my home, but life was moving on, as it does. It was eleven years since the war ended, and rationing of food and materials was well and truly in the past. The wedding of the year 1956 was Grace Patricia Kelly to His Serene Highness Prince Rainer III of Monaco on April 19, 1956. Grace Kelly's wedding dress was designed by Helen Rose, the costume designer for High Society.[3] The dress was made from ninety-eight yards of tulle, twenty-five yards of silk taffeta, and three hundred yards of lace. The veil was covered in a web of thousands of seed pearls with a motif of lovebirds appliquéd in lace.

Grace Kelly was an actress with a lot of class. She made eleven movies from 1950 to her wedding in 1956. Her movies were banned in Monaco by order of Prince Rainer. She won best actress in the 1955 Academy Awards for her performance in *The Country Girl*. In 1950 when my Mum married, brides were still conscious of the rationing and the war years. This is how fast things were changing.

In these times, 1956, people found great entertainment in sport. Boxing was really popular, and my dad followed the boxing. In 1956, the Olympic Games were held in Melbourne, Australia—the first to be held in the southern hemisphere—and were dubbed the friendly games. Because of Australia's strict quarantine rules, however, the equestrian events were held in Stockholm in June. The opening and closing ceremonies were held at the Melbourne Cricket Ground. A ticket for the opening ceremony cost three pounds and four shillings.

Dawn Fraser won her first Olympic gold medal in the hundred meters freestyle.[4] Elizabeth "Betty" Cuthbert won two gold medals in the individual track sprints (100 metres and 200 metres) and a third in the 4 x 100-metres relay. The eighteen-year-old was instantly acclaimed a national heroine and was nicknamed the "Golden Girl."

Seventeen-year-old Murray Rose won three gold medals in swimming.[5] He was known as the "Seaweed Streak." His unconventional diet of vegetarian food—including seaweed—was credited as aiding his success in the pool. Australia won a total of thirteen gold, eight silver, and fourteen bronze medals. This was an event that really brought our nation, Australia, together.

The diet in Australia at the time was meat and three veg at least five days a week for the evening meal, and Murray Rose had the general population looking at alternative diets.

My dad loved his meat. He was from the country and wasn't going to change to this vegetarian diet.

In 1956, television was not happening in Australia, and Mum and Dad listened to the Olympic Games on the radio. They also kept a close watch in the newspapers every day. One thing I do remember is that my dad loved his newspapers, and there were a lot more newspapers in those days.

They even had paper boys on the streets selling them on every second corner calling out the headlines really loudly. The only way I could go on loving Dad after that terrible beating was to block it out and just pretend it didn't happen. So it came to pass that it disappeared from my conscious memory.

I'm not sure when—I think it was early in 1957—I came across this huge truck in our front yard. It was the biggest thing I had ever seen in all my life. I was three and a half. I walked round and round it. It was a Grace Bros removal's truck. They were packing up my/our whole home into boxes. I didn't know then, but I would see this truck many times in my adult life.

I quickly went and rescued Peggy and wouldn't let her go from that moment onward. Nobody explained anything. The next thing I remember, Peggy and I were on a plane flying over land below, and my mother was nursing me.

She pointed down out the window below and told me, "That's Australia, Anthea. That's Darwin where we used to live. We are leaving Australia."

The next thing, there was water below us, which I recognised from the beach. I was wearing a gold bracelet with a padlock and a very pretty dress. My brother was very interested in the plane.

Then the next thing I knew, we were living in a very

different land. My mother and father called it Penang. It was an island off Malaysia. My mother was very angry with me because I had lost the gold bracelet on the plane.

## The formative years of my life spent in Penang

So, what was my father doing in Penang (a small island off the tip of the Malay Peninsula)? In conducting research for this book, I found the following information, taken from *The Macquarie Book of Events* produced by Bryce Fraser and printed in 1983:

> In 1955 Sept 13th "The Advance Guard" of an Australian Army force had arrived in Penang as part of the SEATO commitment. From 1950 to 1960 The British Empire served in Malaysia as part of anti-terrorist forces. From 1960 to 1973 Australians continued to serve at Terendak, Singapore and Butterworth, on the mainland. An infantry company remained at Butterworth after 1973 on short term rotation.[6]

My father was based at Butterworth, on the tip of that peninsula. He was in the air force. Further research, same source:

> In July 1958, no 1 Sqn, RAAF Lincolns (planes) returned to Australia after 8 years active service in Malaya. The Lincolns were replaced by No 2 Sqn Canberras which

> were based at Butterworth. On October 27 1958, The RAFF Operation Sabre Ferry with the departure of the first 8 of 19 Sabres of No 3 Sqn. The aircraft flew from RAAF Williamtown to RAFF Butterworth as a component of the British Commonwealth Strategic Reserve 16 more Sabres of No 77 Sqn flew to Butterworth the following February. [7]

I know that, in 1957, we were living in these very modern flats, nice-looking, with mint and white stucco all over the brickwork on the outside. They were a set of six flats with huge, long balconies at the back that overlooked the ocean. They had lovely architectural facades all around the windows on the outside. It was at the end of the street called Jalan Hashim, not far from the capital of Penang, Georgetown. At the other end of our street was the Indian Snake Temple, which was full of snakes and turtles. At our end, the other side of our flats was a huge, very thick rainforest.

Penang is only a small island, and you could take a cable car ride around the island, even in those days, which we did in the few days after we arrived. There were coconut trees and people everywhere. These were two things I noticed straight away, as that wasn't the case in Australia (or the land I had come from, in my mind).

We lived in the top flat on the left-hand side as you drove in the driveway. I could not remember living in this type of dwelling before in my life. It was really different. So was the climate. It was very, very hot and sticky. The whole of my world had changed. There were all these different people running around quickly, and hardly any of them looked like me.

There were Chinese, Indian, and Malaysian people on the island, all living in the villages in individual thatch huts. Apart from our street, there were villages and shops over the whole small space of the island. The shops had overhanging awnings, and underneath there were markets everywhere. A lot of the markets sold fresh produce, and there were always heaps of chooks scratching around in the dirt and some goats, as well as donkeys and monkeys.

There were a small contingent of white families on the island from the United Kingdom; the United States; and my country, Australia. Jalan Hashim had all white people living in it both sides of the street all the way up to the end, where there was the Indian snake temple. I also noticed that all the other white people sounded different when they spoke because of the accents from their different countries of origin.

I had very fair skin and was a pretty little girl with thin, straight blonde hair falling all around my face and neck. Everywhere we went on the island, the native people would come up and want to touch me, especially my hair to see if I was real. They, with their world of darker skins and black hair, found me like a vision, an angel or something. The Chinese regarded blonde hair as meaning good luck.

My brother had Mum's dark brunette hair and her olive skin, whereas I took after Dad's side. He had blonde hair with ginger in it and red in his facial hair, though he always kept his face cleanly shaved. He was tall and had a slim to medium build and looked quite a striking figure in his military uniform from photos I have seen. In fact, they looked a truly handsome couple, with Mum wearing her hair up in a fashionable bun of those times and her beautiful figure, even after two children. They were in their mid-twenties, and according to later accounts to me, they were both looking forward to an adventure in a foreign land.

It just wasn't like that for me at the time of arrival, though Jack seemed to be coping well. He loved the plane we went on to get there and the cable car following, obviously looking for more. He was happy to play with his cars, and he was twenty-one months older. He was five and a few months, and I was three and a half!

It was a whole different world in every way from what I knew, and I was initially very frightened. We had left Auntie Mabel, Grandpa, Uncle Henry, and Auntie Mescal. Mum and Dad's friends would come over—I didn't really know them, but I knew their faces—and they all spoke like my family did. I even missed our neighbours, the Turnbulls, and that lovely man the doctor who fixed my finger when I was in excruciating pain.

No backyard. I would go out to that big, long balcony with red slate tiles and nothing on it—no clover, no bees, and no butterflies; there was no sandpit or toys, as our toys hadn't arrived. All I had was Peggy doll to tell all my troubles to and talk to. My brother, Jack, and I would run round and round and round the balcony playing chasey. We could not see the sea, as we were not tall enough. His toy cars sped a long way on it as he raced them up and down.

I clearly recall my mother cooking tea every evening in the kitchen, which had a window overlooking the driveway. It was a long kitchen with benches both sides as you walked in from the combined dining room / lounge, with the sink at the end of the kitchen under the window. The whole flat had a musty smell, which may have come from the nearby village, called a kampong (one of many on the island). The kampong nearest us was opposite the flats and down the road a bit. The kampongs didn't have sanitation or rubbish removal. Toilets were a hole in the ground.

The smell of cooking meat or whatever Mum was cooking always smelt nice and made me feel hungry. I just wanted Mum to pick me up and cuddle me, as I was feeling insecure, lost, and frightened. I would hold onto her legs and pull at her close-fitting dress, which went below her knees. I wanted her to pick me up like Auntie Mabel and Auntie Mescal used to and talk to me.

I would pull and pull and then start crying. She wouldn't say a word, not a word, and I would start screaming and screaming. The screaming got louder and louder. I screamed for, say, going on an hour uncontrollably, with everybody ignoring me.

The screaming was so loud every evening for two or three weeks that a British lady—who lived on the other side of the street and up a little in a large mansion divided into two dwellings that were exactly the same—came across one night and knocked on the door. Mum answered, and the conversation went something like this.

The lady said, in a very soft, firm British voice, "I'm Lil O'Sullivan, and I live opposite. I hear your little girl screaming every night, and I would like to help. How can I help?"

Mum replied, quite embarrassed, "I'm not sure. Come in."

This lady replied, "I am happy to take her for a little while and look after her, so you can cook tea. I'll bring her back at 7:00 p.m. and bathe and feed her for you if you like."

Mum was really surprised, as I had stopped screaming and crying once this magical lady entered. Mum said I had to be back at 6:00 p.m. for tea when my father got home.

These were moments I could never forget, as they were

the beginning of a lifelong love with a woman who would give me the love only a mother could give. She would become my Auntie Lilly and her husband my Uncle Joe. They remain the most precious and beautiful people I have ever known in all my life.

That late hot, humid Penang afternoon in early 1957, she scooped me up into her arms and proceeded to take me across the street, cuddling and talking to me all the way to her house. As soon as we got there, she sat us down into one of her sumptuous lounge chair / rockers with me on her lap, talking to me all the time, rocking back and forth. I cannot remember what we spoke about.

I just remember her talking softly and gently while she stroked my straggly blonde hair off my face. She was a strikingly beautiful lady, with blonde hair and fair skin just like me. Her hair was done in an up style, and she had long, beautiful painted nails. She was wearing a lot of beautiful shiny rings on her fingers and very striking glasses. She had a very pretty dress on of a light flowing material. I was soon to learn that she always looked beautiful like this.

We went to her kitchen and got a drink of something pink and sweet. Then she bathed all that perspiration from screaming off me while running a bath. She splashed water all over me, making a big game of it, and the sound of the running water soothed me.

I told her, "I want ducks in the water with me," and she laughed.

She told me I was to call her Auntie Lilly, and if I was a good girl for Mummy, she would come and get me again. It was all right for me to visit her again if Mummy said it was OK. She delivered me back home that night for tea with Dad and Mum and Jack. Mum and Auntie Lilly spoke for some time at the door that night.

The next afternoon, there was a knock at the door, and it was Auntie Lilly. I had been incredibly good for Mum, hoping this lady would come back. She picked me up and again took me to her house. This time she told me about fairies in her house and how they would leave little gifts for good children. Apparently, there was also a tooth fairy who left money; if ever any of my teeth fell out, I was to keep them, as the tooth fairy would take the tooth and exchange it for money.

"What is money?" I asked, so the story goes.

She said Mum had told her I'd been a very good girl. She said, "I have a special place where fairies leave gifts for good children. Let's take a look." She led me into another room, which looked so beautifully decorated (her whole house was). We had a look under the cushion on a special chair like a stool for a piano. There were comic books, and we sat down and read them. I was overwhelmed with wonder. What she had done was introduce me to the world of fantasy, which is absolutely essential in every child's life in their early years for a happy childhood.

She again got me the following afternoon, and that afternoon there was a beautiful brush and comb. She immediately sat me on her lap in that sumptuous lounge rocker and began brushing and combing my hair. The brush and comb had to stay at her house to use when I came over. The next evening, there were toy yellow ducks. That evening, there were toy yellow ducks in the bath, and I laughed and laughed, splashing water everywhere. When Auntie Lilly took me back, she said she couldn't come for a while, and if I was good for Mum, I could visit her again.

Some time went by, and I was good for Mum. In addition, Dad had bought us some new toys from the shops on the Malaysian mainland, as our toys still hadn't arrived.

He went to work every day in Penang, sometimes catching the ferry over to Butterworth.

Uncle Joe, Auntie Lilly's husband, who I was yet to meet, was also British like Auntie Lilly and worked alongside Dad. He was in the army and living in Australia before they went to Penang. He had met Auntie Lilly while they were working in London, and she was about ten years older than him. She had worked as a barmaid in London, and they had married and come on a posting to Sydney before coming to Penang.

Uncle Joe was actually born in northern New South Wales to British parents, and his sister lived in Sydney. They were about late thirties and late forties when I met them, though I never knew this until forty years later. They always had this timeless, ageless quality about them.

On my next visit, I was to meet Uncle Joe, who I saw as a very tall man of big, solid build with a bald area on the top of his head and brown hair at the sides, which he kept very short. He spoke in this soft, haughty male British accent. He smiled and laughed a lot and was always happy. I had tea with them this next occasion of my visit. The fairies had not come this time.

I was told they were busy visiting the homes of other good children, and a lot of children in Jalan Hashim had been good!

Uncle Joe picked me up and played a game with me sitting on his head. That night I went home with Auntie Lilly I was very happy. I was even happier when I overheard Mum telling Auntie Lilly we were moving soon from the flats to across the road, next door to her. We would live on the other side of the wall that divided the two connected houses into two.

Wow, it meant that the families would be even closer. I

was very excited and went out on the balcony to play with my brother. We played chasey for ages.

I was trying to climb up the balcony wall to see the ocean. I knew it was there, as Dad would often pick me up when he got home and go out there to show me the ocean and all the sand. All of a sudden, I slipped and fell down inside on the red slate floor. It really hurt, and I was crying. Next thing I noticed, there was red stuff pouring out of me all over me from my head, my knees, and my hands.

I was to later learn, as a little girl, that this was blood and came out of you if you broke yourself anywhere. Jack helped me up and inside, where Mum and Dad were sitting on this divan settee lounge in an embrace.

Mum jumped up and said, "Oh my God, Charles. What's happened?"

That was the only time in my life I was to see them in an embrace.

I do not recall what happened next. The next thing I can remember was a military truck pulling up outside our flats with big red crosses on it and Dad showing me from the kitchen window, holding me whilst he cleaned me up at the kitchen sink. All the while, he was holding towels on my face where the wounds were on my forehead and chin. Men came in and carried me out on a stretcher, and Dad came with me.

I remember discussion between my parents as to who would come with me and Mum saying, "Oh, Charles. I just can't handle this; you go with her."

Mum started to cry and said, "Be brave, my little girl," kissing my head, which she rarely ever did.

They took me to the military hospital set up on Penang Island. A man greeted us in shorts; an open, checked shirt; and loafers. He said hello to me and told me he could put me back together again like Humpty Dumpty, who fell off the wall. They wheeled me into a room, and Dad stayed with me all the way. That man changed into a white coat over his clothes that seemed to cover a lot of him, and he started washing his hands for a long time, as well as right up his arms.

Dad explained he was called a doctor. He was going to have to sew up the breaks in my head and forehead, and it might hurt a bit, but I had to be good and be brave. The ladies were called nurses, and they were going to first wash and put dressings on my hands and knees, which they did. They then put cold packs on me, and one stayed holding my hand. I was good, as I was scared, I wouldn't see Auntie Lilly again if I wasn't, and the fairies wouldn't visit again.

I stayed at the hospital for a while, and Mum, Dad, and Jack visited. It was fun at the hospital with the nurses looking after me. They played with me and talked to me the whole time, and I was not used to that sort of attention. The doctor in the white coat came again and said I was back together again like Humpty Dumpty. I never liked that nursery rhyme after that. It wasn't long, and I went home.

In the coming weeks, we did move next door to Auntie Lilly. A military truck and military men came and helped us, men in uniforms just like Dad and Uncle Joe. It was nothing like the move from Toowoomba, which was upheaval, and that flat at the very end of Jalan Hashim was never my home. I was extremely glad to leave the flat. Lots of people helped us, as the white people on the island all helped each other.

There were many people who helped us move across the road to the house, and we met new friends who lived on our street. When we got there, all our boxes had arrived from Australia, and unpacking them was such fun. Mum was happy with all her own things, and the house was furnished by the Royal Australian Air Force (RAAF). (Our furniture and a lot of our things were in storage in Toowoomba.)

On approaching the front door of the house, you came to a big cement patio area with an outdoor swinging canopy garden seat at the front entrance and a lattice screen wall to divide us from Auntie Lilly and Uncle Joe's front area. The front door had this huge sliding metal grill door on the outside (so did the back door). All the windows had grills on them too, which could be opened or shut.

On entering the front door, there was a big open space to be used however you liked. Then there was this huge lounge area on the left-hand side. In about the middle of the lounge, a big central staircase swerved around and went upstairs to the bedrooms. Mum and Dad's bedroom was on the left, and there was a little room at the top for a servant.

My brother's and my bedrooms were on the right, with a bathroom and toilet separating our rooms. My room was first on the right upstairs. The wall that divided us from Auntie Lilly was the farthest wall from you when you got to the top of the stairs; in other words, it was at the side of Mum and Dad's bedroom and the back of the servant's bedroom and then the side of my bedroom as you entered it.

At the bottom of the staircase was that huge lounge area, which extended backwards a long way to form the dining room. So, in effect, it was a massive lounge/dining are, combined with a big open space under the stairs, which extended backwards level with the end of the dining room.

At the dining room end of that open space under the stairs, at bench top height, were long round battens, forming a feature screen wall, with a little distance between each batten going up to the ceiling from bench level. There was a door here that led to a massive kitchen, galley style, with a large central bench area.

On the other side, the left-hand side (the other side of that feature screen batten wall), were toilets and bathroom for the servants. At the far back of the kitchen was the back door, which led out onto a grassed garden area. There was this very high cement wall at the end of the garden, and on the other side was the native village, called, as I said earlier, a kampong. I still have fond memories of this house, and I understand it still stands there to the present day.

Every morning, quite early (about six o'clock), we would hear the man in the village at the back saying very loud prayers for the whole village in a language I didn't understand. An old lady from the village who was one hundred years of age who would walk past every evening carrying a large load of sticks, and all you could see was this huge pile of sticks with two feet at the bottom of the pile moving up the road. It was a very funny sight.

It wasn't long before I got to know Archoo, a Chinese lady whose father was the doctor in the village. She would come to work on a bicycle every day and sometimes stay over and look after us on the weekend if Mum and Dad went out. She was our *armar* (Chinese for nanny).

I came to love her very much. She looked after us, Jack and me, in her special Chinese way. She would plait my hair in the mornings as my hair grew longer and longer down my back. I also got to know Sami, who was Indian and was our gardener. We had a Malaysian lady cook who I never really got to know, as Archoo would take care of my brother and my meals.

I'd so badly wanted a cat when I was living in Toowoomba before Penang, so my parents got me a cat. When it got to five months of age, it disappeared. They got me another cat for Christmas that year. I also got a doctor's set from Mum and Dad. Auntie Lilly gave me a Chinese chequers game, and my brother got snakes and ladders.

Following Christmas, my mother was enrolling my brother at the Penang School for the white children. It was late January 1958, and Jack had turned six the previous October, while I was four and a half.

I distinctly remember the teacher pointing to me as I played in the sandpit and saying, "What about her?"

I recall my mother replied, "Well, yes, I guess her too!"

So, I started school at four and a half with my brother, both of us in grade one at Penang School. We had a US curriculum with mainly British teachers, and I was Australian. I loved school. At school, I could draw and colour in and started to learn how to write and count.

My first report card said I was "a pleasure to have in the class" and noted that "at such a young age" I had "trouble handling scissors."

After school, we would go to the beach; Archoo would sometimes take us. My brother and I, despite being told never to go to the snake temple or the rainforest, would go to both places, while Mum and Archoo thought we were playing in the street outside with the other children.

There were the Beaumonts next door from the United Kingdom. They had three girls between six and ten and a boy my age, Harry. There were another family up the street from the United States with a girl and boy, seven and eight. Of course, I visited Auntie Lilly next door often.

I made friends with another girl my age from Australia, who also lived in our street, Zanetta. She and I spent time at Auntie Lilly's, and she was my first real girlfriend who I loved as friends. Auntie Lilly and Uncle Joe loved her too. Sometimes I would get jealous and think they loved her more than me. Zanetta hadn't started school at that stage.

By Easter that year, 1958, my second cat had disappeared. My parents waited till I was twenty years of age to tell me that

Sami the gardener was taking the cats home for tea, which was why they decided to get a monkey. Mum and Dad got a baby monkey. We named him Razoo, probably because he was a rhesus monkey. Oh, how Jack and I just loved that monkey! He grew up with us and insisted on coming on all our visits to the snake temple and the rainforest.

At the snake temple, there was a beggar on every stair on each side of the stairs holding a cup and begging for money. There were a lot of stairs to eventually get to the top and the entrance of this absolutely beautiful temple. I have been terrified of snakes all my life as a result of these visits.

In addition, I have loved turtles, as I felt sorry for the turtles in with the snakes. There were cobras that came out of a hat to special music that a man played on a flute. There were huge pythons and all types of snakes.

We would also go to the beach on the other side of the rainforest. Mum and Dad said we were absolutely forbidden to ever go there or anywhere near the rainforest, but we did. On this beach were bones human bones, probably left over from the war. We did not know that it was wrong to touch the bones. It was an eerie sort of feeling, with the wind sweeping around the point, and no one ever went there. Razoo hated it, and so did I. Once, on going home through the rainforest, this very tall, old, sticklike man came out of nowhere and came for us.

My brother yelled, "Run, Ant, run." And I ran, with my brother running after me. We never went there again.

My parents would go ballistic if they ever caught us outside in bare feet or wearing inside shoes. Due to the risk of contracting hookworms and other diseases through your feet in a Third World country, we had to always wear outside shoes when outside and take them off at the door. Inside, we would wear inside shoes.

This was so ingrained in me I have done this all my life to this day. After returning to Australia, we could have bear feet inside. The more affluent Asian people practised the custom of taking shoes off at the door and inside as well as outside shoes while we were in Penang. Thongs over there were called *gettars*, and we had inside as well as outside gettars.

Jack and I had friends in the village who taught us some of their language, and we taught them some of our language. My brother and I eventually learnt Cantonese from Archoo and our village friends.

One day, Jack went into the village to see a friend, and he hadn't returned long after he was expected back. So, I went looking for him. I found him. The villagers had him tied to a stake, and they were going to burn him.

They accused him of burning their fishing nets, which were on fire at the end of our street in a huge field that separated our street from the beach. We saw the nets on fire when we were coming home from school on the bus. After seeing Peter tied to the stake, I immediately ran home and told Mum. She took Sami, the gardener, and went into the village to get Jack and brought him back. He had a bath and went to bed upset.

Not long after, one of the most frightening events of my life occurred, and for the first time in my life, my boundaries were crossed. The whole village descended upon our house. And Archoo, as well as the cook, Mum, and Sami were rushing around shutting all the grills on all the doors and windows.

There were villagers everywhere all around our house, all putting their hands in through the windows and yelling out in their language in angry voices. All were talking very rapidly, and some of the ladies were screaming.

I was terrified. I simply froze and hid upstairs in my bedroom.

The native police were called, and the military police also attended. A deal was struck that the white people would pay for new fishing nets as an act of good will, but this did not mean my brother had touched their fishing nets. In return, they had to leave the white people alone.

Things seemed to settle down after that, but we remained locked in our home for a few days, and Dad stayed home with us. We all just slept, and Auntie Lilly came to visit. She did my hair in rag curls, and I would have to sleep with rags binding my hair round and round. When they were taken out in the morning, I had long ringlets. She did this often while I was in Penang.

Auntie Lily was always talking about me becoming a nurse. At Christmas this year, 1958, she bought me a nurse's set, which included a red cape I used to wear around. She convinced me I was going to be a nurse when I grew up (and I did).

Mum and Dad gave me a toy tea set and a pram for my dolls. Auntie Lily would do my hair in rag curls for all special occasions. While I lived in Penang, my hair grew so long it fell halfway down my back, but it was very fine and thin. Mum really looked after herself and looked pretty every day. So did Auntie Lilly.

My parents and our neighbours were going to lots of parties and actually holding parties. I do remember my brother and I sitting at the top of the stairs out of view crouched down holding onto the balustrades. This new wave of music, rock and roll, was sweeping the earth like a tidal wave. This new way of dancing rock and roll had even reached Penang.

I think Mum and Dad had a record player, as I remember

hearing *The Platters, with* "Smoke Gets in Your Eyes" and "The Great Pretender." There were also Perry Como and Chet Atkins on guitar. I'm sure I remember hearing them play Frank Sinatra and Louis Armstrong and Bing Crosby, as well as Doris Day and the music from *South Pacific.*

Mum and Dad were not into Elvis Presley or Little Richard or similar music. However, these artists were really big all over the English-speaking world. Elvis Presley was drafted into the army in March 1958, being called up for national service to go to Vietnam, a civil war that had been raging since early '50s.

Marilyn Monroe became even more famous making more movies. Lots of other movies were being made in Hollywood in America and around the world. Television was a pre-war invention but was introduced into America in 1948 and was now well and truly in most homes throughout the states.

In Australia, it was only just beginning, with the opening of GTV-9 Melbourne in 1957. This was the first part of a federal government scheme to extend TV throughout Australia in stages. TV licences were granted for Brisbane (QTQ and BTQ) in 1958, along with Adelaide, Perth, and Hobart.

In 1959, *Ben-Hur* was made, costing $19 million and grossing in excess of $76 million at the box offices which was a massive amount of money in those days.[8] It took six years to prepare the film shoot with over six months of on-location work in Italy. The movie featured more crew and extras than any other film before it. The set for the chariot race was the most expensive set ever constructed at that point in time. Thus, the saying goes "bigger than Ben-Hur."

The race between Russia and America to get to the moon continued. The war between North and South

Vietnam continued to rage, with American and Australian troops stationed there. Protests in both countries continued with national service in both countries, which meant men over the age of eighteen could be called up for service.

The car manufacturing industry grew around the world. Immigration into Australia was at an all-time high throughout the '50s in order to repopulate Australia. A multicultural Australia was beginning to happen.

I was a little girl, and none of this was affecting my life in Penang or the white population in Penang, but it would no doubt affect me once we got back to Australia. We were a small, tightly knit group. Living in Penang, we were somewhat insulated from what was going on in the world. Dad got lots of newspapers sent to him from home and used to spend ages reading them. Mum would write a lot of letters home and also received lots of letters from home.

It was New Year's Day 1959, and I got up to be told Zanetta's parents had been killed in a car accident overnight, wrapped around a telephone pole. I was so sad. It was the first time I had encountered what death meant, though I didn't really understand.

I never got to say goodbye to Zanetta. She was sent to Sydney to live with her grandparents. I did hear about her all my life through Auntie Lilly and Uncle Joe, who always kept in touch. So, it was a long, hot summer holiday that year, and I contracted chicken pox when we were due to return to school. I was grounded and had to stay in my room night and day for six weeks. The doctor visited regularly but I only saw my mother from a distance.

Archoo bathed me daily in a special solution and put pink stuff all over me after drying me. It was all very soothing. I would play with my dolls and have tea parties with them and talk to them. I didn't see Auntie Lilly for six whole weeks and hardly saw my brother, only glancing him from a distance a couple of times.

Razoo was wonderful company. At that stage, he wasn't allowed in the house because he had shaken the pot containing the stem of the climbing plant Mum had growing up the baton screen wall at the end of the dining room, knocking it out of its base. He would come up the drainpipe and in my bedroom window.

As soon as anyone came other than Archoo, he would hide in the wardrobe. Archoo didn't mind, and it was our secret. She spent time talking to me every day, telling me about her family and life. She had to have a shower after she spent time with me. I talked to Peggy, my doll, a lot. At that age, I think I thought Peggy was real. This time cooped up with chicken pox taught me how to be alone.

I eventually got better and returned to school, really loving it. My parents would play Chinese checkers and snakes and ladders with us on weekends. Dad would also, on the weekends, take us to the other side of the island in his Model T Ford convertible he had imported from the States. My brother and I would sit in the little section in the back for luggage.

There was a most beautiful beach on the other side of the island called Batu Ferringhi Beach, and the cable car started and finished there. We would have picnics there, as well as swim in this most idyllic setting. Its beauty was totally unforgettable. (I believe it is on the tourist side of the island and today features a resort.)

Auntie Lilly and Uncle Joe would take us swimming at our beach where we lived on weekends, and I would climb on Uncle Joe's shoulders and jump off, diving in. Once a jellyfish or sea animal of some kind chased me and frightened me of swimming in the sea for a while.

Archoo then decided she would take us regularly to the sea to dig for pippies in the shallow shore to restore my love of the ocean. She would then cook them up for us for tea with rice. She often made fish and rice for us for tea, which we ate out of little bowls with chopsticks, holding the bowl close to our mouths!

My favourite dish ever since, to this day, is fish and rice. The cook taught Mum about Malaysian cooking, which Mum would try out on the weekends. I came to absolutely love all oriental food. My favourite was Penang curry, followed by satay and butter chicken, all of which I have made and eaten regularly throughout my life. Memories of Penang have been like railway tracks going round and round in my mind all my life!

I clearly remember when the hundred-year-old stick lady, as we used to call her, died. There followed this awful ritual, which was the tradition in the village, of keeping a dead person in the for three days house before they buried the dead. The smell was something dreadful, such that I could never forget it. Jack and I did sometimes play with a few of the village children but not for a while after this event.

One afternoon, I was playing over behind the flats, and I accidentally fell over something while playing hide-and-seek with some of the children from the village. I injured my chin, splitting it open again. I remember running home up the street with blood pouring down the front of my body and all these village people running after me.

After I got home, Mum was in shock and upset. She calmed me down and cleaned me up, putting an ice pack on my chin. The military ambulance truck came again and got me, taking me to the military hospital. I took Peggy doll with me. Dad met me on arrival and stayed with me while they stitched me up. They did a good job on both occasions, as I have very little visible scarring. I did have a small bump/lump on my forehead for many years.

Life quickly settled down, and I came to really love Dad for always being there for me and always giving me a cuddle at night when he came home. My dad played competition badminton and won a lot of trophies, which he proudly brought home. Auntie Lilly continued to bring various gifts into my life through the fairies, often comic books or storybooks, which she would read to me.

This included all the classic fairy tales, like *Cinderella* and *Snow White and the Seven Dwarfs*, as well as *Hansel and Gretel*. Mum would read Enid Blyton to us sometimes too.

Razoo continued to be the most adorable pet. He would sit and pick all the salt on your skin off of you. It settled and dried on your skin in the heat. He would climb up coconut trees and shake them and shake them till all the coconuts fell down. We loved eating coconuts and drinking the juice, and so did Razoo.

I fell in love with Harry Beaumont next door, and he with me. We were both nearly six, and we loved building cubby houses up the street with sticks we found in that field that separated our homes from the beach. We would then climb inside to play mummies and daddies, when we would just sit and talk and huddle together and cuddle each other.

The Malaysian ice cream man would come around with a cart selling ice cream wrapped up in banana leaves, and you would simply eat it out of the folded leaf or off the leaf. Harry, Jack, and I would eat ice cream together. The ice cream man also sold chocolate-covered beetles and other delicacies, which we declined.

I turned six on July 22, 1959. Mum and Auntie Lill gave

me this big birthday party with a beautiful cake, and I could not handle being the centre of attention.

We had really settled into this new land, with the memories of the land I had comefrom very distant from my mind, though I still remembered Auntie Mabel.

Penang was vastly becoming the only way of life I knew. In five days', time, on July 27, 1959, my mum had a new baby, my sister, Amy Elizabeth Daley. It was not until nearly forty years later going through therapy that I was to realise this was why I had been cooped up in my room for six weeks. My mum had just fallen pregnant and was afraid for the unborn child with my chicken pox at the time.

My sister came home for a short while and, at only a few weeks of life, fell gravely ill, going into the hospital on the island. They said her bowel wasn't moving at all inside her. It had twisted back inside itself and was now paralysed. She had surgery and remained in hospital for months. They thought she would die.

My mum and dad would be up at the hospital every afternoon and night. My mother practically lived there. She was expressing breast milk for my sister, so I was told. Jack and I would get home from school and go to Auntie Lilly's if Archoo was not home. Sometimes, neither was home, and as night fell, we would sit on the big high cement columns each side of the driveway, one of us on the top of each column.

I felt abandoned. One night, a lady from over at the flats came and got us. She took us home to her house and made chicken alphabet soup. (It had letters of the alphabet in it, made from pasta.)

My new sister, Amy, eventually did come home to us in December 1959. I clearly remember her being in a pram and being told she was behind in all her milestones because she had been so ill but not to worry, as she would catch up. I was told I had to look after her.

I felt totally burdened, as I could barely look after myself. Archoo started staying over a lot and helping with the new baby. I did take her for walks in the pram up the street and would talk to her when she was awake. I would watch Mum bathe her. Mum was not very well after the whole ordeal. I cannot remember Christmas that year except Auntie Lill taking me to the Penang swimming pool. I wanted a Barbie doll (like the girl up the road) but didn't get it.

Soon, it was 1960, and Jack and I were in grade three at school. The Beaumonts next door went back to England, and I really missed Harry. The family from the United States of America up the road had some great toys. Apparently, Lego had first gone on sale in the States in 1958, and in 1959 Mattel launched the Barbie doll in that country. They had some Lego and a Barbie doll, as well as other dolls, and we loved playing up there, even though they were older.

I had gotten used to people going out of my life suddenly so found it difficult to let myself get close to people after this. I could stay at home in my room and play for hours with my dolls, making them cups of tea or rocking them and cuddling them the way I wanted Mum to treat me.

It didn't seem to matter that I thought she didn't love me in Malaysia/Penang because I had Auntie Lill next door, and besides, my best friend was a monkey. I mean I had Razoo. He cuddled me all the time, showing me how much he loved me. And I knew my brother loved me.

Since our new baby sister came home, Mum seemed totally taken with her. She always nursed and cuddled her when she was awake. Mum paid a lot of attention to Jack too. I couldn't work out why she wouldn't notice me or speak to me much or even kiss me or hold me. Though Auntie Lill loved me like a mother, what I desperately wanted was for Mum to love me. I would do anything to get her to love me.

When I grew up, my Auntie Mabel (mum's sister) told me she thought the birth of Amy brought out the maternal instinct in Mum because Amy was so ill. Other relatives thought this too and that Mum and Dad had had two families—in other words, Jack and I were the first, and Amy and the next two, who followed in later years, we're the second.

It was not long after this I had missed the school bus, so Mum was taking me there in a rickshaw. This was a specially made bike with a little enclosure containing two seats on the back; a man peddled the bike, powering the vehicle.

Our rider got near where the school was, and Mum said, "Stop. Stop here."

She pushed me out of the rickshaw and pointed to the school, telling me, "You can walk the rest of the way."

Well, I never made it to the school. I got lost in the streets of Penang. Luckily, this nice, friendly Chinese lady found me and took me home to her house. All her family were quite taken with me and kept coming up and touching my hair. I did not understand why they were doing this.

They apparently thought I was an angel or a spirit or something because I looked so different to them. I kept thinking, *why was I made like this? I must be a freak.* I just wanted black hair and dark skin like them because nearly all the people on the island looked like them! Well, I do not know how many days or weeks I was there.

The family kept me locked inside, and I missed my father and worried I would never see him again. I recall this banging on the front door. When the door opened, it was my father and a native policeman, and I ran to my father. He carried me all the way home from the village. He was quite upset and kept asking me, "What did they do to you? Are you all, right?" and saying, "You are still my little princess."

Apparently, Archoo had found out I was there and had told Mum and Dad. I was so glad to be home again. Getting lost affected my sense of direction, which was forming at that age. I have always had the most shocking sense of direction all my life ever since.

Life continued in Penang for some time, and I was actually quite happy. I really thought that there was no other way of life. I had temporarily forgotten about Australia, except for Auntie Mabel, and always hoped I would see her again one day.

One evening mid 1960, my parents said to Jack and me, "We are going back to Australia."

I asked, "What is that like?"

Dad replied, "Well, you can't take Razoo."

I was horrified and said, "Well, I don't think I like Australia if they won't let you have monkeys!"

They told us that Auntie Lill and Uncle Joe were going back to Australia too. They were going to Brisbane, which was a few hours' drive from where we would be living in Toowoomba back in our old house. I found out when I grew up that Uncle Joe had asked for Enoggera Army barracks to be close to me. Zanetta was still in Sydney. I longed to see her again.

Dad sold his car, the model T Ford convertible, to another family on the island. We started getting ready to leave, with suitcases of clothing and a few toys. My parents found a home for Razoo and we said our goodbyes to him. I was crying my eyes out as he clung to me and wouldn't let me go.

Then it came to pass that a big truck came one day with lots of boxes and packed up our whole house. I left for school, giving special instructions they weren't to touch my Peggy doll, and when I got home the whole house was packed up. We stayed at the military headquarters overnight.

The next day, we were driven by military to the ferry, which took us to the mainland. After that, we were taken to this big ship called the *Willem Ruys*. It was the biggest thing I had ever seen in all my life, reminding me of that big truck I'd seen all those years ago.

## Homeward bound on the *Willem Ruys*

We travelled back to Australia on the *Willem Ruys* which was a beautiful ocean liner. The trip took six weeks. Our cabin had four single bunks in it, and my baby sister slept in a cot in the centre between the bunks. Amy's cot would slide up and down at night with the sea waves when they were rough.

Jack and I and Peggy doll were looked after at the crèche from after breakfast till before tea. I enjoyed being at the crèche, as we played and did craft and things like that. Mum and Dad did take us up on the top deck on some days, and we saw the wide-open sea. I was in awe after living in Penang, and from this, I grew up to love and be fascinated by the sea.

I spent a lot of time in the evenings trying to recall all the memories of my homeland, Australia. I imagined Auntie Mabel with her hair pulled back in a French roll and her lovely melodic voice. I knew I could never forget Penang. I was grieving for Razoo and Archoo. Would I ever see them again? I have longed to go back to Penang ever since I left it.

Memories have remained with me for my lifetime, embedded in my mind like railway tracks and the carriages.

The memories never cease, forever moving through my mind, triggered by different happenings in my life—the same memories over and over again looping round and round.

For now, I was homeward bound on the *Willem Ruys,* desperately trying to accept what was happening. It seemed I would just get happy, and they, my parents, would up and move and take me away to somewhere else. I was somewhat comforted in thinking I was going back to the place I had known before we had gone to Penang. Would I get happy again there? I spent time wondering.

One incredibly memorable and deeply hurtful moment on the ship was when Mum took me to the barber and sat me up on the seat. He put the black cape around me and then, without warning, just cut off my long, plaited blonde hair with one snip. I still have the plait to this day, with its yellow ribbon tied at the end.

My hair was suddenly short, without anybody explaining or warning me. I could never ever forget this. I have never been able to trust hairdressers since. I think Mum was just sick of plaiting it every morning on the ship.

So, it came to pass I had spent the formative years of my life in a foreign land with a different culture and society to the one I was born in. I was now on my way back to live in the country I was born in and had spent the first three and a half years in, and I was now going on seven.

Auntie Lilly and Uncle Joe had already left for Brisbane by the time we left Penang. I felt reassured to be told they would be living not far from us. It would just be a morning's drive in the car.

I have no recollection of the ocean liner docking in Australia or how we got to our house in Railway Parade in

Toowoomba, but we did. Being back in that house is my next memory. It was good we went back to that house, as not long after we arrived, all these memories came flooding back to me of the years before we went to Malaysia. I started remembering Darwin too!

# CHAPTER 2

# Completing Childhood in Australia

## Back to cold, wintry Toowoomba

So here we were, mid 1960, at Railway Parade in this little, wooden three-bedroom house in cold, wintry Toowoomba, with its old wood stove. It seemed a world apart from our palatial home in the hot tropics of Penang. Even the weather seemed the opposite of my beloved Penang. It was so cold in the winter, in Toowoomba that, when you turned the taps on first thing, ice came out.

By early afternoon, my mum lit the wood stove and had to boil up water for our baths, and we all bathed in the same water, which I got to use last! The toilet was up the back path and seemed very strange, not unlike the hole in the ground the villagers in Penang used.

My memories of the next year or so are blurred, with only some clear memories. I remember emotions I had in the next year or so more than memories. I think I was numb, suffering some kind of cultural shock and grieving for my monkey, Razoo, and Chinese nanny, Archoo. I missed the warm climate of Penang and the beach.

It was nice that some things never changed, like the neighbours up the back, the Turnbull family, as well as the doctor next door. It was nice we had the sandpit, but after not being allowed to play in soil in Penang, I could no longer play in it; neither could Jack.

My mum had a new baby, our sister Amy, with whom she seemed totally besotted. The birth of Amy, along with her being so ill, really brought out the maternal instinct in Mum. I wanted Mum's love badly after returning from Penang and would do anything to please her.

I recall Mum enrolling us at Harristown State School and Jack and I having to do a whole series of tests to determine which grades we would be in. I went back down to grade two, based on my age, and he stayed in grade three, which meant we were no longer in the same year at school. I had to walk home from school by myself a few times, as my brother was doing sport, and I felt frightened and unsafe.

I experienced a culture shock. Here I was in the country I was born in, a fair-skinned, blonde-haired young child, and I felt more like a Southeast Asian than an Australian! I have actually been drawn to and had a love of anything oriental all my life. My brother, Jack, also was missing what had become our home in Penang.

Unknown to me, at this time in Australia, due to all the immigration in the '50s, Australia had begun its journey to becoming a multicultural nation. In 1947 post war, under the Chifley government, in order to repopulate Australia and due to shortage of labour, Australia launched a programme aimed at increasing the population by 1 per cent a year through net migration.[9] The White Australia Policy, which had been instituted in 1901 when Parliament first formed in Australia, was still in place and wasn't softened till 1960.

This meant most immigrants were from England. However, Australia was taking persons through the assisted passage scheme introduced for Empire and American ex-serviceman and women who had served in Australia during the Second World War. Later, this was extended to cover members of the resistance movements in France, Holland, Norway, Denmark, and Belgium. Thousands of displaced persons from the refugee camps in Europe arrived in Australia after the war as refugees.

In 1959 the non-Aboriginal population of Australia reached 10 million.[10] In 1961, for the first time, some Aborigines were included in a population count.

Desegregation of black and white people had taken place in America throughout the 1950s, and by 1960 there were still some anti-segregation protests by white Americans. An African American peacemaker who was standing up for his people in America was Dr Martin Luther King.

I will always remember at the age of ten in 1963 his speech in Washington, DC, broadcast all over the world as part of the civil rights movement March for Jobs and Freedom. This speech is recognised as one of the finest orations of the twentieth century.

In it he said, "I have a dream that my four children will one day live in a nation where they will not be judged by the colour of their skin, but by the content of their character."

Meanwhile in South Africa, apartheid had been set up separating blacks from whites. Nelson Mandela, a native South African and another of the great peacemakers of the world, had set up a movement and launched a military wing in 1961 to fight against discrimination of people by race or colour.

For this, he was sent to Robben Island Prison, where he lived in a six-foot-wide cell and did hard labour in a quarry. This sparked a global anti-apartheid movement and a global fight to free him. He was freed twenty-seven years later in 1989.

For me, having grown up as the white minority in a foreign land, I could never understand all this racism in the world and have never been able to comprehend it. I was aware of all the racism going on in the world from listening to my parents talk and from the news but really couldn't understand it. I remember being totally bewildered by racism in the world at a very young age.

It was the beginning of the swinging sixties, a totally psychedelic era. The baby boomers born after the war had hit their youth and led a cultural revolution. Youth made their voices heard all over the world with all their anti-war protests, student sit-ins, and rock festivals. Youth were revolting and changed fashion, music, racism, and politics breaking conservative rules as they went. I recall hearing about all the protests and felt frightened walking home from school!

Space travel was a major step forward, with Sputnik 1 a USSR satellite orbiting the earth on October 4, 1957. On February 20, 1962, Charles Glenn, in his capsule *Friendship 7*, was the first American to orbit the earth.

There were numerous other missiles and rockets launched by both countries in that time, but the race was on to see which country could walk on the moon first. In his world-famous victory speech, President John F. Kennedy, elected 1960 as leader of the Democratic Party, said America would be the first.

This launched a lot of movies, as well as television shows, about astronauts, space travel, and robots. We would go down to the neighbours' house at the end of the street; they had a television we would watch.

Not everybody in Australia had a television at that time, and my parents didn't have one. I recall this lady complaining to Mum we were always down there. And could she keep us at home? We could only go to their house and visit their children when invited by the parents.

Jack and I also played on the high dug-in walls to the railway line, which was at the bottom of these high, grassed walls. I recall clinging onto the walls as trains sped by. My brother took me everywhere he played in our early years.

In October 1961, communist East Germany built the great wall dividing East and West Germany. France, Britain, and the United States were in the West. Communism was still rife in the USSR, and the presence of communist spies in the world was a real threat. This influenced the making of movies for the screen and television, such that the first in the James Bond series began with Sean Connery playing the leading role in *Dr No* in 1962. Another was the series *The Avengers*, which began in 1961 and carried through till 1969.

The most spectacular film of 1962 was *Lawrence of Arabia*, which won Oscars for the photography and the music. Henry Hitchcock had begun his series in 1960 with the film sensation of that year, *Psycho*, and its famous shower scene.

A famous scene featuring Audrey Hepburn in a black cocktail dress was from *Breakfast at Tiffany's* in 1961. Other box office smashes were *West Side Story* and the European hit *La Dolce Vita*.

The dance of 1960 was "the twist," pioneered by Chubby Checker, and in 1963, it was his "limbo rock." I would do both these dances after I left home much later at seventeen. Nightclubs were opening all over the world, places where adults could go and dance, listen to the music of the time, and have fun. Patrons smoked openly inside them.

The Beatles—John Lennon, Paul McCartney, George Harrison, and Ringo Starr—rose from a club in Hamburg to a worldwide audience from 1960 to 1964, backed by their manager, Brian Epstein. They began with *Please Please me*, which was followed by *A Hard Day's Night*, *Revolver*, *Sgt. Pepper's Lonely Heart Club Band*, and on and on.

Beatlemania gripped the teenage fan base and took over

the world. Another UK band, the Rolling Stones, shared almost equal popularity. In the United States, the Beach Boys rose to have a worldwide audience by 1964. The folk music scene had also begun in 1960, with Paul Simon and Art Garfunkel as Simon and Garfunkel.

There was also Bob Dylan and Janet Baez and Peter, Paul and Mary. Then there was Australia's own folk music pop group, the Seekers, with Athol Guy, Bruce Woodley, Judith Durham, and Keith Potger, which Mum and Dad did allow us to listen to, as well as Simon and Garfunkel.

I do not recall hearing any music in that house at Railway Parade after we returned from Penang. I did miss music and noise after all the noise and vibrancy of life in Penang. My parents got the telephone connected. Not everybody had a home telephone those days, and my mother spent a lot of time on it talking to family.

We visited Grandpa, her father, and Uncle Henry, her brother, who lived in Grantham, after Dad bought another car, a light green FJ Holden of which he was very proud.

We went for a holiday to the beach, Caloundra. It seemed a long haul to a child that age, who had to sit quietly in the back of the car for a long time. Mum would play "I spy with my little eye" to keep us amused. Caloundra is north of Brisbane on the Sunshine Coast.

At that time, I preferred Penang, where you could walk to the beach in a few minutes. However, after arriving in Caloundra, we enjoyed a really happy family holiday. It was the first time we had been happy together as a family since leaving Penang.

Caloundra has now become a place of very fond memories, as we went there many times in the future for holidays. And it's now, in the present, where my family has all resonated with. This, to me, demonstrates the power of happy childhood memories and the power of happiness in our lives.

On returning to Railway Parade, an event was to occur that would stay in my memory banks forever and would affect my relationship with my sister Amy. My mother took my dolls and toys, like the tea sets, off me and gave them to my sister; this included my Peggy doll.

My sister, two weeks later, drowned Peggy doll in Dad's fish tank up the backyard. This caused me excruciating emotional pain, which I didn't actually get over till my fiftieth birthday. It sounds weird, but I actually, on a subconscious level, held this against my sister all those years and felt angry with Mum for a lifetime—as crazy as that sounds.

There was just so much happening in the world in those first few years as the '60s took off, and it continued to build momentum. My parents' reaction was to try and encapsulate their children in a bubble and keep the world away from them, except for family and neighbourhood.

I can remember wandering what was happening out there in the wider world. We were only at Railway Parade for such a short period, after which we moved to Amberley Air Base.

I was really only just starting to settle back into life in Australia when we moved.

## Life on Amberley Air Base

It was January 1961 when my parents moved to Amberley Air Base, where my father was stationed. Amberley is twenty minutes west from Ipswich, the nearest town, and about halfway between Toowoomba and Brisbane. We lived on Liberator Street, in a very simple three-bedroom metal house with a metal laundry at the bottom of the back half dozen stairs and ground level at the front.

The garage was a separate metal building in the backyard. All the houses looked exactly the same, side by side. We had an electric stove and toilet upstairs, as well as a hot water system. Dad bought Mum a new twin tub washing machine and a new refrigerator, a Kelvinator, which had to be defrosted every week. They were the latest at that time, and that made Mum happy. At least something made her happy, I thought, as she hadn't been singing or listening to her radio since we returned from Penang.

There were a handful of streets on one side of the main street to enter the community of Amberley and a couple of streets on the other side. The houses on the other side in the couple of streets looked a little more flash than ours but were all the same side by side. They were accommodations for the officers and their families.

We lived in the main housing section. There were two official entrances to the actual air base, with boom gates to where military operations actually took place, and these were manned by military staff night and day. The back entrance to the working base was at the end of our street. The front entrance to the actual air base was right down the end of this road, opposite the end of the school grounds.

My brother and I started school at Amberley State School. I was in grade three, and my brother, grade four. At this school, they had combined classes. Grades 1 through three were in one class; four and five were in another class; and five, six, and seven were in another class again. I did not like the teacher of my class, grade three. The headmaster was Mr Wallace, who took years five, six, and seven. He was very strict, sometimes coming into our classroom to announce something.

He always walked very quickly and, on entering the classroom, would snap in a loud, authoritarian voice, "Now, slates down and hands up those who …" It was invariably about someone doing something they shouldn't have!

I was always scared of Mr Wallace. We had slates and chalk in classes. We sat at long desks, which had inkwells along the top and shelves underneath. The seats were long form style behind the desks. Copywriting was taught using pen and ink. Students took it in turn to fill the inkwells after school in the afternoons.

The school consisted of two buildings, one very high, long room that could be divided into two rooms via a pull-across folder divider. This large, long room housed grades four through seven. There was a large play area cemented under this building. The rest of the play areas around the buildings were dirt.

There was another low ground-level building that adjoined, and it was for grades one through three. The only other buildings were the demountable for toilets set well aside from the main school. There were also huge, open grassed play areas with trees lining the fences all around.

My brother played marbles in the dirt, and I played hopscotch under a huge, hundreds-of-years-old evergreen camphor laurel tree that shaded the main buildings. Under that tree every morning at break, the government provided milk to primary school students in Australia, and we would have our milk from the small bottles near the bike racks. Heaps of kids rode their bikes to school.

We were given bikes for Christmas 1960 from Mum and Dad. That was the first year I found out there was no Santa Clause, as my brother told me he didn't exist. I was quite upset at finding this out.

Dad taught us how to ride a bike, and it wasn't long

before we were riding our bikes to school. My hair had begun to grow again, and though it was not very long by this stage, Mum would plait it in a hurry each morning with me sitting facing the back of a chair.

It was always, "C'mon, Anthea, hurry up. Sit here. I have to do your hair!" every morning.

I would dutifully drop everything and sit up—anything to please her.

In no time, it would be lunchtime, when Jack and I would ride our bikes home for lunch, and Dad came home for lunch too. We had lunch together as a family, which seemed to make Mum happy. Besides her reading and housework, Mum seemed lonely and bored. The neighbours were very close in proximity, but Mum kept to herself.

The lady next door and the lady across the road had both gone back to work after marrying. This was apparently unusual, if I was to believe my parents. According to them, women didn't work after they married. Women working outside the home was a trend that had started in the early sixties and was only going to continue, and eventually, by the mid-seventies, it became the norm.

We were the last on the street to get a television—by mid-1961. It was black-and-white like the rest of Australia's televisions at this point in time. In those days in Australia, you had to have a license to own a television, and there were television license police, who would go around knocking on doors to ensure everybody had their licenses. If you didn't have a license, they would fine you.

For this reason, I was always scared to answer the front door in those days! I didn't get to watch TV, as in the afternoons, I had to take my little sister for a walk in her pram. All around the air base I would go. I often collected mushrooms as we went, and Mum would cook them up for tea that night. There were few flower beds and no parks on the base, which meant few butterflies. There was so little to look at on our walks.

On these walks, the air base struck me as all being made of metal, with metal aircraft hangers and metal aeroplanes; plus, all the houses were made out of metal. The metal was so cold and unforgiving and added to the loneliness of these walks. There was always that smell of aeroplanes in the air or dirt if I went up near the school.

I noticed that the school building, Wilson's shop opposite and the dozen or so civilian houses beyond Wilson's shop were all made of wood and all had their own character. It always felt so different going up near those houses. They signified to me life outside the air force. The wood had more of a human feeling about it, which all the metal didn't have. Those people from those houses had children, some of whom were my friends at school, and I knew they stayed in their houses, not moving around all the time like us. I visited the Illingworths, Denise and her sister; they were of mixed blood, part aboriginal.

On arriving home and telling Mum about my ventures, I was told not to go there and mix with those coloured children. I was bewildered, thinking about Penang, where we played with the village kids, and everybody seemed coloured there.

I started to think I preferred Penang, as it was Amberley that was different and the problem, not those kids. Even once you left the air base, life seemed quite different. Amberley was a small military community set among a dry, harsh Australian bush on flat plains and had horse or cattle farms surrounding it.

It even smelt different once you left the air base, with the smell of the bush and the country. I began to question whether I liked my father being in the air force. But he always looked so brave and important in his uniform. I began to sense that perhaps Mum wasn't so happy. I had felt for some time she was fed up with cooking tea every night. The metal houses were hot in summer and cold in winter.

In the winter, it was very cold at Amberley, and we had a wonder heater that was like an oven with a chimney in the lounge room, where you burned wood. Jack would have to chop the wood for this, and Dad also chopped the wood. I don't recall a lot that year. I have that period in my memory—the first eighteen months after we returned from Penang—where memories are vague and blurry, with only certain memories standing out. I can't recall much about school that year, grade three, 1961.

I do remember going to religious instruction as Roman Catholics, and it was in the lounge area where you went if you were sick. We seemed to be the smallest group in the school. Dad took us to church at the Catholic church on the air base from about this time onwards, until we left the air base four years later.

I recall having to wear a hat and gloves and how you had to go to confession beforehand. They passed the plate around for collections, and I can recall thinking this was a sophisticated way of begging in comparison to the beggars in Penang with their cups.

In 1962, Amberley State School had its fifty-year celebrations, and all the children had to go in fancy dress. I went as a fairy in the most beautiful little black dress that Auntie Mabel had made for me. Auntie Lilly did my hair in rag curls, and I felt very beautiful and enjoyed all the attention. There is a photograph of me that has been displayed in our family many times. I know Mum was very proud of me at this event.

My brother didn't want to go in fancy dress but also seemed proud of his sister. Mum looked beautiful at this function, though she took pride in her appearance every day, wearing her hair in an up style in a bun. She also wore powder and lipstick every day, but most women of this era did. She always looked after her figure and maintained a youthful appearance, despite having three children at this stage.

From about 1961 to 1962 onwards, I went to Auntie Lilly's and Uncle Joe's for all of the holidays. They also visited us at Amberley. Auntie Mabel had married while we were away in Penang, marrying Uncle Reg, and also use to visit us at Amberley.

Auntie Vera, Dad's half-sister, also began visiting us and continued to all my childhood. She would always bring all these second-hand clothes for me— "hand-me-downs," Mum and Dad called them—from a family she knew who had a girl a little older than me. Dad was very restrictive with funds, which made Mum and Dad very frugal. They were saving for the great Australian dream in those days—to own your own home. Mum always complained Dad never gave her enough money. Dad was very stoic and never said much in reply.

I felt humiliated to wear someone else's clothes. Mum was truly glad to have all this family support she hadn't had during the years in Penang. We also continued to go and visit her father, my grandpa, and her brother, Uncle Henry, up on the farm at Grantham near Toowoomba.

We went on our first really big family holiday to Caloundra around this time. Auntie Mabel, Uncle Reg, and Uncle Henry and his wife-to-be, Jenny, all joined us.

We stayed in this old beach house, which had many stairs up to the front door and overlooked the ocean, on

Kings Beach. Caloundra was a sleepy little beachside town in these days with all single-story beach houses. I thought it was the best place in the world—so different to Amberley. It was the second time I had seen the ocean since leaving Penang.

It was hard for Mum and Dad to keep the outside world out. On August 9, 1962, in New York, came the death of Marilyn Monroe after a life of pain and fame. She was just thirty-six years old. At first, it was reported as suicide and was all over the television and newspapers worldwide. Dad explained to me what suicide meant, and it sounded so odd at the time. Conspiracy theorists some years later went to work and traced her death all the way to the White House.

She had apparently had affairs with Kennedys—the president, JFK, and his brother Robert—who at that time was the attorney general. The last person to visit her on the night she died had been Robert Kennedy.

A few months earlier, on May 19, 1962, she had sung "Happy Birthday, Mister President" in a most alluring, breathy voice for the president's forty-fifth birthday at Madison Square Gardens in front of thousands and broadcast worldwide. She was wearing a revealing dress, which made her look as though she were nude and was covered in sequins. It is a famous scene in history and was shown after her death.

Mum and Dad decided they didn't want us watching the violence or women in sexy dresses on television after this, and our TV viewing was cut right back. We watched *The Bugs Bunny Show*, which aired from 1960 to 1972, and *The Flintstones*, running from 1960 to 1966. And there were also some westerns in the afternoon. I was busy taking care of Amy after I got home from school. Australia was a bit behind America in television, as shows on TV had begun over there in the late forties.

Mum watched *Coronation Street* at night, which first screened at 7:00 p.m. on December 9, 1960. It was set in Weatherfield, a fictitious street in Manchester, United Kingdom, and was a serial that ran for many, many years. Dad watched *Doctor Who*, a series that was watched by an estimated 80 million in 206 countries around the world. It has been honoured by *The Guinness World Records* as both the longest running and the most successful science fiction series in the world. I recall Mum and Dad watching these series for many years ahead.

In 1963, I was in grade five and remember it as just another year at Amberley State School, when life at home hummed along. There was still no music in the home. It was as though the music in the world was changing so much that Mum and Dad didn't like it and were unsure which way to go. Not everybody had a record player, and I am uncertain whether they had one after arriving back in Australia.

Still, in Darwin, Mum played the radio a lot but not these days at Amberley. Perhaps it was the television at night that changed things. Mum still read a lot, telling me about the books she was reading. I began writing poetry. I was given two volumes of poetry for a birthday present, one of them by Banjo Patterson. I use to read poetry to Amy at night before bed.

In 1963, the queen and Prince Phillip visited Australia, and they came to Amberley air base. All the schoolchildren went to greet them, and I was in the front row standing with my best friend Julie McKeown. We had the rest of the day of school. It was a very memorable occasion. Auntie Lilly, being British, loved the queen, and I told her all about it.

I enjoyed the holidays, going to stay with Auntie Lilly and Uncle Joe, who did play music and take me on lots of picnics. They also took me to the beach at Redcliffe and fishing out on the Sandgate wharf. Both places are far northern suburbs of Brisbane and not as far as Caloundra to drive from Brisbane. Auntie Lilly lived at Chermside in Brisbane in what I perceived the normal world in a city outside of a military base.

I really loved city life, I decided. I told Auntie Lilly about Peggy and how much I missed her. Auntie Lilly gave me a big pyjama teddy bear, which you are supposed to put your pyjamas in. That soft, beautiful teddy bear has graced my bed for the rest of my days to this day, and I wasn't going to let anybody have him. I told the teddy and Auntie Lilly all my secrets.

I had my first crush on a boy, Barry Fitzhenry, who lived around the corner from us. Unfortunately for me, he did not feel the same away. But I remained a secret admirer. I was really starting to notice boys other than my brother. I liked the male teacher who taught me in grades four and five. He was the first male teacher I'd ever had.

It was this year, at the age of ten, that Mum started me cooking, beginning with jam drop biscuits, as well as coconut biscuits. About mid-1963, Dad went on a posting to Papua New Guinea. and I really missed him. He would send me all these nice postcards and a few letters, which kept the relationship close.

Towards the end of the year, I recall an event that shocked the world. On November 22, 1963, John Fitzgerald Kennedy, the president of the United States, just past his first thousand days in office, was killed by an assassin's bullets as his open motorcade rode through Dallas, Texas. This sort of made me scared going out in the world. I didn't seem to understand that he was famous, and I wasn't, and that was why he'd died!

In January 1964, Mum brought home another baby

daughter, Charlotte Daley. She was my second sister. Dad came home from Papua New Guinea at last! I was so glad to have him home again. I was in grade six and loved to go to the swimming pool after school and ride my bike around the air base. At this time, I was really taking an interest in boys, and there was one who kept leaving love letters under my desk. I thought it was Barry Litton, who lived on the next street from us, and I would visit him. He lived with his Mum and Dad and older brother.

By the time, Charlotte (known to us now as Charlie) was three months old. I had to take the two girls for a walk every afternoon in the pram. I would do anything to have Mum love me, and I learnt in Penang through Auntie Lilly that being good got her approval.

My sister Amy would be in the front sitting in the stroller section, and the baby, Charlie, would be lying in the back pram section. I really resented having to look after another child, such that I was unable to ever love Charlie. The resentment got in the way. I was to find this out going through therapy in the early nineties many years later.

I found walking around the air base so lonely and wondered why nobody else did this; I felt our family was different. I was always very envious of all the other girls at school, whose mothers made their hair really nice or pretty, while mine was always pulled back off my face and plaited with a ribbon at the back. The other girls seemed to have nicer uniforms, as Mum made mine on her sewing machine.

Mum did her best, but she wasn't wonderful at sewing, having been self-taught. At this young age, I was learning the importance of appearance, and I wasn't happy with mine. Auntie Lilly always looked beautiful, and she did buy me some pretty dresses. Auntie Mabel made me some as well. These two aunties showed me the importance of looking pretty as a girl, and Mum always took good care of her appearance. This laid the foundations for later becoming a beauty therapist in adult life.

In 1964 on one of my school holiday visits to Auntie Lilly, she took me to see *Mary Poppins*, and I loved it. it was the first time I had ever been to the movies. On a further holiday in 1965 she took me to see *The Sound of Music* on the big screen. These experiences began a lifelong love of the movies. She also took me to see a play of *Alice in Wonderland*, and that also began a love of theatre.

Every year, she would take me to the Brisbane exhibition in August, and I would end up with all these sampler bags. Life at her house was like a completely different world, where I had fun and knew I was loved, and I always felt happy there.

It was in 1964 that Dad and Mum bought a hundred acres of land at Redbank Plains, which was halfway between Brisbane and Ipswich. We began going for picnics to "the Block," as we called it, every Sunday. It was all red dirt and bush in a large farming area that was all flat land, unsettled other than farms. The land they bought did not have electricity, rubbish removal, sewerage, water, or telephone, and there were no bitumen roads past it. The bitumen road from Goodna ended at the corner of our property. Goodna, an outer suburb of Brisbane, was close to a mental asylum, which meant no one wanted to live there in those days. There were a lot of new immigrants and some aboriginal people.

Redbank Plains was all farms with lots of old dolomite mines through it. There was a small, cleared area just inside the front gate of our property; the rest was bush. Dad and Jack started clearing it with axes, chopping down the trees. My parents saw a Danish architect who lived close by and before long started building a house on this land. Dad and this man, as well as my brother, worked on the house for a long time into the future on weekends.

Back at home at Amberley, I continued to take my sisters for walks in the afternoons. Sometimes, we went all the way up past the school to Wilson's shop, as I loved looking at all the gifts in there. I would get groceries for Mum. It was like a corner store that had everything. Jack and I would also go to visit the Hawthorne family.

The Hawthornes were a big family who had girls and boys our age, and we would play cricket, whilst Amy watched from the stroller section of the pram, and the baby Charlie was in the back. If Charlie cried, I would talk to her, but she was a good baby and hardly ever cried.

Mum always sounded so robotic when I got home saying the same things every night. "How was your walk?" Hardly waiting for an answer, she would continue with, "Well, hurry up now and get the girls bathed for tea."

I would dutifully run along and get my sisters bathed, after which we always had the evening meal as a family with Dad. The pot of tea following the meal was a real ritual every night. One thing I really remember about Amberley life is that we had lots of meals together as a family.

Dad would announce at every meal, "Now, everybody waits until everyone's here, and no one starts until all the family are seated." It sounded like some kind of ritual every meal.

I also recall all the games of Scrabble and Monopoly on the weekends with Jack, Mum, and Dad. These games were so much fun, with lots of laughter.

If I didn't take the girls for walks, I would go swimming some summer afternoons at the pool inside the air base section. I came to love swimming and bike riding, which have stayed with me all my life. I lost a number of pieces of jewellery that Mum had given me in that pool, causing her to become very upset with me. It had all started with losing that bracelet on the aeroplane going to Penang.

In 1965 in grade seven, I sprained my ankle while playing Vigaro, which is like a lady's game of cricket. I recall Dad coming to get me and taking me to Ipswich Hospital. The doctors and nurses strapped it up and gave me crutches. I came to realise that it was always Dad who was there for me when I needed someone.

In the same year, I played basketball at school. All the girls voted for who they wanted as captain, and they all voted me. I played centre. I should have been made captain, but I wasn't. Instead, another girl, Julie McKeown, was given the position, as her father was an officer, and my father wasn't. This had a major detrimental psychological impact on me. Through a child's eyes, I thought I was inferior or didn't deserve to be captain. Many years later, as an adult and going through therapy, I was able to undo this faulty thinking.

It was late 1965 when I was taking the girls for a walk that an almost tragic event took place. We went to the swimming pool, and I took Amy for a swim in the children's wading pool. Charlie was sitting in the stroller section of the pram watching us. She was about twenty-one months old, and somehow, she got out of the stroller. Beyond my view, she had gotten in the pool with us.

All I remember is turning around and seeing her bobbing up and down. She was drowning. I quickly got her out and then Amy out, putting Amy in the stroller. I tipped Charlie upside down to get all the water out and began mouth to mouth resuscitation. Eventually, she came around, and I grabbed everything and raced home. I was too scared to tell

Mum and Dad. The whole incident really frightened me, and Charlie remembers to this day nearly drowning.

Towards the end of grade seven, with only a few months to go before the end of the school year, my family moved to this property at Redbank Plains Road in Goodna. It was about a forty-five-minute drive from Brisbane City and half an hour from Ipswich City. Dad had sold his FJ Holden and bought a Volkswagen for economy with fuel, as he would be driving to Amberley every day for work, which was just under an hour drive each way.

# CHAPTER 3

# Adolescence Living in the Bush

## Isolated as a young teenager on acreage

We finally moved out of that air base, which made me very happy to move on. The base had never felt like home, with all the metal houses looking the same. And the general environment was so uninteresting to me, not like Penang. I had alwaysknown Amberley was temporary—that we would move on one day.

It was a few months following my twelfth birthday in October 1965 when the house at Redbank Plains was finally finished after twelve months of being under construction. I had to go to school every morning with Dad to Amberley and wait on the base every afternoon for him to bring me home from school.

Jack rode two and a half miles on his bike morning and afternoon to a bus that would take him to and from Bremer High School in Ipswich. He was in his first year of high school in grade eight.

Mum and Dad seemed very happy to have their own home. I was aware of all the difficulties they had gone through to build this home. I had watched the house being built through all of the different stages at our Sunday picnics. I had lived through all the years of them being extremely frugal in order to afford the house and Mum complaining that she never had enough money. Dad and Jack had worked hard, but what we didn't know then was that all the work was only just beginning for Jack and me.

It began with daily chores. First, every night, Jack and I had to do the washing up. I washed, and Jack dried. I then had to sweep out the kitchen and wash the floor every night. I truly did feel like Cinderella but would do anything to make Mum happy with me, just for her to love me.

Mum started teaching me how to cook tea, starting with the vegetables. I think I already knew how much she hated peeling those vegetables every night. But by this stage, I was quite desperate for her to love me. This was a change for me, and I was still adjusting to living in this new house and bush environment.

The house was a long, flat cement platform on the ground level with Besser Block walls outer and inner, lined with Gyprock board. There were huge hopper windows to most rooms, with big sliding doors off the lounge and dining room, which was an enormous combined space. The sliding doors led on to big patios that were a continuation of the cement slab. All the inside floors were white vinyl tiles, with the occasional green tile.

The house had four bedrooms with built-in cupboards. The roof was all metal and extended one end to include the garage. It had to be a big space, as it collected all the rainwater that was our water supply into a massive underground tank at the back of the house. Our water supply was then pumped into the house by an outside electric pump. Dad had bought Mum a new washing machine, a semi-automatic that had a water-saving feature that would reuse rinse water.

I was aware of all the insulation Dad had placed in the ceiling and walls to keep it warm in winter and cool in summer after living in that metal house at Amberley. They still had all the same 1950's furniture and frugally got it all recovered.

A china cabinet appeared against the wall between

the lounge and dining, and all these beautiful glasses and china appeared in it. A beautiful old wooden mantel clock appeared on top of the china cabinet and began chiming every hour. There were these ornamental brass figurines that also popped up all over the place, which they had obviously brought back from Penang.

There was a new bookcase in the far corner of the lounge, and Mum had three quarters of it filled with books. They must have had a lot of things in storage while we lived at Amberley to fit into that little house, and I began to understand why Mum seemed unhappy there.

I truly admired my father for creating this house in what I perceived to be isolated bush country. He had solved the sewage problem by taking the sewage away to septic tanks a long way from the house. Waste water went into sumps. It was my brother's job to empty the bathroom and laundry sumps every afternoon, putting the water on the gardens Mum and Dad had started creating.

There was no rubbish disposal, and my brother took all the rubbish down to a gully about half a kilometre from the house and burned it on a weekly basis. They had paid to have electricity and phone brought to the house.

The road in the distance in front of the house wasn't bitumen, and every vehicle that went by threw up all this red dust into the air. Dad was instrumental in forming "The Redbank Plains Progress Association." His first main project was to get the road in front of our house covered in bitumen and the school buses to come in reach of our house.

In the course of the last eighteen months, Dad had cleared a few acres around where we lived and fenced off a section; they soon acquired a cow in calf. A shed, the first dwelling Dad had put on the property, had been there since our early days, with its own water tank and stand. This provided water when we went on picnics. The shed housed all dad's stuff, and there were piles of wood and timber next to the shed.

It wasn't long before they had chooks who lived at the back of the tank to the shed. Snakes were a problem because of the bush being cleared and because they were attracted by the chooks, hiding in the piles of timber and tin. Dad got bees from Mr Guilfoyle, keeping about four hives. I was terrified of snakes from my Penang days and frightened of bees from my early Toowoomba days.

Jack and I would sometimes have to ride our bikes in the afternoon a few miles into Goodna to get Mum groceries at Johnson's shop. It was late 1965, almost the end of grade seven, and I was home from school and unaccustomed to the ride into Goodna. I was by myself on the return journey home when I came off the bike, landing in the scrub. I lay there for some time, later crawling out to the roadway. The spokes in the front wheel had sliced the bottom off my left foot.

A nice man stopped, picking me and my bike up, and drove me home. In some ways, I see I was lucky to strike a nice honest neighbour of ours. When Dad came home, he drove me to Ipswich Hospital, where they did the repairs, putting me on crutches. So, for the end of grade seven at Amberley State School, I was on crutches again. And by Christmas that year, I was fully healed.

Jack and I cut down a Christmas tree from the bush for Christmas 1965, with Amy choosing the tree. It was particularly memorable, with the tree hitting the ceiling in the house, and we all decorated it with a star at the top. The tree was a casuarina from the Australian bush, which looks like a Christmas tree. Amy and Charlie were excited about Santa Claus coming and loved the Christmas tree.

Mum was really happy, and there was music once again in our house, now filled with the sounds of *South Pacific*; the Platters; Perry Como; and, of course, Bing Crosby's Christmas album. That old 1950's radio took pride of place on top of the Kelvinator refrigerator, where it stayed all the years Mum and Dad lived there. Mum would often turn it on and listen to it, especially in the mornings. I began to equate music with happiness.

Mum always made a Christmas pudding, putting money as well as buttons in it every year. If you got a button in your serving, it meant you would be an old maid. I was always scared of getting a button. This year was the last year of shillings and pence, which could be put in a cooked pudding, being made of silver (the new dollars and cents wouldn't be). Mum was, therefore, collecting the old coins to put them in every year here after, cleaning and boiling them in order for them to be recycled each Christmas.

Many of Mum's and some of Dad's family came for Christmas dinner to our new house that year. I received for Christmas a full-length mirror to be placed on the wall in my bedroom. So began a habit of giving me mainly furniture, furnishings, or decorations for my bedroom every Christmas thereafter—until I left home, when I wasn't allowed to take any of them with me because they belonged to the house!

The next school year, 1966, came when I started high school at Bremer High in Ipswich, with Jack also attending. We left at seven thirty every morning to ride our bikes the long distance to the little blue bus. It came from Greenwich Village every day to the Redbank Plains State School and picked us up after dropping the children from the village at the state school. Greenwich Village was a street full of people out in the middle of nowhere.

The bus would then backtrack and pick up the high school students from the village and take us all to the high school. The bus was run by the Rice family, and everybody in the village was related in some way to the Rice family. It was like something you would only see on television.

Amy was six and a half and started school in grade one at Goodna State School. She went by school bus, which picked her up from the very end of our property. She would go with the Parkers, two girls who were one of our nearest neighbours. They were from the United Kingdom and had strong English accents.

There were about four farms between our home and where the little blue bus picked Jack and me up going out on the Plains. Down the other way, back towards Goodna where the Parkers lived, there was a street with a half a dozen house on it. Between our home and the first houses of Goodna, going all the way towards Goodna on Redbank Plains Road, there were three farms.

The year 1966 brought the arrival of decimal currency in Australia. There was a jingle that accompanied the television, radio, and cinema advertisements for the changeover to decimal currency, and it was sung to the tune of "Click Go the Shears":

> In come the dollars, in come the cents
>
> To replace the pounds, the shillings, and the pence
>
> So be prepared when the money starts to mix
>
> On the 14th of February 1966.

The new decimal currency was difficult to adjust to after it was first introduced. Living on acreage on a farm environment was also difficult to adjust to for me, and I never really ever did adjust. The cow, by now, had given birth to its calf and was being rounded up every evening by my brother to be milked by my mother.

Every evening, I would be handed this large bucket of milk, which I had to strain through cloth. By this stage, I was cooking tea every night and had to cook all kinds of different dishes to use the milk up, like custard, creamed rice, and soufflé. My brother had to collect the eggs every afternoon, along with his other jobs, including emptying the sumps and watering the gardens. Jack and I also had to rake up grass and leaves on the weekend, as Dad attempted to keep the grounds under control.

The chores our parents gave my brother and me to do were endless. I was looking after the girls when I got home from school, including bathing them before the evening meal. After cooking the meal and attending the milk, Jack and I had to clean up the kitchen after the evening meal. I washed the dishes; he dried. By the time I had swept and washed the floor, it would be nine o'clock and nearly eleven before I began my homework, as I needed some kind of break and shower after such a long day. I was determined to do well at school. I saw education a way of climbing my way out of the unhappy life I found myself living, which wasn't anything like the lives of any of my friends at school.

In 1966, I was thirteen years of age and got my first period. I had no idea what it meant. I had to wear great big Modess pads pinned to a holder, which was elastic and went around your waste. I found disposing of the pads embarrassing, as we didn't have a council garbage service, and my brother took the garbage down to the gully and burnt it. This was one of his chores.

## A working girl at fourteen

In July 1967, I turned fourteen and started employment at Rosalie Nursing Home as an assistant nurse doing an eight-hour Saturday day shift. My Auntie Mabel, Mum's sister, was a registered nurse and was in charge on the weekend and took me under her wing. I bought clothes and make-up with the money I made, as Mum did not buy me clothes. There was an Avon lady who worked at the home.

Every Saturday, Dad took me to the train. I caught it to Milton and walked to the home a short distance. I thought all the residents of the home were incredibly old and was fascinated by them. I earned five dollars for eight hours work. In those days this was a lot of money. This job started a desire to go into nursing. I saw it as an escape from the life I was leading. I could live in at the nurse's home, be working for a certificate, and earn an income. Work and education were both pathways out of the dreadful life I had at home.

It was after I started work that I began to learn to waterski on the Brisbane River at Goodna on Sundays. For the first time in my life, I felt great passion, and it was for waterskiing. I simply loved the exhilaration—the feeling of fun and freedom. It was like running on the top of the water.

Dad started coming along too some Sundays. It took six weeks to learn how to get up on the skis. I didn't have to cook tea on Saturday and Sunday nights anymore. The elusive butterfly of happiness definitely visited me every time I went waterskiing.

Dad seemed quite devoted to me, taking me to Goodna railway station and waiting for me when I caught the train back every Saturday. I had no idea how dangerous this journey was for a young girl, especially the short ten-minute walk to the nursing home, past and around a school that was closed on Saturday. At the back of my mind, I was aware of young girls being taken and brutally murdered.

I asked my parents what rape was and they explained it was "when a man attacks a woman and does terrible things." I also asked my mother what a prostitute was. She replied, "A lady who sleeps with a lot of different men." And I didn't understand why that was bad.

At school in the science class, we were studying human reproduction, and I asked the science teacher how the sperm met the egg. He told me to ask my parents. When I asked Mum and Dad, they told me to ask the science teacher. I was so naive due to the answers I got when I asked Mum and Dad, I sought answers about the world in magazines and newspapers.

I would go into Ipswich shopping and to see Auntie Mescal, Dad's sister, at times after school. I always took my white beauty case to work. This was very fashionable, for every young girl had a beauty case.

At the nursing home, I listened to the old ladies tell the stories of life in their day—days without electricity and with a toilet in the yard up the back, wood stoves, and an old copper to wash the clothes. The '60s were very modern times for these old ladies. The world is forever changing. It was a huge old home converted to a home for thirty-five ladies.

This was aged care in the late sixties. It was unregulated. I helped the ladies get dressed, some in bone corsets. I helped take meal trays out and feed those who needed help.

My auntie and I turned those who were bed bound every two hours and rubbed methylated spirits on their back and pressure points.

Some were restrained all day in chairs tied with lengths of cotton fabric. It was also my job to hose all the poo off of bed linen. Regardless of what I did, I knew I was happy helping the old ladies.

Eileen Edwards was the Avon lady—an assistant nurse, who looked after the downstairs where, there were seven ladies. Eileen came upstairs to the tea room and joined us for morning tea, lunch, and afternoon tea. On one occasion, Eileen and Auntie Mabel were discussing the contraceptive pill, which was introduced in the United Kingdom in 1967 and Australia in 1968. I said nothing, as I didn't understand. I was fifteen, and it was 1968.

Throughout these years, I kept in touch with Auntie Lilly and Auntie Vera by regular phone calls, and Dad would take the family to visit sometimes on Sunday. We also went to visit Mum's dad and her brother and his wife and children, driving up to Grantham.

In no time, another Christmas came—the Christmas of 1968. I was aware that Christmas was a very stressful and difficult time for our mother. This Christmas was more stressful than others because she was eight months pregnant. Jack and I chopped down a pine tree from the bush, and Amy helped, and we all decorated it. Mum made a Christmas pudding as usual with money and buttons in it. I had holidays from the nursing home over December 1968 January 1969. I had worked there for eighteen months.

## The home invasion and the beginnings of my PTSD

This was the same night that my mother was taken to hospital by ambulance at 3:00 a.m. in labour to have my brother Tony. Dad was in Williamstown on this night of the home invasion and flew up the next day to be with Mum.

What happened was, on January 15, 1969, at about 9:00 p.m., a man in a psychotic state high on drugs was attracted to our house on the outer fringes of town, where his friends had dropped him because he was uncontrollable and had had his drink spiked at a party. This all came out later in court. His name was Keith Joe Burnett. Our house was the only one with lights on, so he came to our house.

I was the first to see him standing in the yard peering at me. I quickly closed my window and ran and told my mother. Then my brother, mother, and I quickly ran around trying to lock all the doors and windows. Memories were triggered of Penang when the village had descended upon us. When he got to the last door, it took the three of us to get it shut and locked while he tried to push it open.

We turned all the lights out down one whole end of the house where the two girls were sleeping to keep them asleep. They slept through the whole night and were told very little in the morning so as not to frighten them.

The man jumped on our roof and walked over our roof. When he got down, he hurled abuse and threats. He thought I was his girlfriend and wanted to get to me. He began throwing pegs in through the open toilet window one by one, with a threat to burn the house down with each peg. There was no 000, and Mum had rung the police earlier.

We decided that my brother Jack would go to the nearest neighbour to get help. At that time, the nearest neighbour was about a kilometre away through bush in the dark. He badly injured his foot doing this. We, my mother and I, kept the man occupied around the back, whilst my brother left via the front.

The man had a branch from a tree and was rushing around madly smashing at doors and windows. Then he left for fifteen minutes and, in his bare feet, ran through the hot burning coals where we had been burning the rubbish near the road. He came back, and we did not know he'd returned. He entered through the laundry door, which must not have been locked properly. Our house had heaps of doors and windows. He picked up a screwdriver on his way through the laundry and came plunging at me with it. A scuffle between me and him took place. Mum ran off, coming back with a rifle I did not know we owned and pointed it at him and screamed, "If you don't get the fuck out of here, I'm gonna blow your balls off."

I was mortified. I didn't know what that meant and had never heard my mother swear.

My mother collapsed on the floor and said she was going into labour. I picked up the rifle; pointed it at the man; and yelled at him, repeating what my mother had said. He ran off back through all the burning coals. Some time went by; I don't know how long. I was helping Mum and frightened. I didn't know anything about how babies were born. I secured the laundry; afraid the man would come back.

Lights came up our driveway. Jack and Mr Parker, our neighbour, arrived. As they made to come in the dining room door, they saw the man hiding in the corner of the patio among the plants. They cornered him and kept him there. Not long after, about 2:30 a.m., the police arrived in two vehicles. They handcuffed him, and eventually, after much discussion, they took him away. They called an ambulance for Mum, and she left about 3:00 a.m. for hospital. The girls were told virtually nothing about this.

A court case followed about eight months later, and the Keith Joe Burnett was convicted of a string of offences, including home invasion. Dad told Jack and I after the incident to just get on with it, and we were told very little about the court case. After the court case, I was unaware I had blocked the whole incident from my memory until I was pregnant with my own child, and vague memories of him outside my window began returning.

After I had my son, I had total amnesia. The only memories I could remember were this absolutely terrifying incident in absolute detail and being beaten by my father in the garage—which I had also blocked out.

After this night, Dad flew up from Williamstown and was with Mum the next day when she gave birth to Anthony another boy, which Dad desperately wanted.

I was told I had to look after the new baby when Mum came home from hospital and could not return to school. Mum had apparently had something wrong with her heart, which was made worse by her giving birth. I pleaded with Dad to go back to school.

Eventually, he gave in—on the agreement I had to make all my own uniforms. So, we went into Ipswich and bought the material, and I got cracking on the sewing machine in late January 1969 and made all my uniforms for senior high school.

## Sweet sixteen and never been kissed

In July 1969, I turned sixteen. And not long after my birthday, man walked on the moon, Neil Armstrong. He said, "One small step for a man but a huge step for mankind." There had been a lot going on all year with the race between Russia and America to be the first on the moon.

I thought everybody had forgotten my birthday. It was two o'clock in the afternoon on a Saturday, and nobody had said happy birthday. Mum and Dad had just gotten home from shopping in Ipswich, and Dad presented me with a gold watch with a pearl face and said, "Sweet sixteen and never been kissed."

It was just after my birthday that year when Dad took me into Brisbane for an interview at Royal Brisbane Hospital for a 1971 intake to study as a registered nurse. I remember it all so well, including the matron interviewing me. Not long afterwards, I got a letter to say I had been accepted. I was thrilled and elated. I put a calendar up behind my door and began to cross the days off one by one. I was to start on January 5, 1971.

Jack had a part-time job at a meat factory and saved the money to buy a fancy stereo with great big wooden speakers, and we would play records. It took up a lot of space in the lounge. Jack bought the Beatles collection and played it often. The Beatles were huge. So were the Rolling Stones. All I knew was that Mum and Dad were heavily against the young music scene, and I was confused. All my friends at school went to record hops on the weekend, where they played spin the bottle. I, of course, wasn't allowed to go.

I couldn't wait to leave home and buy a transistor radio. It was very hip to have a "tranny"—sort of like the phone today. I equated music with happiness. Mum played music when she was happy. I remember the music from the stage play *Oklahoma*. Mum gave me some records for Christmas, little 45s. *Little Boxes*, *Que Sera Sera*, and *Mockingbird* were a few. These stayed in the house when I left home.

It was around this time there was a court case for the home invasion. Mum and Dad never told us much but that Keith Joe Burnett was convicted of a string of offences and that he was a nice young man who had been the victim of having his drink spiked at a party on the night. When he became uncontrollable on the night, his friends had dropped him on the edge of town, and he had gone to the first house with the light on, which was ours.

During the 1969 school holidays, my brother and I played Monopoly, and Mum and Dad played Scrabble as well as Monopoly with us on weekends. I was aware at the time that these were really happy memories.

I also remember the TV shows. Mum, Jack, and I would watch *Happy Days* together, and it was fun. Jack and I also watched *The Jetsons*, which was about space travel; *Bonanza*; *The Flintstones*; *The Munsters*; and *Beverley Hillbillies*. And my brother watched *Countdown*, a show about modern music. *Hey Hey It's Saturday* with Jackie McDonald was also a classic. At night, Mum and Dad watched *Homicide*, which we were not allowed to watch. I would sneak up to the end of the hall and watch it without them knowing. They also watched *Hawaii Five-O* and *'66 Sunset Strip*.

In 1969, Jack turned eighteen, and I was worried he would be called up for national service and be sent to Vietnam. Australia had a system where birthdates for men turning eighteen were drawn out of a barrel, and those drawn had to do national service army training.

I cut Jack and Dad's hair, and Dad also got me to cut his

toenails and massage his scalp and face. These activities laid the foundations for me to later become a beauty therapist.

In 1970, Jack repeated senior year, so we did grade twelve together. He started smoking, as all the rebels smoked. It was very cool in those days to smoke. Some 70 per cent of the population smoked in 1970—and did so in all public spaces.

I was embarrassed by my brother's rebellious behaviour. In 1969 and 1970, the school bus now came within a short walk of our house. So, we no longer had to ride our bikes two and half miles to catch the bus. Dad was instrumental in forming the Redbank Plains Progress Association and getting the bus for us to our house.

Throughout my last two years of high school, I continued to work at the nursing home with my auntie on Saturdays and some Sundays. I went waterskiing on some Sundays. This made me very happy. I had gotten all the confirmation material that I had been accepted into nurse training, and I would get it out at least once a week and read it. I simply couldn't wait.

Throughout my last few years at home, I slept with three Siamese cats. Mum and Dad bred Siamese cats and had a cattery. This began a lifelong love of cats. They also had a bull terrier named Penny, who they got after the home invasion. They then began breeding bull terriers.

In my senior year, 1970, I was elected a prefect—something I thought was such an honour. I also completed the Duke of Edinburgh Award scheme to silver level.

Towards the end of 1970, we had speech night. I was in grade twelve, my senior year, and once again took out the home science prize, having received it in grade ten, my junior year. I had to have a white dress for the night, and Mum bought me one but took it back after the night.

I bought my own clothes, a few, with the earnings from

the nursing home. Most of them I sewed on the sewing machine. Dad bought me a Toyota sewing machine for my seventeenth birthday.

In those last few years at home, I was very aware of my body changing. When I had my periods, it was horrible, without the large array of sanitary products on the market today. I was embarrassed taking a bath, as my brother and father would come in the room to wash their hands, and I had developing breasts.

Our aunties and uncles would drop over to see us, and I longed to meet this uncle we weren't allowed to know. I'd heard them talk about Uncle Mike. I didn't understand what this was all about and why I could not know him.

In 1970, a groundbreaking event happen for the LGBT community, which was to open the way forwards for acceptance and tolerance of the "gay" community. Two lesbians went on ABC television declaring their love for each other. It was never illegal for women, only men. This event shocked Australia.

Auntie Mescal, Uncle Mike's twin, worked at a clothing outlet in Ipswich Rockman's, and I would sometimes go into Ipswich after school to see her. I always wished she was my mother, as my mother didn't seem to want me, and I knew Auntie Mescal loved me. I bore an incredible resemblance to her.

I remember being in Rockman's with Mum and my auntie being fitted for my first bra. My mother screamed loudly, "She doesn't need one. She hasn't got anything." Meanwhile, the science teacher at school peered down the front of my sports uniform at my developing breasts.

I longed to know my grandmother. She was dad's mum, but Mum wouldn't allow us to know dad's mum. Our family was so fractured.

I was aware of what other teenagers were doing, and it was not the life I was living. They didn't have the domestic workload I had; only a few of them worked. The music scene was really big, with the Beatles and the Rolling Stones and the Carpenters, was all I knew.

I was confused by all the negative stuff my parents were filling me with. I couldn't wait to leave home and explore the world. While my friends went to record hops, the only event I ever went to was the end-of-term school dance. In the last term of high school, I was chaperoned by this boy's mother to the pictures with her son.

Happy memories from this era included Jack and my yearly Christmas ritual of going down into the bush and chopping down the Christmas tree and bringing it home and everybody decorating it. It was definitely a family bonding experience—of which we had so few.

Another would be the family evening meal when everybody sat together and ate and talked. There was always a pot of tea served at the end of it, and all my life I have finished a meal with a cup of tea. Dad stopped the traditional Sunday drives once we moved to Redbank Plains. But occasionally, we would do this and visit Auntie Mabel and Uncle Reg.

The last few years at home were hard, studying for my final senior leaving education and working part-time, combined with the heavy workload at home. I was required to look after baby Anthony and the girls when I wasn't at school and do all the cooking if not at work, which meant an evening meal for a family of seven. Takeaway those days was fish and chips, which we had occasionally on a Friday night.

I also had to strain a bucket of milk from the cow every night, do all the washing up and cleaning up, and wash my clothes. By the time I finished at night, it was nine o'clock, and by the time I rested (having not stopped since lunchtime at school) as well as showered, it was 10:00 p.m. to start my homework. I worked until 2:00 or 3:00 a.m., and I had to get up at 6:00 a.m. to start all over again. Mum would call loudly, "*Anthea, Anthea.*" And she would complain I was a sleepyhead and that she couldn't wake me up.

I can honestly say I hated living at home and couldn't wait to leave. Nursing was an escape. School and work were escapes. I really wanted to go to university—free in those days; just buy your books. As I explained in an earlier chapter, early to mid-'60's women were beginning to go out to work. And by the late '60s, there was an acceptance of women going to university. The family unit was still mum and dad and the kids, two or four or more.

Despite all the hardship of my teenage years, the elusive butterfly of happiness did visit me at times. I, by now, knew what happiness felt like. I think because I endured so much sadness as my mother never kissed or hugged me or made me feel wanted. I felt like Cinderella or a slave in a prison released to go to school and work.

I believe that, in many ways, my teenage years were stolen from me. I knew I had to leave, and nursing was the only way out. It gave me a new home in the nurse's quarters. It gave me a job, a career, and a qualification at the end of it.

# CHAPTER 4

# After I left Home: A Babe in the Woods

## Early training days

The day had finally come January 5, 1971, and I was leaving home to start nursing training at Royal Brisbane Hospital. It was the afternoon of a hot, humid January day in Brisbane with a storm on the horizon. I was all dressed in a lilac dress I had made—above the knee, of course, fashionable at the time.

My suitcase was all packed. I wasn't allowed to take books I had been given or ornaments. Other gifts to me belonged to the house—like the bed, desk, bedspread, mat, and full-length mirror. But I didn't care. These were just things, and I could work and buy new things.

It was hard saying goodbye to Anthony, as I had looked after him since he was a baby home from hospital. At 2:00 p.m., Dad drove me to the hospital, and I said my goodbyes. I was, in some way, sad but very excited. I simply couldn't wait to begin a new life. We had to meet in a big hall on the ground level of one of three tall thirteen-story buildings, all shaped like three sides of a box. In the middle of the buildings there was a small office called the reception.

I was shown to my room on the twelfth floor of one of the thirteen-floor buildings. It was a small room with a bed, wardrobe, desk, and chair. You could walk out to an enclosed balcony and hang small washing or sit in a relaxing chair. On the bed was a bag of uniforms, including caps, and a bag of buttons which were reusable attaching to the uniform with a small clip at the back. I proceeded to make a uniform and cap up. It was a plain white cap with no stripes. I noted that it was 4:20 p.m.

Before long, a fifty-something plump lady came. She had blonde/silver curly hair and said her name was Vivienne, announcing she had come to take us to tea. There were about ten of us on the floor, and we followed Vivienne into the lift and down to the first floor, where we joined another group of girls. Then we all took off, following Vivienne through the building and outside through the garden, which was full of white butterflies and some that were gold and black. We then all went down a very steep hill lined with tree, to the dining room.

We all lined up with our trays and chose what we wanted, telling the café attendant, and she put it on a plate. I chose cottage pie, my favourite. You then collected your cutlery and a desert if you wanted it. I chose a table and sat with other girls from my floor. They had come from all over the state—from Roma, Longreach, and Toowoomba.

I felt local, though the hospital was an hour's drive from home at Redbank Plains. We chattered on, all seventeen and were so, soo excited. The dining hall was full of excited chatter. A lady came and took all our dishes. I thought, *how absolutely wonderful.* I didn't have to wash up, and I didn't have to cook either. I didn't express this, as I didn't want to feel different.

Vivienne was waiting at the door for us, and another twenty girls were waiting to come in, standing with a lady who looked similar to Vivienne. So, we all assembled in the foyer of this huge dining hall waiting to go back up that steep hill. Doctors and nurses began coming in to get their tea.

So, out we went still, all chattering, back up that steep hill, which would become so much a part of my life. It connected the nurse's quarters to the hospital. Halfway up the hill was the doctor's quarters on the left-hand side, so we were told.

On getting back up to the entrance to the nurse's quarters, we were shown a small office. This was where Vivienne was stationed when on shift. It was where you signed out if going out, and you had to be back in by midnight or signed out going on days off. It was the headmistress's office where you went if you had a problem. We were taken back to the lift to go up to the twelfth floor to our rooms and told to meet at 7:30 p.m. for cocoa in the big hall we'd first met in, which was in the building directly opposite ours.

So, I made my way back to my room, talking to Dell and Jeanette, who were both on my floor. They were as excited as I was. We continued talking on reaching our floor, standing in the foyer where there was a phone to make calls from and also another phone to take incoming calls, both attached to the wall. We could hear names being paged over a loudspeaker, and if your name was called, you picked up the phone to take your call. The calls were answered in the reception downstairs (the office in the middle of the buildings).

We were standing outside the bathroom, which we all decided to inspect. There were five-bathroom cubicles for the floor. The other girls decided to take a shower, and I thought I would have mine later, so I went to my room. We agreed to meet at 7:20 p.m. in the foyer to go down for cocoa. I was so exhausted I lay on the bed. It was 6:20 p.m., and I thought I would rest until time for cocoa. I couldn't believe I was finally here at the hospital in my room. I thought about home and what I would be doing—washing dishes. The room was small, but I didn't care.

In no time, it was 7:20 p.m., and I quickly got up and straightened my hair, put my shoes back on, and raced out into the foyer. The girls were waiting for me. We pushed the button for the lift, and it made this huge bumping noise as it ascended to our floor, which was to become so familiar in the days ahead.

The lift opened, and a whole group of us got in. Down it went to first floor, and we then walked across the distance of the middle building to the building opposite ours and down some stairs to the hall. It was literally packed with young girls chattering and all drinking cocoa. There were apparently 122 girls and 2 boys in the intake.

I caught up with Gail, who had been at school at Bremer High with me. She had left in grade eleven to start at the hospital, doing a cadetship running mail and items all around the hospital. It was so great to catch up. Gail was a tall, blonde-haired girl who wore glasses. She introduced me to a number of girls, one of whom was Wendy, a short, tiny girl who was to become a good friend. Soon it was time to leave, as there were ladies packing up the cups.

Wendy, Gail, and I decided to check out the TV room, which was on the first floor in the middle building on the way back to the lift for my building. The TV room was close to the headmistress's office. Wendy liked to watch TV and stayed in this room with Gail. After exchanging room numbers, I moved on and back to my room, feeling very clever that I'd found my way back.

I unpacked on getting back to my room and thought about how I could make the room nice. Suddenly, it was nine o'clock, and I thought I'd best take a shower, which I proceeded to do. I met more girls in the bathroom while taking a shower. We all talked while showering.

It seemed I had made a lot of new friends in such a short space of time. I finally got back to my room and got dressed for the night. I decided to sit outside on the balcony and just relax and watch the lights until I was tired enough to go to bed.

Finally, it was 10:00 p.m., and I thought I should go to bed. I set the alarm for 5:30 a.m. so I could go down for breakfast. I got into bed and felt the safest I had done for a few years. I thought how an intruder would have to come up twelve floors to get to my room.

I lay awake thinking about the day. So much had happened. Eventually, I drifted off to sleep with the sound of girls chattering outside my door. It seemed I'd just gone to sleep and the 5:30 a.m. alarm went off.

I got up and got dressed in street clothes and headed down for breakfast with a couple of the other girls. We had cereal and bacon and eggs, as well as toast. We sat talking for a short while before heading back up that steep hill. I finally made it back to my bedroom by 7:00 a.m. and tidied up, making the bed.

I got dressed in the nurse's uniform, tucking the uniform up under the belt, as miniskirts were in fashion at the time. I secured my hair up under the cap and attached the cap with hairpins. I think I looked the part. I then waited in the foyer for Janette and Dell.

Soon, we were all together, commenting on how we all looked. It was time to head off to the big hall, as the whole group had to meet there at 8:00 a.m. We found our way down the lift, across the distance of the middle building, down some stairs, and into the hall. We stood and talked, finding it difficult to hear each other above the chatter of

120 other student nurses, with the noise echoing off wooden floorboards and wooden walls.

A female voice came in over the loudspeaker. "Could I have your attention, please."

Our attention was directed to four middle-aged ladies in nurse's uniforms to the knee and wearing white veils, all standing on the stage section. They were called sisters. "We will be dividing you into four groups. Please come forward when you hear your name called."

So, everybody listened for his or her name and dutifully assembled in front of the stage when his or her name was called. The first group, called group 1, was complete and took off following one of the sisters out of the hall to a classroom.

Finally, my name, plus Dell's and Janette's and those of the two men, were called. And we became part of group 2. Soon we were heading off after another one of the sisters to a classroom. The classrooms were close to the nurse's quarters in the children's hospital. We all found a seat, and I found myself sitting next to one of the men. It was explained to us this was the first day of a six-week "block," meaning we'd spent six weeks solid in the classroom paid study.

Before long, it was announced there was a photographer from *The Courier-Mail* arriving soon to take a photograph, as this was the first intake at the Royal Brisbane Hospital to have men in it. In no time, I was having my photograph taken with this young man beside me. It was going to be on the front page of the paper the next day.

We were then given an overview of the six weeks and a set of books. It was to include medical nursing, surgical nursing, microbiology, psychology, anatomy and physiology, lifting techniques, bed making and housekeeping, observations and documentation, and nutrition and diet and practicals.

We had to pass the exams at the end of the six weeks to be released to the wards. We would then come back to the classroom one day a week for three months. At the end of each three-month cycle, there were two weeks of study block, which meant solid study in the classroom.

The first thing we learnt was handwashing. It was morning teatime, and it was brought to the room on a great big tea trolley. It was a chance to chat and see how everyone was feeling. We were all running on adrenalin, so excited about our first day. More lectures ensued and then a demonstration bed making.

We all took turns teaming up with someone and making the bed in the classroom. It had a life-sized dummy to put in it. Tomorrow, we would learn to make a bed with someone in it.

Suddenly it was lunchtime—twelve midday—and we followed our tutor sister to the children's hospital dining room, which was similar to the main hospital dining room. I really enjoyed lunch. It was roast lamb and fruit salad with ice cream for dessert. I could hear Janette say, "Wow, that was a good lunch."

There was a lady clearing dishes, asking us to move on, as the dining room was so busy. Group 3 was coming at 12:30 p.m., and group 4 would be there at 1:00 p.m. We left, going to the reception, which was that small building on ground level in the middle of the three tall buildings. I had a message from home asking me to call home and tell them how my first day had gone.

We quickly headed for the classroom, as it was almost 12:30 p.m., and we were due back. Back into lectures, and I found my mind drifting somewhere else—to the garden with the butterflies. I found it difficult to focus. Had I found happiness? I certainly felt very happy.

I started taking notes, as I had to pass the exams at the end of these six weeks. Soon following afternoon tea, we did practicals. We had to wash our hands and make a bed. We all passed, and it was 4:30 p.m.—time to go back to our rooms and, afterwards, the evening meal.

I collapsed on my bed and awoke a short time later with Gail knocking on my door. "C'mon, Ant. Aren't you going to join us for tea?"

I quickly got myself together and, still in my uniform, went with the girls down in the lift through the middle building, down out into the garden, and down the steep hill to reach the main dining room. We all got our tea and sat at the same table. Gail and Wendy were in a different class to me, so it was good to compare notes.

We once again found our way back to the nurse's quarters, and Gail showed me her room so I could visit her. She and Wendy were going to the TV room, and I went back to my room. On the way, I rang home, telling my family my picture was going to be on the front page tomorrow. I rattled on to Mum about the day and all I had done, saying I had learnt to wash my hands and make a hospital bed.

I went afterwards and had a shower. I waited till 7:20 p.m. to go down for cocoa at 7:30 p.m. in the hall, after which I went up to my room, got into my nightie, and went to bed. I sort of felt uncomfortable and discovered someone had short-sheeted my bed. I had to get up and make it again.

It was 8:30 p.m., and I found myself drifting off, only to be woken by two girls in the bedroom, Sue and Anna. I had met them the night before whilst taking a shower. They were one year ahead of me in training, and it was obviously them who had short-sheeted my bed. Both asked, "How's your bed, Ant, comfortable? How's your day been?"

We sat talking some more for half an hour. They then left, turning the light back out, and I finally fell asleep.

The next thing I knew it was 5:30 a.m., and the alarm was sounding. I was in the middle of a dream and momentarily went back to sleep. I awoke to Janette knocking on my door. I said, "Come in."

Janette poked her head around the door and announced, "Dell and I will meet you in the foyer in ten minutes to go down for breakfast."

I said, "OK. Sounds good."

In no time, we were sitting at breakfast, and then back we went up that big hill. I soon was once again in my room preparing for a new day. Sue walked past my door and knocked, saying, "Have a good day." She was just finishing night shift.

I yelled out, "Thank you. Have a good sleep."

I continued to get ready and managed to make it to the classroom by 8:20 a.m. for 8:30 a.m. for the second day, Tuesday. We sat in the same seats. The morning was three hours of anatomy and physiology, separated halfway by morning tea. This was very tough going. There was a real-life full skeleton in the room. I looked forward to lunch this day. Everybody said at lunch how they'd found the anatomy and physiology tough and difficult to remember.

In no time, the day was over, and I was having tea with Wendy, Gail, and a girl called Jill. After tea, Gail decided to show us the hospital kiosk/shop. It was at the Gilchrest Avenue entrance to the hospital not far from the main dining room. There on a stand was *The Courier-Mail* newspaper, and right on the front page was a picture of myself and Robert beside me. I was staggered. I bought two copies.

Gail took us back to the quarters through a different route. She knew her way around, having been a cadet at the hospital for twelve months before starting training. We went up Gilchrest Avenue and then through the children's hospital, entering where casualty was and going up about fifteen very long cement stairs in a pathway to reach the top, not far from the reception at the quarters.

I left the girls there and went to my room. The week just flew by. And before I knew it, it was the weekend. It was Saturday morning, and I was sleeping in. I missed breakfast. I went down for lunch and sauntered through the garden with the butterflies. It was a hot January day, and there were plenty of butterflies and bees. I felt so free and so happy. On the way back, I picked a few daisies to put in my room, which I did on arriving back at my room. I rested for a couple of hours.

Then I decided to check out the swimming pool. I arrived down there at three o'clock and stayed till 5:00 p.m., either swimming or lazing beside the pool. I spent time in reflection, thinking over the past week. The following day, Sunday, I spent the whole afternoon at the pool. I loved swimming after the beach at Penang and the swimming pool at Amberley and then waterskiing in my teens. I spent a lot of time at the pool in my training years.

Sunday came, and I spent all morning sleeping; I was utterly exhausted. I attended the laundry of the uniforms, putting them in the laundry bag with a laundry form to say who I was and what was contained. You had to take all the buttons off and then put the bag down the laundry chute. I got an early night after going down for cocoa and catching up with some of the girls.

The second week came and went so quickly. A highlight of the week was collecting our first pay on the Thursday. We had to go down the main hospital to the pay office and all line up to receive our envelope with cash, signing for it. I received $279 after board and lodging were deducted and was absolutely over the moon with happiness. I had thoroughly enjoyed the two weeks; getting paid seemed a bonus.

Before long, it was the weekend. I decided to catch a bus into the valley shopping hub on the Saturday morning. The shops were only open to midday on a Saturday and closed on a Sunday. Going shopping in the valley was something I did regularly throughout my training days. There was this big department store called McWhirters, where I visited the music and clothing sections. I bought a transistor radio and a maxi dress, which had just become fashionable.

The mini had gone as high as it could go in 1970, and fashion designers brought out the maxi dress. I looked at the boots that were very popular. I put on layby a pair of suede knee-highs with tassels down the side. I checked out the record shop. There were several with listening bays that had headphones, enabling customers to listen to music before buying it. But there wasn't time. I headed back to the hospital in time for a late lunch.

The third week flew by, just as the second had. And on that weekend, I went out to visit my Auntie Lilly and Uncle Joe, catching a taxi there to Chermside, ten minutes from the hospital. Uncle Joe met me at the taxi, carrying my bag into the house, which smelt like freshly baked muffins.

Auntie Lilly was known for her delicious muffins and greeted me with a big hug and a kiss on the cheek. "How are you, darling?" she asked and continued with, "Why don't we go out on to the veranda and have a drink?"

Uncle Joe piped up. "What would you like, my dear, Cinzano or Pimm's?" Both of these were popular drinks for ladies at the time. I opt for a Cinzano, as this was their way of showing me, they accepted me as an adult. Going out to see and stay with Auntie Lilly and Uncle Joe was something I did regularly throughout my training days.

The fourth and fifth week was heavy going with study and doing practicals down on the wards. On the fifth weekend, I went out to Rosalie Nursing Home to visit my Auntie Mabel and all the old ladies. I arrived at lunchtime and brought a cake from the pastry shop. It was great catching up with Auntie Mabel, who I knew loved me to bits, and I loved her heaps too. This was something I did as often as I could when I had a Saturday off.

In the sixth week, we sat exams on the Tuesday and Wednesday, getting our results on the Friday. I passed, thank goodness. Eleven people failed and consequently had to drop out. We all had our photos taken as a group on the Thursday in the grounds of Lady Lamington Nurses Home.

On the Friday, we got our allocation to the wards and were able to visit the wards for our next two-week roster. I got sent to the radium institute and had the Monday and Tuesday as days off, giving me four days off at the end of the six weeks. I decided to go home to Redbank Plains to my family.

I signed out of the nursing home at Vivienne's office then went shopping on the Saturday morning. Afterwards I caught the train from the Valley to Goodna, which took thirty minutes. Dad met me at the station, and I got home at 1:15 p.m. Everyone was excited to see me and congratulated me on passing my exams. Mum, Dad, and I sat out on the front patio and drank cider to celebrate.

I stayed in Jack's room, as he had moved out, and Amy had moved to my room. Mum treated me well on this stay. She cooked, and I washed up. Mum and Dad took me around the garden, showing me all the new plants, they had planted. I played hide-and-seek with Anthony. He was so happy to see me. Charlie had drawn some drawings for me, telling me how much she had missed me.

I went home about every six weeks.

## My first day on the wards

I arrived back at the nursing home Tuesday afternoon late, just before the evening meal, about 4:30 p.m. In my room were notes from girls who had visited me while I was away on the days off. One was from Gail Shepherd asking me to leave her my roster in her room and leaving me her roster in my room. Another was from a girl in my class, Carol Watson, saying she had organised some ten-pin bowling at Exhibition Bowl just up the road and was getting together a group of twelve interested girls. I was invited to join. She asked me to let her know.

I went down to tea. On the way back, I visited Carol and Gail's rooms. I ran into another girl from our class, Carol Symons, who told me she was joining the bowling nights.

On getting back to my room, I took a long hot shower in readiness for an early night. The next day was a big day, my first day on the wards at the Radium Institute.

I shined my brown leather nursing shoes and prepared the heavily starched uniform cap and belt. I put out a petticoat, which was compulsory to wear under the uniform. I went to cocoa in the hall, catching up with a lot of girls. I called into the TV room on the way back to see if Wendy was there, but someone said she was working.

I got back to my little abode in which I was so happy, so high in the sky; I felt safe. It seemed no time, and the alarm went off at 5:30 a.m.—in time for me to work my

6:30 a.m. to 3:00 p.m. shift. I dragged myself out of bed, getting dressed. I was so proud, wearing the uniform and white cap. I was down to breakfast by 6:00 a.m. and then up seven floors on B Block, arriving ten minutes early as we were told to do.

Handover by the night staff to the day staff was at 6:30 a.m. sharp. Then the sister in charge showed me around the ward. She showed me a time sheet, on which I had to have a nursing sister (called RN today) sign me on and sign me off.

She showed me the ladies in bed with big thick lead barriers each side of the bed, which rolled up and down the sides of the bed. These ladies had radium inserted vaginally. I never really understood why, and the barriers were to protect the nurses. I know the radium had something to do with cancer of the reproductive organs.

She showed me the oncology section, split into a male and female section. There were women who'd had breast cancer and had consequently lost an entire breast. These were days when, if you had breast cancer, you underwent a full mastectomy, losing the whole breast. You stayed in hospital for three weeks, went home for three weeks, and then came back in again for chemotherapy, which was very heavy duty.

There were men who'd had prostate cancer and who'd had surgery. They had an indwelling catheter (IDC) inserted into the bladder, as well as a bag hanging up to irrigate the catheter every four hours. There were patients with leukaemia who were dying, and I found that difficult. But I found the ladies who were bed bound behind the lead barriers the most difficult of all. They required pans for toileting and had full bed baths. I was worried I would become infertile from the exposure to radium, so I kept behind the barriers.

The sister in charge went back to her duties, telling me to get everybody ready for breakfast, which arrived in a big food trolley at 7:00 a.m. It was the job of the sister in charge to serve the meals from the food trolley to plates on trays, which nurses then took out to bed-bound patients. Ambulant patients lined up and got their own breakfast given to them. I had to assist a couple of the oncology patients to eat their breakfast.

After breakfast, it was clearing the dishes into a very high silver trolley, which all the trays slid into. Kitchen staff came up and collected the trolleys and took them to the kitchen. We just pushed them outside the ward into the corridor. Then there was writing up the fluid balance charts. All the patients had a chart at the end of their bed on a clipboard. The sister was giving out tablets on a tray of medicine cups with each patient's name above their medicine cup of tablets.

I was busy giving out pans and taking them away, as well as cleaning them. The pans were never-ending in this ward. It was hard finding time to go to the toilet myself. The bed bath basins of warm water with towels were given out so that people who couldn't shower could have a bed bath. The curtains were all pulled around them.

All the beds got linen changes daily. Changing all the sheets of the beds with ladies in them was quite time-consuming. We worked in pairs for bed making, taking a dirty linen skip with us. Everybody helped with bed making, even the sister in charge.

Soon it was 10:00 a.m., and I went for morning tea at the main dining room. I was so relieved to get a break. I sat with the sister in charge (with whom I was not on a first-name basis) and a few of the other nurses at the same table.

I met an assistant nurse Sandra Bussey (known as Bussey), who wore a green cap for assistant nurses. She was permanent at The Radium Institute. She and I were to become friends and stayed that way the whole of my training days. Sandra lived in quarters down at women's hospital.

In no time—ten minutes goes fast—it was time to go back to the ward so others could go for morning tea. On arriving back, I was shown the instrument steriliser and asked to do some sterilising, after being shown how to operate it. I was petrified of this medium-sized metal tunnel with steam blowing out of it.

The cheatles, huge forceps/tongs, with their container had to be sterilised daily. They were used for lifting things in and out of this steriliser, and the container they lived in, had pink chlorhexidine with anti-rust in it. So, I dutifully washed them in detergent and water, dried them, and placed them in the steriliser, doing up the door as hard as I could. =

I then, as scared as hell, turned the steriliser on. It made a huffing and a puffing noise, blew steam, and then kinda hummed. I came back fifteen minutes later to find they were all done and was rescued by Bussey telling me not to open it until it cooled down, or it would blow steam at me!

I was told to shake all the thermometers down in readiness for the two o'clock "obs" (observations). All these mercury thermometers sat in two little oblong metal containers soaking in pink chlorhexidine. I was required to shake them all down one by one and told, if I broke any, it would be deducted from my pay. My wrist ached at the end of prepping forty thermometers.

The meal trolley for lunch came to the ward at 11:30 a.m., and the same procedure as breakfast followed. At 12:30 p.m., I was sent for my lunch with Bussey and another nurse with two stripes on her cap. She was in her second year and seemed to be doing a lot of the medications, as well as looking after the drips (intravenous fluid administration).

I was told to call the sister in charge, Sister Armstrong. I really enjoyed lunch. I had roast lamb and fruit salad with ice cream for dessert. I saw some of the other girls from my class, and there were a lot of quick hellos.

Twenty-five minutes went quickly, and it was time to get back to the ward by 1:00 p.m. There were still fluid balance charts to write up. It was an opportunity to talk to the patients about lunch and anything else they wanted to discuss.

At a quarter to two (1:45 p.m.), the 2:00 p.m. "obs" started, with three nurses helping. There were two thermometer trays, each holding two small oblong metal dishes a little bigger than a thermometer and five centimetres deep. One metal dish held shaken down thermometers; the other metal dish was half full of pink chlorhexidine for the dirty thermometers. Each thermometer tray was set up like this.

So, we began. I helped Bussey. The thermometer was placed under the tongue. Then the pulse was taken, pressing two fingers just inside the wrist down from the thumb and counting silently using a nurse's fob watch, which was pinned up high on our uniforms. We counted for a minute, noting the quality of the beat and any irregularities. We then counted the respirations (breaths) for a minute. By this time, the thermometer was ready to be read, and this took some practise. It was then all recorded on a chart at the end of the bed.

The nurse with two stripes took any blood pressures that had to be taken. Not everybody had blood pressure taken. It was taken using a cuff and a sphygmomanometer, which is something that puts air pressure into the cuff and slowly, in a controlled way, lets the air down whilst the operator listens with a stethoscope to the pulse beat in the blood vessel.

When the air pressure equals the pressure in the vessel, the beat will cut out and come back in again when the heart is at rest, measuring the lower reading.

The afternoon staff came on at 2:15 p.m., when they got handover. At 2:30 p.m., the day staff all went to afternoon tea. When we came back, the afternoon staff went to afternoon tea. While they were at tea, I put my request in the roster request book to have Monday evenings off to go bowling.

I also did a swap shift request form to have the coming Monday evening off. Three o'clock came, and it was time to go home to the nurse's home. I had done many things in my day that I would do hundreds and hundreds of times in my training days and in nursing years beyond training.

## Freedom at last and nursing days

The next day was Thursday, and I was back in the classroom for a study day. This happened every Thursday for our group from 8:30 a.m. to 5:00 p.m. It was difficult to adjust to sitting all day and concentrating after being so physically active the day before. We spent the first three hours on anatomy and physiology. After lunch, we studied microbiology before afternoon tea and medical nursing after tea break, learning about diabetes.

The study of diabetes hasn't changed a lot to this day. What has changed is that better insulins are available, in addition to better ways of administering insulin with insulin pens and better drugs for non-insulin-dependent diabetes. Better diet control and meal preparation is also present today.

Study days were a good way of catching up with all the girls and guys. Also, it was one night you always knew you had off. I took heaps of notes. I wrote everything down to stay awake. When 5:00 p.m. came, we all headed off to the main dining room for our evening meal through the garden with the butterflies and down that steep hill. A few of us walked back via Gilchrest Avenue to get some exercise, calling in at reception to pick up our mail and messages.

The next day, Friday, I was working a late shift, the first of six shifts in a row. That meant working the weekend, which was at a higher pay rate with penalties.

I spent the whole morning down at the pool covered in coconut oil and basking in the sun. I just loved this pool. I listened to my transistor radio on station 4IP, "the station" that all young people listened to. Every now and again, the news would come on about all the war and unrest in the world. The IRA was throwing bombs in the United Kingdom. There was the war in Vietnam, which polarised the world with different opinions. The PLO was creating war in the Middle East in Lebanon and Israel. I didn't like hearing about all this war.

I loved listening to the music, especially Creedence Clearwater Revival with "Bad Moon Rising" and "Lookin' out my Back Door" and any Beatles or Rolling Stones songs, as well as Bob Dylan with "The Times They Are a Changin'." There were updates about peace protests, which were happening all the time. Though I wanted peace, I didn't want to go to a protest. There was a punk music movement starting, and I really wasn't into this sort of music.

I went to lunch at the children's hospital dining room, which was very close—a five-minute walk and no hill. Then I went back to my room, showered, and got ready for my first evening shift. I arrived at the Radium Institute ward at 2:05 p.m. for a 2:15 p.m. start.

After handover, we said hello to all the patients, and

then it was time for afternoon tea. At 3:00 p.m., the day staff went home, and Bussey and I collected all the water jugs and glasses. Washing, drying, and returning them with fresh water to the lockers was an evening staff duty. Every ward had a kitchen attached.

We had to clean and tidy the top of the lockers before returning the jug and glass to the locker. There were always pans to give out and take back on this ward. At 5:00 p.m., the tea trolley arrived. The sister in charge served up the meals from the trolley. The first lot of staff going for tea went at 5:00 p.m. I was with the second group and went at 5:30 p.m.

On arriving back to the ward, there were charts to write up and final clearing up after tea. Then we gave out bowls of warm water to everybody to wash and get changed into their night-time attire. Some patients needed help. At 7:30 p.m., the supper trolley came around.

We had to go around to all the patients and ask them if their bowels had moved and document it on the chart at the end of the bed, reporting to the sister in charge anyone more than two days not opened. We were allowed to have our supper in the kitchen due to staff shortages, in case we were needed. I had tea and toast, sitting in the staff room to eat it.

It was 8:30 p.m., and we were due off at 10:45 p.m. We spent the rest of our shift sitting in the office answering buzzers. Before we went off, the pan room had to be cleaned and the dirty linen skips had to be emptied, putting the full bags down the laundry chute. A new bag was placed on the skip. We had to do regular checks of patients with a torch, attending to people who couldn't sleep and asking them if anything was wrong. Any pain was reported to the sister in charge, along with reports of who was awake.

The night staff came on at 10:30 p.m., and in no time,

it was 10:45 p.m. Finally, it was time to leave and go up that steep hill back to my room. I was working an early shift in the morning on Saturday, starting at 6:30 a.m. This was often the way the rosters were done—a late shift followed by an early shift. I found it really difficult, as it took me a couple of hours to unwind to go to sleep. Then, in no time, it was 5:30 a.m., and you had to get up to go to work again.

I managed to get to sleep after a hot shower and sitting on the balcony just in reflection. I awoke the next morning feeling exhausted at 5:30 a.m. and managed to get to work in time to do another day shift. I collapsed on my bed that afternoon after work and fell asleep, missing the evening meal. There were weekend penalty rates for the shift I had just worked and that was the only consolation.

It was Saturday night, and Dell and I decided to go to the TV room and watch the black-and-white TV before cocoa. Colour TVs were just becoming popular. Most people had black-and-white sets. We watched *Hey Hey It's Saturday* with Jackie MacDonald. A cocoa trolley came to the TV room.

I was working a late shift Sunday, and so was Dell. So we decided to spend the morning at the pool, which we did. I worked the late shift and then the morning shift on Monday so I could go bowling. I got my shift swap. I was going to have Tuesday and Wednesday as days off and study day Thursday, which was payday. I got all dressed to go bowling. We were all meeting outside Vivienne's office, where we had to sign out at 6:30 p.m. to be at Exhibition Bowl by 7:00 p.m.

Tenpin bowling was very popular in the '70s. As a consequence, there were bowling alleys all over the city. There were twelve of us, and we did the ten-minute walk to Exhibition Bowl. On arriving, we had to get our shoes from the service desk. There were special shoes for walking on the floor of the bowling section. I then got an orange drink. Most of the girls got Coca-Cola, which was very popular. We were divided into four teams, three girls in each team. We were playing teams of guys.

In the team we were playing against was a guy, Barry Jaimeson, who took a fancy to me, asking if he could call me. I gave him the number of the nurse's quarters and told him I was off duty the next three nights. He was about five foot nine inches of slim to medium build, with wavy brown hair. He smoked and had his own bowling ball and shoes. He told me he was an apprentice carpenter. I thoroughly enjoyed bowling, especially on this night. I think it was love at first sight between Barry and me.

We left at about 9:30 p.m. to go back to the nurses' quarters, arriving before 10:00 p.m. and signing ourselves back in at Vivienne's office. We were all so excited. Many of us had met interested guys who had asked if they could call. I went back to my room and couldn't sleep thinking about Barry and bowling.

I waited and waited for my name to be paged the next evening, and finally at 7:00 p.m., I heard my name called. I raced to pick up the phone, and the operator put me through to him. He said, "How's your day been?"

I told him I had spent it at the pool.

He then asked me, "Anthea, would you go out with me?"

I didn't know what to say. I said, "I would like to get to know you better."

We arranged that Barry would pick me up outside reception at 6:30 p.m. the following evening, and we would go to a milk bar in the valley and have a milkshake. This was the "in" place to take your girl in the early '70s. There were milkshake bars all over town.

The following day was Wednesday, and I got up early to

go into the valley shopping. I picked up my boots on lay-by, also buying a suede drawstring bag with tassels to match the boots. The midi (mid-calf) had just come into fashion, and I bought a green and white one with a split up the back. Green was very fashionable at this time. I was all set to go out with Barry in my new outfit.

I was nervous and excited. I couldn't wait for 6:30 p.m. to come. It eventually did, and I was waiting for him to show wearing my new outfit. He met me and took me to his car, a blue Chrysler. Not all young men had their licence or a car. He was wearing cream corduroy jeans and a cream and burgundy check shirt. I was totally taken with him. We talked for a while in the car and then headed off to the milk bar. We did some window shopping in the valley after having a milkshake.

We got back to the nurses' quarters about 9:00 p.m. and just sat in the car and talked. It wasn't cool those days to kiss on your first date. That night back at the nurses' quarters, everyone wanted to know how my first date had gone. I was over the moon. Barry and I arranged to meet again the following week on my days off, and it became a regular thing. We started cuddling and then kissing and then heavy petting.

Barry became my first real boyfriend. I was determined to be a virgin when I got married, as sex before marriage was frowned on in those days. So, we never actually went "all the way" but got very close. I was terrified of becoming pregnant, so the relationship was never consummated. I honestly didn't know about sex—how it happened—so it didn't happen. I came to really love Barry. I got very wet vaginally after seeing him and didn't understand why.

Work on the wards continued with me completing eight weeks at the Radium Institute. Then it was a study day and

Easter time. I had Easter Sunday and Monday off. Barry drove me up to my parents' house on Easter Sunday and met my family. Mum was actually really nice to Barry. I met Barry's family on the Easter Monday. He had a sister who worked at a high-class restaurant in the city. His family lived at Aspley, not far from Auntie Lilly.

After Easter, we did two weeks of block study in the classroom. Most nights, I saw Barry. One night he took me to the drive-in movie cinema to see *Love Story* with Ali McGraw and Ryan O'Neil and the famous line, "Love means never having to say you're sorry."

Drive-ins were very popular, and they were scattered all over the country. They were like great big, cemented parking lots sloping down towards the screen, which was massive out the front, all open air. You drove in, found a bay, and hooked the speaker in your window, turning it on. Every parking bay had a speaker. You usually arrived early and bought some tea, most often a hamburger with chips. This was what Barry and I did the night we went. I loved the movie. It made me cry, and Barry cuddled me the whole time we were there.

The two-week study block was very useful, as I was going to the male medical ward following it. We studied the anatomy and physiology of the heart, lungs, gallbladder, and pancreas, as well as diseases of these organs. We sat exams at the end of every block, which I passed.

On the Thursday payday, I visited the ward to get my roster and had already put in a request for the Monday evenings off. I received an amazing pay after working Good Friday, which was triple time.

I decided to do some regular banking and opened a Commonwealth Bank account because they had a branch at the post office at the hospital. Everything was cash. It was a different world to today. I had four days off with the Monday and Tuesday off on the ward, so I decided to go home to Redbank Plains.

On arriving home, Mum was in a rage because I had a boyfriend, telling me I was too young. She said I had to be a virgin when I got married and told me I would get pregnant. I left early and went back to the nurses' quarters. I walked out on the Monday with my bag hitch-hiking it back to the hospital with a truck driver. Young people hitch-hiking was common in those days.

This was followed by Mum's regular phone calls to the hospital abusing me, telling me the same things. This really interfered with my ability to go on seeing Barry, but I did.

Nursing days on the male medical ward were interesting. There were a lot of heart attack and stroke victims. Patients who'd had a stroke and couldn't swallow had a nasogastric tube, a tube from the nose to the stomach, inserted. If the tube dislodged, the feed could potentially go into the lungs.

Many of these patients died. This tube was replaced in the early '90s with a gastrostomy tube, which went directly from the abdominal wall to the stomach with a plate on the stomach side so it couldn't come out. These became known as "peg feeds."

I still remember pathology coming up to take blood on the heart attack patients. After heart attack, a small area of the heart dies and this dead tissue releases enzymes after so many hours and peaks in a day after. Cardiac enzymes blood taken has to be put on ice, and this is one aspect of diagnosis that hasn't changed to this day.

What has changed are the drugs used to treat heart conditions, with some amazing drugs available for doctors to prescribe today, including preventative treatment. For the last thirty years, the statin drugs have been available.

These reduce cholesterol in the blood vessels, so the walls don't become clogged up, causing an occlusion and blocking the blood vessel that supplies the heart with blood (with no supply due to a blockage, it dies).

The statin drugs were discovered in 1976 by a Japanese biochemist. In 1981, Merck, a pharmaceutical company, began clinical trials, which were fraught with difficulties. On September 1, 1987, the FDA (Food and Drug Administration) approved Lovastatin, and it was then on the market in the The United States. It wasn't till the late '80s that it was approved for use in Australia.

Drugs used then that are still used today on a medical ward are Lasix to rid the body of excess fluid and potassium to replace what is lost with the fluid. When the heart doesn't function properly, fluid builds up in the lungs and body.

Today, more is known about diet and effect on the heart and body. These were days of high meat consumption in Australia. The evening meal was typically "meat and three veg." Diets have changed as knowledge of nutrition's effect on health grew. There were more heart attack cases in those days due to both the diet of the day and the absence of statin drugs.

Today, more is known about disease, and the amazing technological advances in imaging have led to the availability of the equipment to diagnose it. During my days on this medical ward, the ultrasound, developed in 1963 and introduced to the Royal Brisbane in the late '60s, was relatively new at the hospital.

Surgery has changed, with open-heart and closed-heart surgeries now in use. From my memory, insertion of a pacemaker was the latest in these days. Since then, coronary care units (CCUs) have been set up with sophisticated monitoring devices. The ECG was used then and now. I learnt how to read it. I was forever fascinated. Today, there are automatic monitoring devices for the ECG. The hospital then only had the intensive care unit (ICU).

So, working on this ward was completely different to what it is today. There were more stroke patients, and more died. There were a lot of nasogastric tubes. Just about everybody had a "drip," which was a cannula going directly into a vein, usually in the arm. The arm was splinted with splint and bandaging. I learnt how to look after these drips by counting the number of drops per minute. It is totally different today, with equipment that automatically monitors, and today the drips are no longer in the arm but, rather, through a central line.

There were also diabetics on this ward who had short-acting insulin before every meal in the days before long-acting insulin was discovered. I learnt how to test urine with a dipstick. There were lots of men with gout who had diets high in red meat and dairy. At that time, it was thought that alcohol was the main cause (it certainly contributes).

There were also men with high blood pressure, and Aldomet was the drug of the day for reducing high blood pressure. I mastered the art of taking blood pressure with a sphygmomanometer and a stethoscope.

I enjoyed my days on the medical ward. I was very interested to learn about disease and disease management. I thought I worked in one of the most up-to-date hospitals in the world, and I probably did at that time. Medicine, surgery, diagnostics, and treatment has come a long, long way since the early '70s.

At the end of eight weeks in the medical ward, I entered two more weeks of study block with the weekends off. Barry and I went up the coast on a day trip to my favourite beach, Kings Beach, at Caloundra. On the Sunday, I lazed about at the nurses' home reading weekend papers. In those days, everybody read the weekend papers.

Barry came early Sunday afternoon, and he took me and showed me some of the houses he was helping to build. He said he wanted to build me a house and get married. He asked me to marry him. I didn't know what to say but said I would think about it.

The next two-week block was spent studying psychology and mental health, as well as emergency nursing and anatomy and physiology as always. The exams at the end of this were important as they marked the six-month mark. If you passed you got your first red stripe on your cap, and of course I passed. I was thrilled and excited and had a real sense of achievement.

After the block, I had four days off again but didn't go home due to the tension between Mum and me over me having a boyfriend. I spent the weekend seeing Barry and the Monday and Tuesday at Auntie Lillie's; she was accepting of Barry, who came for tea one night. After block, I went to a male surgical ward, and life cruised on, with Monday bowling nights, time at the pool, time shopping in the valley, and visiting Auntie Lilly and Auntie Mabel. Plus, there was all the time chatting to different girlfriends at the nurses' home.

Shopping in the valley was a favourite pastime. I bought nice clothes and was building an incredible wardrobe, but Barry and I never really went out, other than to the milk bar and the drive-in. I longed to go out nice places and wear my clothes.

I also bought an acoustic guitar and began lessons on a Thursday evening because I knew I always had that evening off, as it was our study day. An instructor, Sarah, came to the nurses' hall opposite the reception and gave me instruction between 6:00 p.m. and 7:00 p.m. on the Thursday evening. I also bought a lot of 33 LPs. These were records, and I also bought a record player.

I put in a request to move to the end of the corridor on the opposite side of the nurses' home, as Sue had moved out to Lady Lamington Nurses' Home now in her third year. I moved down to this room. It was great, as it was two rooms joined. The first room had lots of lock-up cupboards, enabling me to lock up my records and player and the guitar.

The second room had the bed and a large table on which I collected potted plants. This second room had louvers overlooking the whole car park below. It was the highest corner room of this entire block, where I felt so safe.

The surgical ward was certainly different to the medical ward. It was full open-abdominal surgery for operations. Patients having an appendectomy (removal of the appendix) stayed ten days till the sutures were out. Patients having a cholecystectomy (removal of the gallbladder), considered major surgery then, stayed three weeks.

These operations are now done by keyhole surgery and patients stay a few days.

There was investigative surgery, where the whole abdomen was opened up to investigate, often resulting in bowel resection, and patients ended up with a bag on the outer abdomen to take the faeces.

On this ward, I learnt how to do dressings and how-to take-out sutures and Michel clips (like staples). There was no pre-packaging of dressings. They all came from the CSD (Central Sterilising Department). The forceps and scissors were autoclaved in the ward steriliser and constantly reused. Dressings were limited to combine gauze. It was nothing like the amazing array of pre-packaged dressings available today.

On this ward, I met Peta Tall, who became my best friend, and we were to stay connected for life. We had not long met, and we were given the task of laying out a young man of twenty-six. He had died of septicaemia (blood poisoning) after a burst appendix. It was the first time I had ever laid someone out, the first time I had seen a man naked, and the first time I had seen someone dead. We completed the task, wrapping him up in a sheet and sticking pieces of plaster all along the sheet to keep it secured.

We then looked at each other and quietly burst out laughing, which was a dreadful mark of disrespect. But we both realised at the same time we had left the scissors inside the sheet. We had to undo the sheet, retrieve the scissors, and stick it all up again.

There were always patients coming back from theatre who had to have post-operative observations done. Many of them vomited, for anaesthetics have come a long way today. Intramuscular Stemetil was the drug of choice to prevent nausea. There were last meals of tea and toast given out by night staff for patients going to theatre.

It was our job to get them ready by giving them paper cups filled with pHisoHex (medical washing soap) and instructing them to wash all over with this, including their hair. It was what staff used to wash their hands. They then dressed in theatre clothes, which haven't changed much to this day.

Something that never changed at all through all my training days was how much I enjoyed walking through the garden at the top of the hill seeing all the white butterflies flitting about among the flowers. I felt happy, and somehow this was a sign of happiness to me. I often picked a few of the flowers for my room, though you weren't supposed to.

I was making music in my room strumming my guitar

and listening to music on my record player. This all made me happy too, as did swimming in the pool and listening to my transistor radio. It seemed I had finally found some happiness, which was a continual state of mind, something I had searched for all my life.

The eight weeks in male surgical flew by so swiftly, and we were back in block studying pharmacology and psychology. We were learning how to give injections practising on oranges. We were learning all about different drugs. In our second year, we would be giving injections and medications, as well as checking drugs. So, we had to pass the final year exams at the end of the next block in order to do these tasks.

At the end of this block, I went to Lowsen House, which was the mental health facility. It was a detached building down towards the women's hospital at the back of the main hospital. The placement was sort of indicative of society's attitudes towards mental health at the time, when mental health was not talked about in public but, rather, tucked under the carpet. The general public's approach was to lock people up in institutions and forget about them—just "throw away the key."

I worked in the female section, which was upstairs, with the male section downstairs. Both were lock-up wards, where patients were locked in. There was overcrowding, which was present in all mental health institutions at the time. It got to terrible overcrowding by the '80s.

In the early '80s, government campaigns to raise public awareness and acceptance of mental health began. By the very late '80s, government funding to set up community support programmes for the mentally ill was granted, and these were set up progressively—with a view to releasing a lot of the patients in mental health institutions back into the community.

Their release began in the very early '90s across Australia and coincided with dramatic changes to psychiatric drugs available for doctors to prescribe. Second-generation (newer) atypical antipsychotic drugs with fewer side effects were approved for use in Australia. The newer antidepressant drugs, the SSRIs (serotonin reuptake inhibitors) with fluoxetine (better known as Prozac) were approved for use.

Consequently, homelessness started to become a real issue by the mid-'90s. And so did the use of street drugs. Over time, both became more of a problem like they are today, while more and better drugs came on the market to treat the mentally ill.

So, what do we do with our mentally ill? We can't go back to the way it was in the '70s when I worked in Lowsen House! It was a madhouse, with crowding and people screaming and dragged off and given intramuscular Serenace (haloperidol,) a first-generation typical antipsychotic with heaps of side effects. Chlorpromazine, marketed as Largactil, another in this family of drugs, was given out like lollies in attempt to sedate the agitated and psychotic patients. Tofranil, a very old drug, was being used as an antidepressant.

ECT (electric convulsive therapy) was widely used, and I helped on many occasions. This involved placing an electrode on each side of the head and passing an electric current through the brain. It was believed to help with depression.

Lobotomy was still used in some mental health institutions then. It involved passing an instrument that resembled an ice pick through the eye orbit into the frontal lobe and stirring it around. I never saw any of these done and do not know whether they were being done at the RBH when I worked there. I don't think so.

I spent much of the time in introspection when I worked at Lowsen House. Working there really caused me to question my own sanity. This is certainly not the effect it had on everybody, but it was how it affected me. I spent a lot of time talking with patients, as this was said to help the patients. We learnt the basics of reflective listening. I couldn't wait to finish there and made the decision mental health was not for me.

I finally finished working there to do another two-week of block the last for the year. It was early December 1971, and Barry and I planned to go to Cairns in the first few weeks of January, which we both had off. We were going to stay in separate rooms, as it was taboo those days for unmarried couples to stay together in one room.

I made the mistake of telling Mum we were going away on holidays to Cairns. She was absolutely livid, and I was so upset I broke it off with Barry. That was a decision I have regretted all the days of my life. In a Rod Stewart song, I found "The First Cut Is the Deepest," and I played this song over and over.

So, I completed the last block for first year and passed my exams just before Christmas 1971. This gave me a second stripe on my cap when I returned from five weeks of holiday, with Christmas and the first three weeks of January off on holiday.

The trip to Cairns with Barry was cancelled. I booked seven days on South Molle Island on the barrier reef in the first week of January and travelled to Cairns in the second week, going by myself. I booked accommodation through the Queensland Tourist Bureau.

## A babe in the woods

I went home for Christmas 1971, and it was a lovely time. Mum was happy because I had broken it off with Barry. I didn't tell her about South Molle Island. Auntie Vera (Dad's sister) and Uncle Cyril spent Christmas Day with us. On Boxing Day, we went up to Grantham to visit Mum's family—her father (my grandfather) and her brother and his family (my uncle, auntie, and cousins). It was lovely seeing everybody on the farm.

During Christmas and New Year 1972, we visited Auntie Lilly and Uncle Joe, as well as Auntie Mabel and Uncle Reg and my cousin Ann. Auntie Mabel had just had a new baby, Damian, to replace Scott, who they had lost. It was a truly wonderful family Christmas.

I got back to the hospital on New Year's Day, January 1, 1972. Dad drove me. I hastily packed for my big adventure to South Molle Island the next day. In the morning, I caught a bus into the bus depot very early. All aboard the bus, and it took us on a six-hour bus journey north to Mackay Harbour. We then caught a medium-sized boat out to the island. I loved the boat trip, as I always do.

On arrival, we disembarked and then walked up a long jetty to the island. People were waterskiing out on the bay, and I decided I would do that every day. It was 1:30 p.m. in the afternoon, and we were taken to the dining room for a late lunch, which was scrumptious—all seafood. We were then shown to our chalets. I had a whole chalet to myself. There were about forty chalets, all going back from the beach.

At my table in the dining room was seated a nice couple, Charles and Lyn, on their honeymoon from Brisbane and a guy about my age on holiday from New Zealand,

Charles. He was tall, dark, and handsome and dressed quite nicely. Their chalets were near mine. I spent the rest of the afternoon exploring the island and in the island pool. The chalets were self-contained, and I quickly got ready for the evening meal. After tea, Charles asked me if I would join him in the entertainment area, where there was a bar, tables, and chairs, as well as a dance floor. This became a nightly occurrence, after which he would escort me back to my chalet.

I spent the days waterskiing, swimming at the beach or pool, or going out on the reef on one of the boats. I attempted snorkelling but wasn't good at it. The mealtimes were pleasurable, with us all talking and sharing wine. The food was out of this world—it was so delicious. Every night dancing with Charles on the dance floor was much fun. On our last day, we went out on the reef in a glass-bottom boat, which enabled us to see all the beautiful fish and coral.

Our last night was particularly memorable. Charles and I danced the night away to some amazing music, which finished at 2:00 a.m. I usually limited my alcohol but had had a few more this night. Charles escorted me back to my chalet and asked me if he could come in. I said yes.

I found myself in bed with him, cuddling and kissing, and before long, I had lost my virginity. I did not know that would happen. My goodness did it hurt, and he was upset that he had hurt me. Charles had to leave early in the morning on route back to New Zealand. I awoke, and he was gone. We had already exchanged contact details.

I got up and packed up attended breakfast, after which I boarded a boat back to Mackay. I then got on board the bus on route for Cairns, stopping over at all the towns on the way. It was a ten-hour journey. I sat next to Gordon on this journey. He was a guy twenty years of age who lived with his parents in Cairns.

On arriving in Cairns, I caught a taxi to my booked accommodation, the Cairns Country Inn. Gordon was on holiday and took me out on day trips exploring all of Cairns and the surrounds during the following week. I went to tea at his parents' house a couple of nights, and he took me back to the inn afterwards. Nothing ever happened between us, as I was too scared after what had happened with Charles, and I felt I didn't really know him.

The time came for the big journey overnight back to Brisbane. I managed to get two seats to myself and slept most of the way. I finally made it back to the nurses' home and slept for two days and one night without eating. I was simply exhausted. I got up and unpacked. I then did all the washing in the laundry upstairs on the thirteenth floor. I had my meals at the children's hospital dining hall that week because it was so close, avoiding the hill. I had about five days of holidays left, and I spent it in reflection.

I thought about how unprepared I was for adult life on leaving home. I was "as green as grass" or "a babe in the woods." I had no understanding of adult life, no money management skills, and no real knowledge about sex. I thought about how emotionally screwed up I was. I had maternal feelings for Tony, my brother, who I had looked after since he was a baby for two years. I was extremely angry at my mother for not loving me. And I put my father up on a pedestal over-loving him. I was very confused about many things in the world.

I spent the fourth week of January and the first week of February in the infectious diseases ward, whose roster I was on for the holidays. At the end of the second week in February, I decided to see a doctor in outpatients at Cowlishaw. This was the ward for sick nurses.

I hadn't had a period for over a year since leaving to go nursing, and it was over a month since Charles and I had slept together. The doctor said it was the massive change for me of going into nursing, combined with the enormous fear of getting pregnant that had prevented a period. He did a pregnancy test, and it came back negative. He gave me some tablets to take to bring on a period and then some oral contraceptives. So, I started on "the pill." I returned every few months to get a new supply. I had put on two stone in weight (twenty-eight pounds) since starting nursing.

I spent only three weeks early 1972 in infectious diseases, which made me happy because I didn't like it. There were a lot of cases of gastroenteritis and a few cases of whooping cough. Almost everybody was vaccinated against known communicable diseases. The vaccination compliance rate was very high in those days.

The ward was made up of single self-contained rooms. Outside each room hung long-sleeved white gowns you had to put on to enter the room, and inside the room were gloves to put on. We wore a mask the whole time and booties on our shoes. I was glad to finish there.

I then went to casualty, now known as the ER (emergency room). This was over ten weeks, as I had study block after four weeks in casualty and another four weeks there after the classroom study block. Casualty was amazing. Every shift was different, and you never knew what each shift would hold when you went to work. Working there really opened my eyes to the world.

Friday and Saturday evenings were always busy with car accidents and drunks. There was a room called the "pink room," where they put all the drunks on trolleys. I swore I would never drink more than two drinks at a time after this experience of looking after these people.

There was a bay just for eyes to administer eye washes when patients had gotten something in their eyes. There was a collection of seats for the asthmatics to have nebulised Ventolin and oxygen. Sometimes these patients needed a drip (IV infusion) to have steroids and Ventolin IV.

There was a plaster room for stabilising and fixing broken and dislocated bones. I learnt what rape was from helping rape victims. I learnt about prostitution when these ladies came in to get tests done for STDs (sexually transmitted diseases). I learnt how to calm upset people, about chaos, and about life.

It was an absolutely amazing experience, and I loved it. It involved absolute teamwork, all of us in casualty working with each other, as well as radiology, pathology, and the ambulance officers and, at times, police. Jeanette was working there at the time I worked there. She began dating an ambulance officer Glen Collier. They later married, had a family, and stayed together for life.

While I worked in casualty, I went out at night "clubbing" with Bussey and whoever else wanted to come. We went to nightclubs in the valley and city. We always all came home together. There were bars with dance floors, and I would dance the night away. We would sneak out without signing out and sneak back in really late about 2:00 a.m. through an open door at the end of the hall.

Peta and I both wanted to lose weight, so she suggested we join up with Janet Drew Figure Clinic in the city, so we did. Both of us took out a six-month membership. It had a sauna and a spa, along with gym equipment and, in addition, ran exercise classes. It was ladies only and the only clinic of its kind in Brisbane, a real forerunner in fitness services in

Brisbane. The clinic was open seven days a week from 7:00 a.m. till 9:00 p.m. I went as often as I could. The buses from the valley to the city dropped you at the door.

After block and casualty finished, I went on six weeks night duty on a relief pool, where I went all over the hospital. I actually loved working night duty too. It was the peace and calm of the night. Yet at times, you could be run off your feet. There were only two nurses per ward at night. I liked the relief pool—the variety of working somewhere new every night or every couple of nights. No two shifts were the same.

On my nights off, I went to the movie cinema at Windsor, the Crystal, during the day. I saw *The French Connection* with Gene Hackman and *Dirty Harry* with Clint Eastwood, as well as *The Boyfriend* with Lesley Hornby, better known as Twiggy, a well-known model in the United Kingdom. There were privately owned suburban picture theatres in most suburbs all over town and only two big movie houses in the city with lots of seating. There were no movie chains like today.

During the day, I also went tenpin bowling if there were enough girls off duty who wanted to play. I kept the nights off for sleeping in the dark. I went to Janet Drew's many of the afternoons or evenings. I missed a lot of meals on night duty. I was exercising in my big double room. Consequently, I lost considerable weight, as I couldn't eat at night anything more than tea and toast.

At the end of night shift, it was another two weeks of block, the last two weeks in June 1972. Study block was every ten weeks in second year, with a study day once a fortnight. We learnt pharmacology, psychology, and microbiology, as well as paediatric nursing. I sat and passed the mid-year '72 exams.

Following the classroom, I went to operating theatres, which I absolutely loved. I felt it was my niche in nursing and put in for an extended stay for ten weeks, which was granted. I would "scout" a lot of the time, which meant you had to get the scrub sister what she wanted for her trolley.

I occasionally got to scrub alongside a fully trained nurse. Sometimes I got to assist with the operation, which often meant holding a retractor for hours. But you got a bird's-eye view. A retractor holds back the abdominal organs so the surgeon can work. Sometimes, I worked in recovery waking patients up. The other role was "anaesthetists' assistant."

Anatomy and physiology became clearer when you saw it in the flesh. I learnt all my instruments and what the names of all the different operations meant. Most surgery involved full open wounds before the days of keyhole surgery and lasers. I learnt a lot about drugs used in theatre.

I had all the weekends off while working in theatre, which meant less pay.

Peta wanted to go on a cruise to see the South Sea Islands and asked me to come with her. So, we booked it for the first two weeks in November. We paid for it and saw the matrons' office about ensuring we had the first two weeks in November as annual leave. The cruise was fourteen days and went to Wellington in New Zealand; Vanuatu; Tonga; and two stops in Fiji, Noumea and Suva. We really looked forward to this cruise.

Early September, I was finished operating theatres and back into block again, studying hard for two weeks. I went shopping on the Saturday mornings. I bought a pair of corduroy hot pants to match my boots. These, a little pair of shorts with a bib at the front and straps at the back that attached to the bib, were the height of fashion. I had no idea how sexy I looked.

I went out one Saturday night at the end of block wearing these and my boots to the National Hotel with a whole big group of girls including Carol Watson. On this night, I met Zach DeVito. He said, "Would you like to dance?"

I said, "No thanks."

He replied, "What's wrong with you? Do you have a wooden leg?"

So, I got up and danced with him. He told me his name was Zach. His friend Ryan Boston had a bet with him he couldn't get me up to dance, as I was knocking back dances. Zach was a tall, well-built, well-dressed man, with brown hair and a receding hairline. He had long sideburns and a moustache, which were fashionable. He was four years older than me. I thought he was incredibly handsome.

I went back to his flat that night and ended up in bed with him fully clothed. He respected that I did not want to do anything. As soon as he fell asleep, I got up and left via the front door. I walked a couple of streets and hailed a taxi back to the nurses' quarters. I sneaked back in, taking my boots off. I was so relieved to get back to my room.

For the rest of September and October, I worked for six weeks in the gynaecology ward. There were women coming in to have curettes for various reasons. Other women were having a hysterectomy (removal of the uterus). Some had a full clearance, which resulted in a surgical menopause.

There were women being investigated for infertility, having laparoscopic investigation. This was a surgical procedure that had only just begun using a long telescope connected to a fibre-optic tube that carried a light source, entering through the abdominal wall via a tiny incision to investigate. I didn't really enjoy the "gynae" ward.

Zach began sending me bunches of flowers, such that they filled the reception area. He was telephoning the nurses' home frequently and sending beautiful cards. I eventually went out with him. He took me to a couple of upmarket coffee shops in Piccadilly and to Rowes Arcades. There was someone playing on a piano in both. It was very romantic.

Next, we went to the Shingle Inn for pancakes and coffee. I told him I was about to go on a cruise with my friend. He said, "I've only just met you, and you're going away."

I reassured him, saying I would see him when I got back.

Peta and I flew to Sydney and were met by a travel guide who took us as a group to a bus. The bus drove us to the ship *The Princess.* This was the forerunner of Princess Cruises. We were ever so excited. Once on board the ship, we found our cabin and unpacked. It was then time, we decided, to check the ship out.

There were two pools like a beach on the top deck. There were bars and entertainment areas with dance floors on the next deck. The deck below that had a movie cinema, as well as a theatre for live entertainment. We decided to have lunch, as we were with the second round for lunch, and it was 1:00 p.m. In our cabin, we found the daily guide telling us what was on. We met our steward for our cabin.

We had an absolutely wonderful two weeks going to lunch and dinner every night and eating scrumptious food. Breakfast was served in our cabin. We went dancing every night and had a pact that we would always go back to the cabin together at the end of every night. We hopped off the boat in Noumea (Fiji), hired a car, and drove to Suva (also in Fiji) on the other side of the island. We drove all around the island, having a beach party on the final night with some island residents who kept asking us if we wanted Bacardi. We said no, not knowing Bacardi meant "to make love." Thankfully, neither of us drank Bacardi.

We bought a lot of souvenirs, including carved wooden items in Tonga and paua shell from New Zealand. It was difficult getting our suitcases shut to get off the ship, but finally it was time to disembark and say goodbye to all our new friends. We exchanged contact details, especially with those who sat at our dining table

Back we went to Brisbane for the last two weeks of November 1972. Peta went home to the country to St. George, and I spent a week home with my family and a week at the hospital. During the week I spent at the hospital, I saw Zach. He took me out to dinner on the Wednesday night to a very romantic restaurant, which had a dance floor. Afterwards, we went back to his new flat at Merthyr Road New Farm (he had moved), and we slept together. It was so wonderful—something I had never experienced before. As I was taking "the pill," I wasn't worried about getting pregnant.

After holidays, it was the first two weeks of December, and we were in block again. I spent most of the nights at Zach's, and he would take me in the morning to the hospital. I knew I was really in love with this man.

Christmas came, and I had to work it in the "gynae ward." Zach took me home to Redbank Plains between Christmas and New Year on days I had off to have dinner with and meet my family. Mum and Dad were totally enamoured with Zach.

## My relationship with Zach and nursing, 1973

New Year came, and it was 1973. I had been rotated to the children's hospital, where I stayed until mid-May. I now had three stripes on my cap. I was rotated around the different wards. There was a respiratory ward with patients who had croup nursed in steam tents and asthmatics, as well as children who had breathed in an object. They required a bronchoscopy to remove the object, often a peanut. There was a cancer ward, where I found it very difficult to watch a young person, who had not had a life, die. There was a surgical ward, with most patients having tonsils and adenoids out.

There was another ward, with babies and children with a deformity who had been abandoned and became a ward of the state. Some of these children had hydrocephalus, where the spinal fluid builds up on the brain and a shunt is put in. They have really big heads. Other children had anacephalus with little or no brain, often with the top of the head exposed. Some of the babies in this ward had spina bifida, where the base of the spine is exposed. All were lovable, beautiful little people. There was also an orthopaedic ward and an eye ward, as well as a medical ward.

In the third week in January, Zach took me to see my grandfather, who was dying in the Hospes Perpetual General Hospital. It was a two-hour drive in his Plymouth Valiant car. I saw my grandpa and said my final goodbyes to him.

On January 26, 1973, I went to work and was told to go to the matron's office. When I went, I was told my grandpa had passed away overnight, and I was given three days of bereavement leave.

That February, Peta met a friend of Zach's, Len Thomson. It wasn't long before they became a couple. Back at Zach's flat, there was Zach's friend Ryan Boston, who had a girlfriend, Marie Valentine, and the six of us would go out to restaurants, nightclubs, and bars. We had the most amazing times.

On March 7, 1973, a Wednesday night, Zach wanted to take me to the Whiskey A-Go-Go nightclub to meet his friend Charles Runner, along with his girlfriend. I had a bad headache and didn't want to go, so we didn't go. Zach got up early that morning and got the paper off the lawn. (It was common in those days to have the newspaper delivered.)

On the front-page news was that the Whiskey A-Go-Go nightclub had been firebombed and burnt down at 2:08 a.m., March 3, 1973. Fifteen people died in the fire, including his friends and friends in the band. Charles had been having an affair and was there that night with his girlfriend. The fact that we weren't there was luck better than winning the lottery. As we drove up Brunswick Street that morning, we could see the burnt-out front entrance.

Not long after this, Peta and I were both shifted down to the Lady Lamington Nurses' Home. It was for third years and newly trained nurses. I was squashed into a little room after being in my big room. The building had only two storeys, and we were on the first floor, two rooms apart. I didn't feel safe at all, as the front door was always open, and it was close to the entrance to the nurses' quarters. We decided to move out and get our own flat.

Our flat was a five- to ten-minute walk from the main hospital. We moved there in May after I finished at the children's hospital. We had to get a letter from our mother to say we could move out, and Mum reluctantly wrote one. I had the main bedroom with a big queen bed, and Peta had the single room with a single bed. The flat was at Windsor right on Bowen Bridge Road next to Sam's takeaway store. It was sixty-five dollars per week, and we found it in the newspaper in "flats to let." We still had a lot of our meals at the hospital.

Peta and I enrolled in a modelling course at June Daly Watkins. It was the top modelling agency in Brisbane at the time. We requested Tuesday evenings off so we could do the course. We caught the bus there to the city. There were often anti-Vietnam war protests in the city, and Peta told me her only brother, Jack, had been called up for national service and was killed in Vietnam.

The course ran from 5:30 p.m. till 9:00 p.m. and covered many subjects, including deportment, make-up, and dress sense. Zach and Len picked us up after the classes, and the course ran for ten weeks. At the end of the course, I was offered a modelling contract but declined it, opting to finish my nursing instead.

Following this, Peta and I took up jazz ballet, held at Mt. Gravatt, not far from where Len lived. Zach picked me up and took me to this every Tuesday night. We usually called at Len's with Peta afterwards. Jazz ballet was done to music, "The Lion Sleeps Tonight." I have continued throughout my whole life to do the routine we learnt to the same music in my bedroom to keep fit.

On July 22, 1973, it was my twentieth birthday, and Zach organised a surprise birthday party for me at his flat. He gave me a beautiful Swiss gold watch with engraving on the back. I was to wear this for the next forty years. Ryan and Marie gave me a beautiful gold bracelet. It was an amazing party that night. I met Suzanne McPherson, who was going out with a guy who also lived at the flat, Charles Bishop. Suzanne and I became lifelong friends.

In July, August, and the first few weeks of September, I went to the female surgical ward, spending the first six weeks in the ward and the last four in the new burn unit attached. I was the first nurse to work in the burn unit at the Royal Brisbane Hospital.

To begin, we had one patient, Mrs Curtis, who had burns on 90 per cent of her body. She wasn't expected to live. She was burning some letters in the sink of her home wearing a flammable nightie, and she went up in flames. She was running a bath at the time. The tap kept running, eventually alerting neighbours to a problem above with water dripping through.

She lived for two weeks, and I "specialled" her, looking after only her, one on one. Her feet were not burned, so an IV (intra venous infusion) was placed in her foot. She was given salt baths every day in a special bath in the unit. New and innovative equipment was used, hoist lifters, with two wardsmen to lift her into the bath every day via a sling.

When she was first admitted, she looked like a piece of blackened charcoal, and I did not know whether she was male or female. While in the bath, I had to debride the dead skin with scissors and forceps, removing only the dead skin.

When Mrs Curtis spoke, I realised a real person lived inside that blackened body. I became professionally very close to her. After she died, I was called to the matron's office and thanked for my service. Her family had bought for me the biggest box of chocolates I had ever seen, as well as a silver pen with my name engraved on it. I was taken aback. I didn't know what to say. Her death affected me, and I was given three paid days off to debrief. I was advised to visit the doctor for the nurses, and this I did.

The rest of September was spent in block, and then I went to the orthopaedic ward. The first week in October, Zach took me to see *Jesus Christ Superstar* at the SGIO theatre, and my love of theatre was cemented.

Following this, he went to Rockhampton to start a new contract, as he worked as a contract's administrator. His contract in Brisbane had come to an end. I missed him very much. I would catch the bus to Rockhampton to see him and stay for the weekend.

On the first trip, he drove me to Yeppoon, which was on the coast and very close to Rockhampton. We stayed at Yeppoon the Friday and Saturday nights. On the Friday night, we were in bed and had just made love, and he said, "Anthea, will you marry me?"

I didn't know what to say. I said, "Can we talk about this in the morning?"

The next morning, we were up early into town and looking in jewellery shops. We finally chose a beautiful ring that showed the whole diamond. And that was it; we were engaged to be married.

On October 20, 1973, Queen Elizabeth II visited Australia and officially opened the Sydney Opera House.

In November, I was transferred to the ICU (Intensive Care Unit). I didn't really like it. Patients were "specialled," meaning one-on-one nursing. All the patients were unconscious and required frequent sucking out of secretions.

While I was in this ward, Dad rang me at work, and I spoke to him. He said, "Anthea, do you really want to marry this man? Are you sure?"

I said, "Yes, of course I do. I am sure I want to marry Zach."

He said, "OK, then I will pay for the wedding."

Mum rang Zach at his work and said all these dreadful

things about me and tried to talk him out of marrying me. He hung up on her and was horrified.

We were originally to be married on January 19, 1974, but brought it forward to January 5, 1974, because Zach had found a wonderful opportunity for our honeymoon. This was a cruise on a cargo ship, which had two decks for cruise passengers. It stopped for a few days at every capital city—Brisbane, Sydney, Adelaide, and Perth. We could disembark at Perth and spend time with his family in Perth. After that, we could fly to Darwin to start our married life, as Zach's next contract was in Darwin.

I bought a chiffon-over-satin wedding dress off the rack from a valley dress shop. Peta and Marie were my bridesmaids and chose lime green dresses from the same shop, and I paid for them. I ordered a round two-tiered cake with a bride and groom figurine on top and lacework around the side from a cake shop in Rowes Arcade in the city.

I chose frangipanis for the flowers, as Mum had had these at her wedding, and organised them from the florist down from the hospital not far from our flat. On the next weekend that Zach came down, we organised the reception at the restaurant across the road from the hospital for fifty guests. Zach organised a band to play, as the restaurant had a dance floor and a garden area out front for pre-dinner drinks.

I finished in the ICU and went into the final study block when we would sit our final exams. After block, I went on five weeks of paid annual leave. The results were published in *The Courier-Mail* just before Christmas. I passed every subject with honours. I was elated, and so was Zach and my family.

On January 3, 1974, we were presented with our nursing certificates and on Friday January 4, 1974, I went into the city and registered for the first time as a state registered nurse. Peta was three months behind me and still had her exams to sit.

# CHAPTER 5

# My Marriage to Zach (January 1974 to January 1982)

## The wedding and the honeymoon

Peta and I got up early and picked frangipani fronds and did them up with aluminium foil on the stems to put in the centre of each table at the reception. I walked up to the reception room and took the flowers and the place cards, putting these all-in places on the tables.

I checked that the cake had been delivered. It had arrived and looked spectacular. I took my going-away outfit and left it in a room upstairs. There were butterflies—gold and black—hovering over the garden beds at the front of the restaurant / reception room. This to me was a good sign.

I washed my hair and blew it dry myself. I did my nails. A friend of Zach's from his work arrived about midday to take myself, Peta, and Marie up to my parents' house at Redbank Plains, where I would leave from for the church. We had to be there at 3:00 p.m., and it was a fifty-minute drive. When we arrived there, the photographer was waiting for us. I got changed into the white wedding dress, and Peta and Marie helped me with the veil. I did my make-up.

Some photographs were taken, some in my parents' bedroom and some in the lounge room. I am unable to remember the exact arrangement with cars that day. All I remember is a friend of Zach's owned a white Rolls-Royce, and he drove Dad and me to the church that day. We arrived a little late. Dad walked me down the aisle. Zach looked so handsome, and so did Ryan, his best man, and Len, his groomsmen. Peta and Marie helped me with the veil, which was full length, as I walked down the aisle.

The ceremony was held in Lady of Mt. Carmel Church, a Catholic church that was walking distance from where I currently lived. It was a church I'd regularly gone to and would continue to do for years (I still do as of this writing). At that time, Marie lived two doors up from it. Father Vince O'Shea married us and saw us a number of times beforehand. It was a beautiful ceremony in the most beautiful church.

Afterwards, there was signing documents. Then more photographs were taken. The gentleman with the white Rolls-Royce drove Zach and me to the reception room, which was directly opposite the hospital. He was the master of ceremonies at the wedding reception. We were handed a glass of champagne on arrival. Hors d'oeuvres were being served in the garden area, and they looked delicious. The photographer kept wanting to take photographs, to the extent it was disturbing my enjoyment of the reception. Finally, he left after taking a photograph of my whole family.

A delicious three-course meal followed, with wine and champagne for toasting. The reception room allowed Zach to supply wine and champagne, which cut the cost somewhat. Zach and I had silver champagne glasses to toast with. This beautiful round cake was cut with the smallest tier being kept for us to cut on our first wedding anniversary. Peta and Marie handed the cake around. After the speeches, it was time for the first dance. One thing Zach and I always did well together was dance. This was a particularly romantic shoulder to shoulder dance. Then everybody followed and danced too. All the gifts were in a room upstairs. Ryan and Marie with Len and Peta would take these to our flat after the reception was over, along with anything else, like my wedding dress.

I got changed into the going-away outfit. Everybody got in a circle as "Auld Lang Syne" played. Zach and I went around the whole circle saying our goodbyes. I got to my mother last, and she grabbed me and hugged me for the first time in my life and kept saying over and over, "I'm sorry. I'm sorry. I'm sorry."

I was so shaken and affected by her doing this I cried all the way down the coast to Surfers Paradise, an hour's drive.

It poured with rain the whole way down there. I don't know how Zach managed to drive there. We were shown to our room. Zach immediately crashed on the bed, fell asleep, and snored the whole night. There was a very noisy air conditioner outside the windows of the room. I did not sleep at all the whole night. I was very disappointed and upset, as I thought you were supposed to make love on your wedding night.

The next morning, I went down early by myself to the pool and had a dip. When I got back to the room and showered, we got dressed for breakfast. This was a smorgasbord with plenty of fruit. We ate well and then sat by the pool, after which we went back to the room for a late checkout at twelve midday. After that, we drove to Burleigh Heads, where Dad had taken the family towing the caravan and set up for a holiday at the caravan park. We spent a few hours with them and then drove back to the flat (Peta's and mine).

On arriving back at the flat, late that Sunday afternoon, we looked through all the beautiful gifts people had given us and then collapsed on my big bed. We planned the next few days as the ship for our honeymoon was leaving Wednesday January 9, 1974 at 2:00 p.m. We had Grace Bros coming Monday the next day to pack everything to go overland to

Darwin, where Zach's next job was and where we would start married life. We had to pack separately a suitcase for the ship and our stopover in Perth to visit Zach's family.

Peta and Len, along with Ryan and Marie, arrived, and we all chatted about the wedding. We all had fish and chips for tea from Sam's Takeaway next door. Monday came, and all the packing got done. Auntie Lilly came collecting my wedding dress and veil; she wanted to pack them in blue tissue so that they'd stay white. Zach had arranged to drop his Valiant off to Carol Runner, the wife of Charles, who died in the fire. Carol bought the car for $1,000.

Auntie Lilly and Uncle Joe came on the Wednesday about midday to take us to the ship. We were standing on board as the ship pulled out, waving goodbye at 2:00 p.m. We stood there until the ship reached the mouth of the Brisbane River and then went down to our cabin. There were six single bunks in the cabin.

We met our steward, who said he would bring us orange juice early, followed by breakfast. We just had to fill out the breakfast form each day. We checked out the ship and had a celebratory drink in the bar upstairs. We then went out on deck and stood for about two hours watching the ocean. It was then time to have a shower and get ready for dinner. As the only honeymooning couple on board the ship, we were sitting at the captain's table, our steward told us.

So up we went to the dining room, as we did every night and had a scrumptious dinner. After dinner, there were games every night—crazy, fun games, like pass the parcel and musical chairs. There was dancing once the band started. We had so much fun night after night. We slept in a different bunk every night, and the poor steward never knew which bed he would find us in the morning for the orange juice.

The stopovers in each capital city were fun. In Sydney, we walked the Rocks, took a boat around Sydney Harbour past the opera house, and went to Chinatown for lunch. In Melbourne, we hired a car and drove all around. It was hot when we left the boat, and I was wearing a little summer dress. By the time we got back, it was cold, and I was freezing. Apparently, Melbourne weather was like this—so quickly changeable. In Adelaide, the city of churches, we simply took a day trip around the city and outskirts looking at some of the churches.

In Perth, where Zach's family lived, we disembarked the ship on the January 19, 1974. His Auntie Lucy and Uncle Bill Martens were there to meet us and drove us to Zach's parents' house at Gosnells. Zach's mother was lovely, and his father a bit overbearing. They all spoke in another language, Polish, including Zach, and I found this somewhat disconcerting. His mother had cooked a big lunch for us, with the table all set so beautifully. She was a very loving lady, and they had given up their main bedroom to accommodate us.

On arrival in Perth, Western Australia, we learnt that Brisbane and surrounding towns were well and truly flooded with the great 1974 floods. I rang home and found out my family were fine, but Goodna was all flooded. The day we arrived was the day we were originally going to marry but had brought the wedding forward. This was the day the floods peaked.

We believed that luck like this was better than winning the lottery—for the second time in the space of a year. We stayed in Perth for ten days and met some of Zach's friends, including Rob and Sarah. We also saw his brother, Willy, and Willy's wife, Pat, and their children.

Ten days went fast; soon it was January 29, 1974, time

to fly to Darwin, in the Northern Territory, on the top of Australia about central on a map of Australia.

On stepping of the plane in Darwin, I immediately noticed the heat and the humidity hitting me in the face.

## Early married life in Darwin

We were met at Darwin Airport by a person from Zach's work, who drove us to our new house, a company home, at 26 Westralia Street, Stuart Park. It was a fully furnished, two-bedroom duplex with front and back yards, complete with some butterflies.

Zach organised for Grace Bros to deliver our boxes of belongings to us the next day. They had apparently just gotten through inland Queensland before it flooded. Zach went back into work with this colleague. He would be officially starting with the mining company on Friday, February 1, 1974.

On arriving home, he told me he had organised to buy a vehicle from a work colleague who was leaving to go back to Adelaide. This colleague would drop the car over the next day, Wednesday. It was a green station wagon, which would be great for going camping and fishing, as they did in the Territory.

The next day, Grace Bros delivered all our boxes, and our car arrived for $1,000. We took a drive around the town, stopping at Fanny Bay. Zach took me to the hospital, and I got the application forms to work there, as well as an interview for the following day.

Zach took me to the interview the following day, Thursday. I got entry into a nurse graduate programme for newly trained nurses. It was commencing on Monday,

February 4, 1974, and ran full-time for twelve months. I would be rotated around all the different wards and attend a lecture afternoon once a week, which would include videos.

On that Thursday, we went into the city of Darwin and did a big food shop, as well as had a good look around. Darwin was like a big country town with an incredibly relaxed and informal way of life. There were a lot of aboriginal people around, something you didn't really see in the other capital cities. I had to buy uniforms, as I didn't have any; in addition, I bought some paper veils because then trained nurses wore veils.

We both settled in to a working life. I was working shift work and weekends, which Zach did not like. So, after about eight weeks, I reverted to part-time, which worked better for us.

We both had some major adjustments to make. There was, firstly, married life and, secondly, living in Darwin. On weekends, we would go "down the track," as they say in Darwin. There is only one road out of Darwin, and it goes through central Australia to Adelaide; taking it is called going "down the track".

On one weekend, we went fishing to the Mary River. All of the rivers there had crocodiles in them. We were fishing with a great big throw net—a huge net with lead weights on the bottom of it. I was using the throw net, putting it over my shoulder and then casting it into the water.

Unfortunately, the net was so heavy I went in the river with the net. I panicked and began screaming very loudly, totally hysterical that a crocodile would get me. Zach went out on the branch of a tree to get me and yelled at me "Swim, swim."

I thought, *yes, why didn't I think of that?*

I swam to the edge of the river but couldn't get out. The banks were just thick, soft mud. Before long, boats were coming from everywhere to see what all the screaming was about. Zach eventually pulled me out, and I was covered in mud with a small blond section on top of my head.

Zach exclaimed, "Don't worry. They wouldn't have eaten you. They don't eat fresh meat. They would have dragged you off and hidden you under a log." He then said, "I've lost my watch, my sandals, and my throw net getting you out of there."

Over Easter that year, we went on a four-day camping trip. We went down to Katherine, where we went on a day trip of all the gorges by boat, leaving the boat at the end of each gorge and walking up to the next gorge to catch another boat. All of the waters and land had crocodiles, and we were in little boats. We saw a few crocodiles in the water. The gorges were absolutely spectacular, high rock faces with water at the bottom.

We left Katherine the next day and drove west across the West Australian border to Kununurra and the Ord River irrigation scheme. I shall never forget seeing fields and fields of white cotton and also fields and fields of rice being grown. It was an amazing sight. We camped here two nights. We then drove back east along the coastline to Darwin, arriving late Easter Monday afternoon in time to unpack and clean up.

On another weekend, we drove to Fanny Bay to simply watch the water over the bay. On this weekend, there was a boat moored that was taking people out waterskiing on the bay. I decided to go for a ski, and Zach went in the boat while I skied. I came off once, and Zach yelled to me, "Get up quick. There are tiger sharks and crocodiles in this bay." Apparently, the man in the boat had told him this.

I got up very quickly and signalled to be taken into the land. I never skied there again. I was terrified those few minutes in the water.

While in Darwin I got my driver's licence. Zach pushed me to get it, enrolling me in lessons and paying for them. It was so easy getting it in Darwin, a big country town. I feel I wouldn't have gotten it if I had gone in a big city like Brisbane.

Nursing at the hospital was interesting. I learnt to look after the aboriginal people. One ward was for tuberculosis, and I must have breathed in the tubercle, as my lung encapsulated it so that it shows up as a white spot on my lung to this day. The emergency room always had snakebites, as snakes thrived in the heat. I met Pauline Lyons, who was from Brisbane, at the hospital. Zach and I went out to dinner a few times with her and her husband Phil.

I missed my family and friends. We didn't have the phone connected, and I had to walk to the shops up the road to ring home. Mum and Dad sent me cassette tapes with recordings of everyone talking on them, and this was great. We also exchanged a lot of letters, as you did in those days.

Dad had been in a work accident in June. His arm was drawn into and crushed in a conveyer belt. I did not like being so far away from him with him having this sort of injury and being in pain.

For my twenty-first birthday, I had my eyelashes tinted at a little beauty shop in the Darwin Hotel. It was a life-defining experience. Because of it, I knew I wanted to become a beauty therapist and have my own little shop on a shop front one day.

On my twenty-first birthday, July 22, 1974, we held a party underneath the next door of the duplex. While the party was going, the next-door gentleman screamed out, "There's smoke coming out your back door!"

We raced upstairs to find the underneath of the overhead cupboard on fire. I had put the birko cooker on to boil water to make coffee and forgotten about it. It had boiled dry and burnt the kitchen shelf, which had also caught fire. Zach put the fire out.

After the party that night and after everybody had gone home and we were in the lounge room, Zach started bashing me, blaming me for the fire. "You're dumb," he said. "You're stupid. You're an idiot. You nearly burnt the house down." He was slapping my face back and forth, hitting me all over the lounge room. I was falling down, getting up, falling down.

I was shocked and numb after this happened. All I wanted to do was leave him.

On the Monday, I resigned at the hospital, giving two weeks' notice. I told Zach, "I am going back to Brisbane."

He replied, "Can I come too?"

I said, "I suppose so."

He resigned from his work, and we sold the car, as well as packing everything up.

We flew out of Darwin on August 9, 1974.

## Back in Brisbane, August 1974 to May 1977

We arrived that day in early August 1974 at Brisbane Airport. Zach hired a car, and we drove to a motel at Hamilton on the north side of Brisbane. Zach had an interview the next day for work as a contract's administrator with Rob and Brown builders. We lived at three different addresses in two months. First, we were at Coorparoo on Rutland Street.

Then we were at Hendra, near the airport in half a house, with an old funny couple in the other half of the house. Both of these were fully furnished. Finally, we were at Ascot at 152 Crosby Road in an unfurnished house that had a flat at the back.

While we were at Coorparoo, I visited Marie Valentine, who had a unit on Shakespeare Street. She had organised all the photos from the wedding, which we had paid for. We had left her this task. The photos were beautiful.

While we were at Hendra, Zach bought a white Datsun Fairlady sports car. We had so much fun in this car. It had a soft top, and when it rained, the roof leaked in several places. We kept plastic cups in the car for when it rained. Zach started work while we were at Coorparoo (on the south side of Brisbane). We moved to Hendra to be near his work on the north side.

Zach had said he didn't want me working shift work and weekends, so I went for an interview at Turrawan Private Hospital at Clayfield (near Hendra) as a theatre sister. This involved working mainly day shift Monday to Friday. I started there in mid-October 1974.

We then moved to Ascot, walking distance to the hospital. This house/flat was unfurnished, and in no time, Zach had all the furniture organised for it through the "for sale" column in the newspaper, *The Courier-Mail.* Zach had a real knack of organising things like accommodation, cars, and furniture very quickly.

We bought a dining room table and six chairs, a bar and two bar stools, a three-piece lounge with a big settee, and a queen bed with bedside tables, as well as a long oblong china cabinet, which had recently come back into fashion again. There was also a nest of tables for the lounge. I was very happy with our new house at Ascot.

It had white carpet throughout, so we bought a carpet sweeper and a vacuum cleaner. Not everybody had a vacuum cleaner in those days. We often had Peta and Len over for dinner, and Marie visited. She had broken up with Ryan. We also bought a colour TV, as they were just taking off, with everybody giving up their black-and-white.

I retrieved my sewing machine from Mum and Dad's, and I managed to re-cover the lounge in a blue snakeskin-like fabric. I made curtains for the bedroom and the lounge. It was such a great place. It was built into the side of a hill, with the garage under the front yard and the back yard higher than the house, with views of Brisbane City.

That Christmas Day, 1974, Cyclone Tracey hit Darwin, demolishing it. A lot of people thought we were still in Darwin. This was the third time in twenty-one months' when we were supposed to be somewhere but weren't and terrible destruction occurred there, causing loss of life and property. They say things happen in threes.

I had Christmas and January on holidays as the two theatres didn't operate. We took the sports car up the coast to Maroochydore and visited the couple who lived next door to us in Darwin with their four boys. On another day we went to the Glass House Mountains and also visited Montville, a beautiful country town known for its art and craft. We bought a pottery bread crock. On another day, we went up the coast to Noosa to visit Ryan Boston, who had moved up the coast to be with his new girlfriend, Trisha, a teacher.

We had been visiting Dad for all of his operations on his arm in Princess Alexandria Hospital, on the south side of Brisbane. He kept having microsurgery to restore all the physiology of his arm. Zach took me in the evenings. Ferrying me around everywhere was getting difficult for Zach, so he bought me my first car, a little silver Bellett.

This car sat parked on the edge of the one-way road below our house.

In February 1975, I went back to work at Turrawan Private Hospital. There was a great deal of plastic surgery performed at this hospital, including breast enhancement with silicone implants; breast reduction for oversized breasts; lipectomy, which is removal by surgery of excess abdominal fat; and facelifts and rhinoplasty (surgical cosmetic correction to the nose).

General surgery was also performed, including appendectomy and laparotomy (fully opening the abdomen to investigate), as well as bowel resection. Gynaecology included removal of the uterus, removal of tube and ovarian cyst, laparoscopic investigation of the pelvic organs for infertility, and (D&C) dilation and curettage. Orthopaedics was also performed at these two theatres.

In late February, two weeks following Valentine's Day, Zach came home one Friday night intoxicated. He began bashing me about the head and face. He seemed very angry. I had no idea what I was supposed to have done wrong. On the Monday, I went to work with bruises on my face and neck, including a black eye. When I told the girls I had been bashed by my husband, I was shunned.

There was a real stigma attached to domestic violence. It was a cultural issue that was taboo—simply not talked about except in hushed tones behind closed doors. I was given the rest of the week off, I think so they didn't have to look at me.

In March 1975, I believe Zach was unfaithful to me because this girl Sherry kept telephoning our house. If I answered, she would straight away ask to speak to Zach—no how are you or anything. Zach kept playing The Four Seasons song "Sherry" and acting indifferent towards me. He didn't have sexual relations with me all month.

In April 1975, he once again came home after drinking about 6:00 p.m. on a Friday night and began bashing me about the head and face. This time, it was my body too. I was so frightened, I jumped out of an open window in the bedroom and began running up the road. I had no shoes on, and the small stones from the road on the footpath were hurting my feet. Zach came running after me and dragged me back by the hair and continued bashing me once back inside the door.

In May 1975, Zach apologised for his unacceptable behaviour and a honeymoon-like cycle followed, where he took me to a romantic dinner. He also took me to see two movies, *Chinatown* and *The Godfather Part* II, at the Village Twin at New Farm. I found it very difficult, as I was still very much in love with this man. Only someone who has been through domestic violence would understand. Another number of "good" months followed this. He swore he would never bash me again.

I was aware Zach was gambling heavily on the horse races every Saturday, as he played the races very loudly, and I came to detest this on the radio. He placed bets through the TAB. An organisation all over Australia with outlets everywhere where anyone over eighteen could bet on the horse races in person or by phone.

I found out through a friend who had been at the wedding that Noel, Zach's friend, had told everybody except me at the wedding about Zach's past. This being that he had spent time on a prison farm at age sixteen for embezzling money from a bank he worked in and using the money to place bets. At twenty, he had declared himself bankrupt, as he'd had no way of paying the debt off, and it was the only way to get out of it. I was so embarrassed to think everybody at the wedding knew he was bankrupt at the time he married me. In those days, bankruptcy carried a real stigma and was for five years, not three.

In June 1975, The Family Law Act was passed through Parliament in Australia, and this was to forever change the family unit. It was meant to protect children when marriages broke up. This act acknowledged de facto couples, which precipitated a slow acceptance of couples living together before marriage. The act also did away with "blame" being needed to get divorced. Bringing in the "no blame" divorce made it easy for abused wives to leave their husbands, but they still had no economic support.

It is interesting that, in 1978, social services (Centrelink) brought in the sole supporting parents' pension. This paved the way for women with children in unhappy, abusive marriages to leave their husbands. And this is what happened, slowly changing the nuclear family as we knew it in 1975. Slowly, as these people remarried, blended families started happening.

Another interesting thing happened in mid-1975 that was to, in time, change the face of the family unit. With Don Dunstan as premier of South Australia, the state became the first state in Australia to decriminalise homosexuality. Slowly, the other states followed, with Tasmania being last, over twenty years later in 1997. The gay "Mardi Gras" in Sydney, an annual event that was really about LGBT rights, began in the late seventies.

On April 30, 1975, the Vietnam War finally ended, after polarising the world for so many years.

In October 1975, I began training for my second nursing certificate, midwifery, at Royal Women's Hospital. It was a twelve-month course, and I had to wear a half veil height veil on my head. The training was tough. Zach didn't like it as it meant I was back to shift work and working weekends.

So the tension began to rise between us again. He wanted to start a family, and I wasn't ready, after having looked after my siblings till I'd left home.

On Tuesday, November 11, 1975, the famous "dismissal" in Australian history occurred when Governor General Sir Charles Kerr sacked the then Gough Whitlam government, dissolving the Whitlam government. Labour had been able to push through a wide range of policies in its time. During his time in office, Whitlam had led one of the greatest reforming governments in Australian history. Malcolm Fraser headed the caretaker government, and then there was a new election in December.

In December 1975, my family spent Christmas at our house at Ascot. Zach and I cooked Christmas lunch, and I had to work a late shift that day. Mum and Dad seemed extremely happy, for they loved their new son-in-law, which was another reason why I couldn't leave Zach. I also had this strong belief that you only married once and that I had to make it work. I took my vows seriously. There was such a taboo around domestic violence, and my parents wouldn't have believed me if I'd told them anyway.

In February 1976, Zach found a house for sale that was a deceased estate. It was being sold with vendor finance. A deposit of $5,000 was required, and I put in $2,500. It was right at the top of the hill on Alderley Avenue, number 36. I cannot remember the price, but it was something like $169,000—worth $1 million today.

Our moving there was difficult; it was fully furnished and had everything left in it by the person who had died. I didn't really want to part with our beautiful furniture, but I did in order to move. It had lovely old furniture and effects in it. We set it up really nicely. It had a front and back yard. The back yard ended in a cliff face overlooking to a quarry.

Just after moving, mid 1976, Zach sold the Datsun sports car, as it was quite aged and getting too difficult to get parts for. He bought a gold Holden Monaro. It was a beautiful car. He was very proud of it, frequently washing and polishing it. I had my Bellett and was driving to and from work at the hospital in it.

I found midwifery difficult, due to the attitude of administration at the hospital. The work was very rewarding, but it frightened me off having a baby of my own. In order to gain your certificate, a lot of practicals were involved, including the requirement to deliver one hundred babies and perform fifty vaginal examinations on women in labour to determine the position of the baby. I also worked in antenatal, helping women to fall pregnant by knowing their cycle.

Around this time, on a Friday night, Zach came home late, intoxicated, and began bashing me around the head and face. He was swinging me around the lounge room by my hair and arms. After he stopped, he went to bed and started snoring heavily, smelling of alcohol. I was so deeply upset I just wanted to die, and I put my head in the gas oven with it turned on. After a while, I felt like vomiting and decided I wanted to live. I told no one about this incident or the violence. It was taboo in society at this time.

Peta and Len got married and we were bridesmaid and best man at the wedding. I made the dress, a Japanese-style gown, on the sewing machine in a beautiful blue fabric. We often held dinners at our house. We met a couple at tennis lessons, Leigh and Don, and they came over for dinner, along with Pauline and Phil Lyons from Darwin. Marie had joined the Department of Foreign Affairs as a diplomat for Australia in other countries. Her first posting was Paris, and she wrote to me often. I played tennis regularly with Leigh.

One evening, we went to Leigh and Don's for dinner, and they had cooked a meal for us in their microwave, which I thought absolutely amazing. I had not heard of a microwave until this. The microwave, though developed in 1970, did not start to sell until the mid-'70s. And even then, sales were very slow. It was not until the early '80s that sales took off, with TV shows on how to cook in a microwave and microwave cookbooks being released.

Music was something that bonded Zach and me. We loved our music—the Stylistics; the Four Seasons; Linda Ronstadt; the Everley Brothers; the Doors; Creedence Clearwater Revival; the Beatles; Charles Lennon; and Paul McCartney's band, Wings. The Beatles had broken up in the 1970s, citing Yoko Ono as the cause. The Bay City Rollers and the Osmonds were big bands dominating the '70s, but neither Zach nor I liked either of them. I still listened to Carole King and Rod Stewart, as well as Carly Simon, which weren't Zach's favourites.

It was around this time that I met Maurie Doss, a friend of Zach's from work, along with his wife, Nerida. She had a baby girl, Natalie, and I became the godmother. Maurie made lots of cassette tapes for us of some great music.

Also, around this time, I had a falling out with Peta. Zach had told me while I was on evening shift and Len was away that he and Peta had made love on her couch. I stupidly believed him, realising many years later it was just his jealousy over me being so close to anyone else; he wanted to separate me from her.

We also visited Auntie Lilly and Uncle Joe often, and they came to our house for Sunday lunch sometimes. I wrote to my Auntie Mescal, who was now in Perth. We visited Auntie Mabel and Uncle Reg occasionally in the evenings.

Zach took me a couple of times to visit my family at Grantham—a two-hour drive. They had an emu, which met you at the gate, and I found this really scary, with his big, long neck and standing taller than the car. He was overly friendly.

In October 1976, I completed midwifery, gaining my second nursing certificate. Not long after that, I began work at the Prince Charles Hospital at Chermside in a coronary care unit, which I loved.

About this time, Mum and Dad were planning a world trip spanning three continents for ten weeks away. One day when I was visiting in late November, they were discussing the trip, and Dad asked me if I would come and look after the property, as well as Charlie and Tony, my younger siblings, while they were away.

I said I was undecided, and Mum stormed out the front door onto the patio, exclaiming, "I just won't go unless my daughter is here while I'm gone!"

I then said I would.

This meant resigning from my position at Prince Charles Hospital, as I hadn't been in the position long and couldn't get the leave. We had a mortgage, so Zach was not very happy. I resigned to finish mid-January 1977, and they were leaving early February 1977.

Looking after my younger siblings was not that easy. Charlie made it impossible for me. She was a rebellious teenager; at thirteen, she already had a boyfriend. She did not help in the house or with cooking or washing up. Tony missed Mum and Dad and seemed sad and unhappy. I think he was worried they wouldn't come home.

Dad left me a book of signed cheques with arrangements for the local convenience store to cash them. In those days, there were a lot of convenience stores and no big shopping centres. I remember clearly that, after buying the groceries and putting petrol in my car, there wasn't much left over from the cheques. Zach came for dinner a couple of nights, and the dinners were full of tension, as he just wasn't happy at all.

Mum and Dad came home eventually, and Mum hugged me. This was only the second time in my life that she'd hugged me. She had brought me a pair of pearl earrings from a pearl farm in Los Angeles. After hearing many stories about their trip, I finally left that night in my Bellett for home in Brisbane, an hour's drive. I got home to a very angry husband.

He exclaimed, "I am taking you to Perth! I am sick of your parents interfering in our marriage! We will be there in a fortnight!"

I thought I would go with him because I was scared of being alone.

We sold all the beautiful old furniture and my beloved Bellett. We got Grace Bros in to pack everything up in boxes. I found the whole ordeal heartbreaking. We would rent the house out, putting it in the hands of a real estate agent. We would drive the Holden Monaro overland to the opposite side of this vast country to Perth on the southern tip of Western Australia.

We drove the inland road through country towns in New South Wales. It was not without event. The car suffered a tyre burnout at high speed just out of Dubbo. Zach managed to slow the car, and we did not roll thanks to amazing driving skills on his part. But the burnout slowed us down, as we spent the night in Dubbo to recover and get a new tyre.

We hardly stopped. Zach just drove madly towards his target, Perth. We did stay in a little hotel in Eucla, a very small town on the border of South Australia and Western Australia, which advertised "hot showers." This was a dribble of water!

We drove over the Nullarbor Plain, which was thousands of miles of perfectly flat road with no vegetation other than the odd little flower and no sign of civilisation. We did stop at the Great Australian Bight and walked towards the edge with signs fifteen metres back that read, "Do not proceed. Ground gives way." It was an absolutely stunning sight, a cliff face with a sheer drop-off for thousands of metres, which gave way if you walked on it. It took us a full day to travel the Nullarbor Plain.

The first and only town we came to was a mining town, Kalgoorlie, a few hours' drive out of Perth, known for its prostitutes. We stopped for tea and stayed the night in a little motel, as Zach just couldn't drive any more that day after the flat forever miles of the Nullarbor. We headed off early the next morning for Zach's parents place at Gosnells, a suburb going inland from Perth, arriving mid-morning on that day, end of May 1977.

## The other side of Australia, Perth, May '77 to August '79

We stayed with Zach's parents for about one week. They gave up their double bed for us, and I didn't feel comfortable about the arrangement. Zach was applying for jobs and going for interviews. He secured a job with Rio Tinto and was to start in two weeks. We looked at flats and found a very cheap one at Innaloo that was still nice, probably because Innaloo smelt awful, like being in a loo. We moved there in late May 1977. Before moving. I went to visit my

Auntie Mescal, who lived two train stops up from Gosnells with her new husband and children.

I got a job at a nearby hospital, Osbourne Park Hospital, in a surgical ward. My brother Jack stayed with us for about six weeks while we lived there. I would go up to the public phones to ring home, as we didn't have the phone connected.

We would visit friends of Zach's, Rob and Sarah, and through them, we met Lou and Aaron Tall. Rob and Sarah lived in a big brick four-bedroom, two-bathroom house with a fireplace. This was typical of Perth, so different to Brisbane, with its wooden three-bedroom "Queenslanders" up on stilts.

The houses in Perth were built of brick—double brick—for the Perth weather; it was freezing cold in winter and sweltering hot in summer. Most of the dwellings in Perth had air conditioning, unlike in Brisbane. Rob and Sarah had twin boys, and Sarah was pregnant again. Lou was a hairdresser with her own shop, and she and Aaron had a great big docile Alsatian dog. They, too, had their own house.

Zach and I looked at houses to purchase. We looked at one at Scarborough, just out of the city on the beach. Perth is built around the Swan River and on the beach. I regretted not letting Zach buy this property. It had a pool and a barbecue area and was fully finished. I think he would have been much happier had we bought this place. Instead, we bought a house at 46 Cutter Crescent, Beldon, walking distance to the beach and not far from Mullaloo. It was a new home, just finished by A. V. Jennings. The yards were not finished at all.

While at Osbourne Park Hospital, I met Mellissa Johnson, and we started going waterskiing with her and her husband, John, in the dams just out of Perth. Zach liked to go marron fishing in these dams with cray pots. Marron are freshwater creatures like crayfish, only smaller and absolutely delicious. They are unique to Western Australia. Zach would boil them up in pots at home and shell them for me.

We moved to our new house in September 1977. There was a lot of work to be done in the yard, and I wondered whether we would ever do it. We got a loan of $5,000 to do the landscaping and planted a lot of plants, especially down the side, and had the driveway put in, as well as paving out from the dining room.

Rob and Sarah gave us a lounge, and Zach's parents bought us a fridge. We purchased the most beautiful dining room setting from Zimmpel's Furniture in Perth. It was black painted burnt timber in a Spanish style, a six-seat setting. We bought a wall unit in a walnut veneer, which was beautifully crafted. We also bought a new bed and bedside cabinets with lamps.

Zach wanted to start a family, so I went off the pill but didn't fall pregnant straight away. But we kept trying.

I had applied for a position of theatre sister on the commissioning staff of a new hospital that was going to be built at Glengarry, close by to us at Beldon. When Matron Margaret Connor first interviewed me, it was just a vacant block of land, and she was employing two trained nurses for each section to work with the architects in the design stage.

I got this job, partly because I had midwifery, and she wanted this sister to relieve in labour ward. Ellie was the other girl employed for theatre, and she and I never really got on.

This was the most challenging job I have ever taken on. But it was by far the most satisfying and would be one of my career achievements. My name is listed on a plaque in the foyer entrance to the hospital as one of the commissioning staff. We watched the hospital being built and had a say in what materials were used in the theatre section.

Once the hospital was built, we had the task of fully equipping the theatre complex, buying everything from operating tables and trolleys to instruments, linen, and sutures—absolutely everything to fully set up the theatre. After fully equipping the theatre complex, we had to design theatre trays with instruments and theatre linen packs, as well as write policy and procedure manuals. We had to set up systems. Four more theatre staff members were employed. And just before Christmas that year, we officially opened.

That Christmas was particularly memorable at Zach's parents. Zach gave me a long, peach-coloured nightie with a brunch coat to match. Zach's Mum was an excellent cook and put on a traditional Polish spread. His parents gave us a beautiful stainless steel silver cutlery set, all boxed. I missed my family and rang them from the shops at the end of the street. I had Christmas off duty, and we had a party at our new house for all our friends to see in the New Year 1978.

In 1978, I worked at the Glengarry Hospital all year. I also spent the whole year trying to have a baby.

On July 25, 1978, three days following my birthday, the world's first test-tube baby was born. Louise Joy Brown was born at Oldham Hospital in Manchester, United Kingdom. And here I was trying to have a baby.

It took twelve years to perfect the method of conception outside the human body called in vitro fertilisation (IVF). This, in years to come, would massively impact the family unit, giving LGBT people the ability to have their own children and changing the nuclear family as we knew it then.

In August 1978, I spoke with a doctor, Malcom "Mal"

Washer, who I worked with in anaesthetics about my inability to fall pregnant. He was a general practitioner in practise at a clinic near where I lived. I decided to see him as a patient.

He examined me and took some swabs and slides. When the results came back, they showed I had chlamydia, a common sexually transmitted disease (STD) and bacteria. He said my husband had to provide a seminal specimen, as he would have the infection too. When I told Zach, he blamed me and said I had given it to him. I was very upset. The results of his tests came back showing he had the infection too and that, as a result, he had a very low sperm count. It would return to normal after medication, which we both commenced on straight away.

To distract us from the mission of trying to have a baby, we went to the movies often and saw *The Towering Inferno*, as well as *The Poseidon Adventure*. In 1977, *Star Wars* was released by Twentieth Century Fox and was still playing at the cinema in 1978, so we saw that.

We also saw Sylvester Stallone in the Oscar-winning *Rocky*. We had game nights at our house. Couples would come, and we'd play cards and, afterwards, serve supper. We had dinners at our house and went to other couples' houses for dinner. Zach watched his favourite TV shows, *Colombo* and *Kojak*. In November 1978, we took up golf lessons.

On November 28, 1978, a Saturday morning, we went to a golf lesson and, afterwards, went to a seafood restaurant with a couple we met at golf and had the most delicious meal. Afterwards, we went home and made wild passionate love, and following I hung my legs up on the wall above the bed, hoping to get pregnant.

I missed my next period. And on December 21, 1978, I took a urine sample to the doctor for testing. I couldn't believe it—it showed I was pregnant. The baby was due on Zach's birthday—August 21, 1979.

I told Zach that night, and he walked out of the kitchen; out onto the patio away from me; and said loudly, in not a nice tone, "Well I don't *know* where I will *be* next August."

I was truly upset.

We had friends staying with us at the time who'd come over from Brisbane, Maurie and Nerida Doss, with their two-year-old daughter, Natalie, who was my god-daughter. They were in the bedroom at the time this happened and didn't understand why I was so upset.

To see the New Year 1979 in, we had a party at our house. Zach had been really awful to me, so I sat in my bedroom. He came in and started bashing me across the face and head and told me I had to come out of the bedroom. I was so deeply upset I found it difficult to function that night. Zach had organised the party, not me.

I didn't want him to be the father of the baby with the way he had treated me. So, I stupidly told him he wasn't the father of the baby. I was just so angry with him.

Later that night, I told him he was the father. I was just angry with him. He wanted this girl, Janet, who he knew in Brisbane who worked for Rob and Brown to come over and stay with us. I said, "No. She can't come and stay with us."

He started going away on business trips up north to the Pilbara region with his work.

While I was alone in the house, vague memories of the night that man stood outside my windows in 1969, the home invasion, started resurfacing. My mother was very pregnant that night and went into labour. I would just sit and look out the windows into the dark space outside. I felt frightened being alone.

These people started ringing in the evenings saying

Zach owed them money. One said he would put Zach in cement boots at the bottom of the Swan River if the debt was not paid. When I approached Zach about these calls, he fobbed me off.

I found out from the bank manager who had lent us the $5,000 for the landscaping that Zach had increased the loan to $10,000 without my knowledge and had forged my signature to do it. The payments were behind on the loan, and the bank manager had rung me at work to ask me to make payment. I started investigating my tax cheque from last year, which, to my knowledge, hadn't arrived. I found out it had been cashed. And written on the back was, "Pay to Z. DeVito," with my forged signature on it. I had been giving him nearly all my pay since I'd worked at Glengarry.

Zach eventually came clean and told me he had gambling debts and asked me to take over our all of our financial affairs, which I did.

I kept working at the hospital in theatre till May 1979, when Matron Connor said her insurance didn't cover pregnancy beyond six months. I got everybody paid and up to date. As I resigned, Margaret Thatcher had been elected as the first female prime minister of the United Kingdom in May 1979. In the same month, my sister Amy in Townsville, Queensland, had given birth to a little girl and called her Christina.

We spent May, June, and July getting the nursery ready. Zach bought a baby's cupboard and painted it white. We bought a beautiful cot, with two drawers underneath. I had bought some beautiful clothes for a baby. The nursery looked beautiful, and so did our house. I was happy with both, though I didn't feel very happy, and I hadn't seen any butterflies since leaving Brisbane.

On the morning of August 1, I started having

contractions and rang Zach to let him know the baby was on its way. I had decided early on on falling pregnant that I would have a gynaecologist/obstetrician S. O. Lim, who I worked with, deliver the baby. And on that day, I rang his rooms.

Zach came home from work and stayed with me. In the afternoon when the contractions got closer, he took me to Osbourne Park Hospital to have the baby.

## The birth of Steven and suffering amnesia

On arrival at the hospital labour ward at about 2:00 p.m., I was shown to a bathroom and asked to shower and put on a labour ward gown. I was given a small enema and used the toilet. After this, I was taken to a labour ward room to have the baby. The contractions at this stage were not strong and ten minutes apart. They firstly took the foetal heart rate, which I could hear on a machine. It was nice to hear, like galloping horses. The contractions stayed like this until teatime when Dr Lim came to see me. He decided to break the waters to try and speed things up.

This made the contractions a lot stronger and closer together. About 7:00 p.m., they started to get quite painful, and I was firstly given the nitrous oxide gas to breathe on with the contractions. About 10:00 p.m., I was given an intramuscular injection of a narcotic drug to relieve the dreadful pain. I felt I was going to roll off the narrow couch I was on with each contraction. Zach threatened me, saying, if I rolled off the couch and harmed the baby, he would harm me.

The never-ending, continual pain with each contraction just kept on coming over and over again. I thought it would never end. The narcotic drug had dampened the pain, but I was worried about the effect on the baby. Dr Lim had been in to see me a number of times.

At 3:00 a.m., I was having trouble pushing the baby out. I had been pushing for some time with each contraction, so Dr Lim decided to deliver the baby with forceps. At 3:10 a.m. on August 2, 1979, a baby boy was born. We had decided to call him Steven Anthony.

As Steven was born, I ripped vaginally, and it felt like someone had put a hot knife in my vagina and taken it up to my stomach. I had a post birth haemorrhage and lost a significant amount of blood. I then felt a tremendous heaviness on my chest and the most excruciating chest pain that came in spasms. I'd had a heart attack.

The next thing I remember is my legs up in stirrups and being stitched up vaginally. I do not remember anything else until the next morning about 9:00 a.m., when I woke up to the baby beside me. That was the first time I remember seeing him. I couldn't believe how perfect he was, and it was one of the happiest moments of my life.

Zach was then brought into me, and I didn't recognise him. I had complete amnesia. All I could remember was what my mind had blocked out—the home invasion and being beaten by my father in a garage when I was three. I knew I needed help and asked to see a psychiatrist. Dr Lim found me one. He said he was the best in Perth.

I lay there for two days remembering all these dreadful memories over and over. They plagued me night and day. What I actually had was post-traumatic stress disorder, but it wasn't a diagnosis in those days. It was known as "shell shock" in 1979 and usually only diagnosed in returned soldiers who had fought in a war.

On discharge from hospital, Zach took me to my home

at Beldon. But I did not at first recognise it. The memories did slowly come back after a few days. I saw a cardiologist, Dr Lane, who diagnosed me with Prinzmetal angina, a rare form of angina where the coronary arteries go into spasm when under extreme stress or in deep rest. They are not clogged with cholesterol.

I saw the psychiatrist, and he wrongly diagnosed me with bipolar disorder and put me on medication for this, which made me feel absolutely dreadful. He made his diagnosis based on everything Zach had told him about me; he hardly spoke to me at all.

I couldn't cope at home with Zach, so my Auntie Mescal suggested I go and stay with her, which I did. I found it very hard at her house with the memories of the home invasion plaguing me. My cousin, her daughter Rhondda, was born deaf, as Mescal was exposed to German measles when pregnant with her, and Rhondda was very loud and didn't speak in clear English. I found this nerve-racking, along with the dogs up the back barking. I felt I was losing my mind and so agreed to go back into hospital at Glengarry because it was familiar surroundings.

I spent two weeks in Glengarry. The medication made me feel awful, and I had to stop breastfeeding the baby because of the medication, which truly upset me. I couldn't sit still, and I felt rigid. I had an allergic reaction called tardive dyskinesia to one of the drugs. With tardive dyskinesia, the head arches back, and the tongue curls up, and the spine starts to curl up. Dr Mal Washer came from the theatre and gave me an intravenous drug to neutralise the reaction.

When I arrived home at my house, Zach told me he was taking me to Karratha in the Pilbara in the north-west of Western Australia, where his work had posted him. He was advised by doctors not to take me but, rather, to leave me in Perth, where there were familiar surroundings to help my amnesia. He told me the house had to be sold to pay gambling debts. I was heartbroken when Grace Bros came the next day to pack up the whole house. I felt like squatting in a room and refusing to go.

On September 1, 1979, we boarded a plane for Karratha.

## Living in remote Australia: Steven's early baby days

On stepping off the plane in Karratha, the heat hit me; the temperature was high—38 degrees Celsius—and this was springtime, September. We were met by company personnel and driven to our house on the edge of this small town. Almost everybody who lived in the town worked for the company, Rio Tinto, or for BHP.

All the houses were built to take cyclones. They were of metal fabrication, bolted down, and had metal screens on all the windows. All of the buildings in the town were air-conditioned because of the extreme heat. There was little vegetation in the town, with some trees beyond the town. In town, there was no vegetation, just red earth and rock. It was iron ore-rich country. There definitely were no butterflies in sight the whole time I lived there.

I was faced with all the boxes of our belongings in the house, with no inclination to unpack them or set up a house. I enjoyed baby days with Steven. He had his bath every morning, and I would feed him breakfast and formula in a bottle. I talked to him all the time, as I had no one else to talk to— except the maternal and child welfare sister, occasionally, and Ann next door, who worked in the office at Zach's work full-time.

On weekends, I would ask Zach to take me for a drive (we had a company vehicle). The drive seemed fruitless, as there was just miles and miles of red earth and red dust. After a while, I began to see beauty in the different red rocks. On Saturday nights, he would take me for fish and chips at this restaurant on the coast at the port of Dampier, an hour's drive away. The restaurant sold amazing seafood at sit-down tables, and we took Steven in his bassinet.

For me, life was very difficult with the PTSD. All the memories of when I'd thought my life was threatened were coming back to me, including incidents of domestic violence, as well as falling in the Mary River with the crocodiles and waterskiing in Darwin at Fanny Bay. I wanted the good memories of my life to come back and knew, for this to happen, I had to get home to Brisbane somehow.

There was also the economic abuse. I had no money and no income other than the child endowment, about twenty dollars every month.

Christmas 1979, we flew to Perth and stayed with Zach's parents. We saw Lou and Aaron, and after seeing them, I remembered them. Lou told me Zach wanted to have me incarcerated in a mental asylum and have the baby all to himself. We saw Rob and Sarah, who were Zach's loyal friends.

On returning to Karratha, the outside temperatures were in the forties from January onwards. It was too hot to take a baby outside in the sweltering heat. There was a small group of four shops for the town and one a supermarket close to where we lived. I would walk there with Steven in the pram just to get out. For something to do, I sewed three summer dresses on the sewing machine, which was satisfying, as I hadn't sewn in years.

One day in mid-March, I was in the storeroom outside the garage just looking around, and what I found terrified me. In a box was a plastic container of kerosene with some rags and newspaper and a tomahawk axe. I immediately thought, *My God, is he going to kill me?*

I went to see the maternal and child welfare sister right away and told her I thought my husband was going to murder me. I mean, who else did I have to tell? I rang my mother and told her, but she never believed anything I said, so that was fruitless.

On the evening of March 29, 1979, I was talking to Lou on the phone, and she said, "Anthea, you have to get out of there. He is going to have you committed."

Zach overheard us talking and rushed into the kitchen where the phone was and pulled the phone out of the wall. He then began bashing me about the head and face. I immediately ran out the back door to Ann next door, hurting my foot on the way. I told Ann and her husband that Zach intended on murdering me or having me committed to a mental asylum. I spent the night at her house.

The next morning, March 30, 1979, someone from the company came to see me, and I spoke with him about what was happening. He said the company would fly me out of Karratha to Perth at 1:00 pm. I was to go home and pack a suitcase and the pram and they would pick me up at twelve midday. I did this and brought the suitcase and pram and Steven to Anne's. I left Karratha at 1:00 p.m. Company personnel met me at Perth Airport and drove me to our home at Cutter Crescent.

Lou met me there. She said, "Anthea, you have to leave Perth ASAP. Zach is going to have you committed. We are prepared to lend you $2,000 and have booked a ticket for you on the midnight flight to Brisbane tonight because we know you're not crazy." They rang the real estate representative for me, and he met me at the house.

Zach always accused me of having sexual relations with this man, but nothing ever happened. I simply spoke to him about the house and my position in terms of what I was doing.

Lou and Aaron took me to the airport at 11:00 p.m., and at twelve midnight, I flew out of Perth for Sydney. The plane was refuelling in Sydney. I had one suitcase of clothes, which had only two changes of clothes for me and was full of nappies and two teddy bears, mine and Steven's. I also had a pram and my baby, Steven.

Dad said he would meet me at the airport and had invited me to stay at home. By the time I reached Brisbane Airport, I was so weak I was wheeled of the plane first in a wheelchair.

## Marital separation, Brisbane, March 1980 to December 1980

Dad met me at twelve midday on Wednesday, March 31, 1980, when the plane got in from Sydney. He was pleased to see me. Steven had spent a lot of time in the cockpit on the journey up to Brisbane. The captain had taken a shine to him. We got my luggage, the pram and a suitcase, and we then proceeded to the car. Dad drove me home to Redbank Plains, and all the memories of my teenage years came flooding back, as well as memories of the home invasion. On seeing Mum, I instantly remembered a mother who, all my life, had not loved me.

Never in my life was her seething hatred of me more evident than in the next fifty hours. As soon as Dad left to go back to work, she started saying, "Anthea I don't believe a word you've said about Zach. You're telling lies. You're lucky to have such a good man marry you." She also said, "Don't you have somewhere else to stay? Don't you have friends you can stay with?"

She completely ignored her new grandson and did not even acknowledge him the whole time I stayed with them. No arrangements had been made for me bringing a baby, and I had to sleep in the same single bed as him.

Mum continually kept saying, "Anthea you should go back to Zach. I don't know what you're doing here."

Steven was crawling around the floor, pulling himself up, and she refused to put anything up so he wouldn't break it. I unplugged an electrical cord to a huge lamp on a low table, which Steven was pulling, so he couldn't pull the lamp off, and she kept plugging the lamp back in.

Charlie hadn't spoken to me since I'd looked after her in 1977 when she was thirteen years old; she'd harboured a grudge against me since then. She was clearly on Mum's side and treated me without love and without respect and, if anything, with contempt. She also ignored Steven, failing to even acknowledge him.

I was standing on the back patio on Friday, and when no one was looking, Mum picked up the rubber doormat and started belting me around the body with it and yelling, "Will you please leave?"

I ran inside crying and immediately rang my girlfriend Suzanne (who I'd met on my twentieth birthday at Zach's flat).

She said she and her boyfriend, Benedict, had rented a flat a couple of streets away from her mother at the Grange, but they both basically still lived at home with their parents. It was so they could have a private relationship. Suzanne said I could come and stay at the flat, which had two bedrooms.

I rang Dad and asked him if he would come home as soon as possible and take me to Suzanne's. He said he would, and he arrived not long after. I was all packed up and ready to go.

Suzanne was very welcoming and glad to see me. Both Suzanne and Benedict took an active interest in Steven. I went to the Department of Social Security (now Centrelink) on Monday and put in a claim for the sole supporting pension.

I went to see a doctor on Monday, as I was passing blood in my urine and had terrible back pain. I had bruises all over my body. He ordered an ultrasound, which showed I had bruised BS swollen kidneys. I needed a lot of rest and drank a lot of water.

I took Steven for walks in the pram and went into the local Grange real estate looking for accommodation. I met Mr Ray Green and his daughter Janet. They were really nice to me, and I became friends with them.

Dad came to visit on the Thursday but said I was to say nothing to the family of his visits and that this was the way it would be from now on if I wanted to know him. So began a secret relationship with my father, which was to continue till 1996, when I said, "I cannot play the game anymore." I showed Dad the bruises and told him about the ultrasound results. Then he realised that Mum really had beaten me. He told me that Auntie Mabel had offered me a place to stay if I wanted to stay with her. I stayed with Suzanne and Benedict at their flat for a number of weeks.

Maurie and Nerida from Coorparoo came to visit and offered for me to come and stay with them to give Suzanne and Benedict a break. So, I did. One night I prayed and prayed for my own little place with a fence and some grass for Steven to crawl on—something I could afford. I was crying so much I cried myself to sleep.

The next morning, my prayers were answered. A friend of Nerida's, Desley, with her husband, had moved out of a small flat, which was a third of a house. In the other two-thirds lived the owners, an elderly couple. It was on Kitchener Street in Coorparoo, on walking distance to Nerida's and to what was then Myers (now Coorparoo Square and high-rise). It would be like living in a house and was fenced in and had grass.

I met the couple that morning and moved in that afternoon. It was fully furnished with a little black-and-white television. The bedroom was massive, so I divided it into two with the big wardrobe cupboards, giving Steven a third of the room. Maurie and Nerida got me a cot. The house only had one front door with a little room inside that served both flats. It had been several weeks since I'd slept in a bed without Steven, and to sleep in the bed by myself seemed like a luxury.

Dad visited me every week at the flat. On his second visit, he brought a Russell Hobbs electric kettle because, on his first visit, I was boiling water for a pot of tea on a gas stove. Nerida got together a whole lot of kitchen things for me. I took Steven for lots of walks in the pram, and I either visited Nerida, or she visited me most days.

Steven had his first birthday on August 2, 1980. Dad visited that day, and so did Nerida with the girls Natalie and Susan.

After a couple of months, a relief night duty RN position came up at Dolcie Domum Nursing Home (which later became Coorparoo Nursing Centre), and I got the job. I then had to find someone to look after Steven, which I did through the East Brisbane family day-care scheme. They found me Anne Whitehead, who lived in Shire Street Coorparoo. I could walk to Anne's house and then to the nursing home on Shakespeare Street, leaving home at 9:15 p.m. I did this in winter for the three months relief during July, August, and September.

The Walkman with a cassette tape plus headphones was released in 1979, and with my earnings, I bought one of these. I wanted a colour television and a video recorder, which came out in 1978. But I believed that, while I was living in poverty with few possessions, I'd never afford these things. As a result of the release of the video recorder, there were video hire shops popping up all over town.

I caught up with Colleen from school and Gail with all the nursing girls, and this helped a lot of my memories to come back. I wrote to Lou and Aaron, and they wrote back. I saw Peta regularly at Nerida's place.

Both houses in Perth and in Brisbane sold late this year and were settled. I did not receive any proceeds. All monies went to pay off Zack's gambling debts.

In October and November, I felt trapped into a life of poverty. I played with Steven on the grass and in the house. I talked to Steven a lot. The lady next door crocheted Steven a Santa Clause and a stocking in December.

I got a surprise just before Christmas. Zach came to the front door and knocked. The elderly couple, of course, let him in once he'd told them he was my husband. He took off his big work boots and left them in the lounge.

He stayed that night and we did not have sexual relations but slept together. The old couple must have rung Centrelink, as the next day, there was a knock on the back door, and it was an investigation officer from Centrelink.

He came into the lounge room, which was at the back entry and said, "Who do those boots belong to?"

I said, "My husband he is just visiting."

The officer then said, "We have been told your husband is living here with you, and I am to further advise you that your next Centrelink payment will be stopped."

I was flabbergasted.

In that moment, I decided to go back to Zach. I thought I would give the marriage one last try so I could be absolutely sure I was doing the right thing if I left for good.

Zach was now working for Ranger Uranium Mines, living in the temporary town of Jabiru while the permanent town of Jabiru was being built. Jabiru is on the edge of Arnhem Land in the Northern Territory, sacred aboriginal land, about a three-hour drive out of Darwin.

Zach stayed with me until the first few days of January when Grace Bros came to pack up the belongings I had. On January 3, 1981, I handed back the keys to the flat. Maurie and Nerida took us to the airport, and we flew out for Darwin. We were met by a Ranger Uranium personnel, who drove us to Jabiru.

## A reconciliation: The edge of Arnhem Land, 1981

On the way to Jabiru, we went via Coles and got a huge shop—enough for six weeks, as apparently, there was only a convenience store at the temporary town of Jabiru where we would be living. We arrived at the house after three hours of driving. The house was a demountable on steel poles with the garage and laundry underneath.

It was fenced off about a half an acre of bushland with

metal poles and wire meshing. On the other side of the fence were kangaroos and dingoes, which could be seen from the back veranda. The demountable was fully air-conditioned, as it was very hot and humid outside, a January day. We had a company vehicle built for the terrain.

Zach bought two mountain bikes on our next trip to Darwin. Mine had a seat canopy on the back for Steven. Zach also organised a big sandpit in the backyard for Steven. I was worried about snakes and watched him very closely. We got a black and white, medium-sized dog, and Steven loved to play in the sandpit with the dog.

I went for walks to the swimming pool and then rode once we had the bikes. I rode all around Jabiru with Steven on the back through beautiful pristine bushland. I didn't like to go too far, as there were buffalo, and I was scared of them.

We didn't go swimming in the natural waterways, as there were crocodiles in the water. They also travelled over land. I met the policeman's wife at the swimming pool, there with her little one. She and I started playing tennis twice a week at the courts on site with our babies in prams. I wrote a prolific number of letters, as you did in those days.

I wrote to Suzanne and Benedict, Lou and Aaron, Nerida and Maurie, Colleen from school, and Gail from nursing, as well as Mum and Dad and also Auntie Lilly and Uncle Joe and Auntie Mabel and Uncle Reg. I occasionally rang home in the evenings when Dad was home. I'd call from the shops up the road, as we did not have a phone connected.

Zach did not give me money, and I had no income. I had money saved from the year before in the Commonwealth Bank. There was nowhere to spend your money, except when we went to Darwin every six weeks. The convenience store was everything—a post office, agent for the Commonwealth Bank, a petrol outlet, a newsagent, and a convenience store. Everything was frightfully expensive, especially if it was cold or frozen at this store.

While we were in Jabiru, Zach did a lot of fishing on the weekends. One Saturday on one of these trips, I sat on a big flat rock with Steven just watching. We caught some delicious fish. The next day, Sunday, we returned to this same spot, and there was a four-metre crocodile sitting on the rock where I had been sitting the day before. We didn't go there again.

We went for lots of four-wheel drives into the bush, and there were always lots of buffalo and some kangaroos. In one area, there were original rock paintings thousands of years old. In another area, there was a high density of very high ant hills.

By April, the wet season had hit. It just rained day and night for five months, and everything flooded. I stayed indoors much of this time, just going to women's craft days held at the new town of Jabiru. Zach showed me around all the new houses in the new town, and they were really beautiful.

At craft days, I learnt pottery on a wheel, making a pen holder and a bowl, as well as an ash tray. We also learnt basket weaving, and I made some mats that I still have today.

On May 2, 1981, Suzanne and Benedict got married in Brisbane, becoming Mr and Mrs Banning. I was unable to attend the wedding. Suzanne sent me photos. In mid-May 1981, my dad's mother, my grandmother Louise Dagan, passed away. Dad was feeling unsupported as Mum hated his mother (who she continually said I took after her). Though I wasn't allowed to know her and only saw her once, I felt sad for the loss. I was even sadder when Dad told me they piled most of her possessions in the backyard and burnt them all, keeping some pieces of furniture for restoration.

In June, there was a taipan snake, a small very deadly snake in my washing machine that came out every time I did the washing. Zach got the natural elders, aboriginal people, to get it out and relocate it. I worried the snake would come back, so I lit a match when going near the washing machine. Snakes have heat sensors, and this would bring him out if he was in there. This was what the aboriginal people said to do.

Zach was receiving death threats from anti-uranium mining protesters. His role at the mine was contracts administration for the construction of the mine; once built he would move on to the next mine being built. These people had also threatened to harm his family.

In July 1981, I was fed up with the heat and the rain, as well as these threats and asked Zach if I could go back to Brisbane. I was having difficulty sleeping with him given all that he had done to me. I asked him when he came home at lunchtime as he did every day.

He opened up the front door and bundled me up and threw me down the front stairs, a flight of fifteen stairs, onto a cement landing at the base of the stairs. This fractured my third and fourth lumbar vertebrae and ruptured the disc space between, depositing spinal disc fluid like gel onto the spine. This I was to discover on getting medical treatment back in Brisbane.

The injury caused me permanent disability for the rest of my life, with back pain and inability to sit for more than a few hours in one position. At the time it happened, I could barely walk and couldn't sit and just lay flat in bed.

The next day, he came home at lunchtime to no lunch prepared, telling me he had organised for me to leave Jabiru and would spend ten days in Brisbane with me to set up accommodation. He had booked flights out of Darwin to Brisbane on my birthday, July 22, 1981, a week away. I spent the week in bed. I was fed up with all the moving around and just couldn't do it anymore. My birthday came, and we drove to Darwin and then flew out after lunch; all the sitting was extremely painful.

On arriving in Brisbane, Zach hired a car, and we drove to a fully serviced guest house at East Brisbane where we had a booking. We stayed there all week. We looked at houses and flats to let and found a nice house at 214 Jones Road Carina Heights, which we could move into on Saturday. It had a nice garden, and I thought I could grow some flowers to attract the butterflies.

It was about five- to ten-minute drive from Nerida in Coorparoo and the other side of town from Suzanne and Benedict. We had gone during the week and organised beds, wardrobes, a dining setting, and a fridge, with all being delivered on Saturday, July 29, 1981. On this day, Prince Charles married Princess Diana, and I managed to watch it on the television in the afternoon.

Zach organised for my belongings—both in storage in Perth and in Jabiru—to come to this house. He flew out of Brisbane for Darwin on the Thursday, putting money in my bank account for food and living expenses. That Wednesday was Steven's second birthday, August 2, 1981, four days after moving to the house.

Zach continued to put support in my bank account every month August, September, October, November, and December. I saw a doctor and found out the extent of damage to my spine after medical imaging. I became very good friends with the elderly couple who lived next door, Doreen and Frank West. Nerida came over often in her old Holden Kingswood, bringing my god-daughter Natalie, who had started school, and her sister, Susan, born July 25, 1979, about a week before Steven. Nerida was pregnant again. I took Steven for walks to the Carina Library, the shops, and the park often.

In December, Zach's work had paid for us to go to Hayman Island on the barrier reef for Christmas. I bought a new bikini and two new outfits with money I had saved in 1980. We were going to Townsville afterwards to see my sister Amy. On arriving on the island, I decided to go waterskiing every day, which I did with great difficulty with my back. On getting in from skiing, I had a gin and tonic to refresh me.

Zach and I argued a lot of the time. I couldn't bring myself to have sex with him after all he had done to me, especially my spine. Seeing him brought back all the memories of domestic violence in the past. Christmas lunch was nice on the island, and going out to the reef on the boats was lovely. I attempted to learn to snorkel in the swimming pool and nearly drowned.

We got to the hotel in Townsville, and I was talking on the phone to Amy, who I dearly loved, and she me. Zach couldn't stand me being close to anyone, so he grabbed the phone off me and ended the call. Then he slapped my face and threw money at me, walking out and saying I could find my own way back to Brisbane.

The next day I was standing in the children's pool with Steven, wearing my new "itsy bitsy"—a leopard skin bikini. I had no idea how sexy I looked. I met a very handsome man, Bob De Bernardo, who was separated from his wife and from Brisbane. That night, after Steven was asleep, we sat outside the room windows eating Asian-style prawns and drinking wine. Later that night, we quietly made love in my hotel room, and I thought, *Wow! If this is what it can be like, I am never going back to Zach.* Zach was all I had ever really known.

I saw Amy while in Townsville, spending a week with her, as that was what was paid for at the hotel. I met her husband, Mark, for the first time and my new niece, Christina, who was born in May 1979.

Bob spent another day in Townsville and then flew out to Brisbane, with arrangements we would meet up in Brisbane when I got back. At the end of the week, I flew back to Brisbane.

# CHAPTER 6

# Making It on My Own: The '80s

## Making it on my own, 1982

We got back on a Sunday afternoon at the end of the first week in January 1982. Steven was very tired but loved seeing his cousin, Christina. Australia was experiencing one of the worst droughts on record, said to be a result of the El Niño effect. It was first time El Niño had been spoken about in Australian weather history.

In Las Vegas, the Commodore 64 computer was released and appeared in shop windows in the United States. Back in Australia, we were becoming a multicultural nation, with the push in the '70s of Asian and Chinese immigrants. Zach's parents had come from Poland in the early '50s.

Zach came back the end of the second week in January on a Saturday. He had gone to Adelaide. I think he had a girlfriend there. We were in the bedroom talking about 1:00 p.m., and I told him I wanted to permanently separate—that I wanted to break up for good. He picked me up; carried me into the spare bedroom, where there was no furniture; and started throwing me around the room.

He would pick me up and toss me around like a heavy parcel. I screamed for him to stop. He kept just continually doing that until Steven came in the room, crying and screaming, "Don't hurt my Mummy! Don't hurt my Mummy!"

At that, Zach just dropped me mid-air on to the hard floor and screamed out taking his bag and the car.

I crawled into the main bedroom to my bed and pulled myself up onto the bed. My body ached, and I was very sore. I just cried and cried with Steven lying beside me. Doreen, my elderly neighbour, called out at the back door (the houses were very close). She offered to take Steven for the afternoon and give him tea, which I agreed to. She handed me the daily newspaper. I said, "Thank you so much." And Steven was happy, as he was growing to love this elderly couple next door, Doreen and Frank.

In those days, everything was in the newspaper, especially on. I looked up the "positions vacant" column and found there was a job advertisement that suited me: "Wanted, theatre sister for Fertility Control Clinic, Greenslopes." This was only one suburb away, and though I didn't have a car, it was doable. I thought I would ring on Monday.

Then I made a list:

- Get a *job*
- Find a *babysitter* for work and for night-time
- Find out about buses
- Save some money
- Apply for legal aid
- Buy a *car*
- Buy a microwave and learn how to use it
- Join some social groups
- Set the house up nice

So now I had a plan, which was making me feel better. On Sunday, I would get outside and spend time in the garden and take Steven for a long walk. I was determined to make it and recover from this failed marriage. I did not have the support of my family or my son's family, as they were in Perth. I made a pledge for Steven's sake that

I would always keep in touch with them, keeping them in the loop.

Bob rang me on Saturday evening suggesting we go out. I simply told him I wasn't up to it. We arranged to meet at my house on Wednesday night and have a nice Chinese meal together after Steven had had his tea, as I didn't have a babysitter organised at that stage. Steven came home about 8:00 p.m. and was ever so happy. I thanked Doreen and Frank profusely, telling them what a difference they had made in our lives.

On the Monday morning, I rang about the job, securing an interview that afternoon. I rang the East Brisbane Community Centre about accessing the family day-care scheme. A woman rang me back in a few hours and set up an appointment for Tuesday morning for me to meet a mother who she thought might be suitable. She said she would come to my home first at 9:00 a.m. and pick me up and take me there.

On that Monday morning I also rang legal aid, who said, as the matter was urgent—my need for a restraining order—they would process the application over the phone. This they did and said they would phone me back Tuesday afternoon to let me know the outcome.

Doreen looked after Steven for me while I went for the interview. I told her I was meeting a babysitter in the morning to look after Steven while I worked. I caught a taxi to the interview. I took my very impressive résumé with references for theatre work from both Turrawan and Glengarry. I met a doctor who had a GP practise at the clinic, and he interviewed me. He told me he performed vasectomies, and I would have to scrub and assist with these.

He also told me I would be working in a day surgery that was an abortion clinic. This set me back a bit, as though I had always believed women should have a choice and I certainly wouldn't be judging anybody, I hadn't thought I would ever work in an abortion clinic, possibly because I didn't want that for me. I recognised how imperative it is that we as a society have safe, legalised abortion available to women sixteen weeks or under; otherwise, backyard operators that are not safe will exist. The doctor said he would get back to me in twenty-four hours and told me to think about it and be sure I could do that before accepting the job.

On Tuesday morning, Steven and I met Melanie Bernardo at her house. Melanie had nine children with a little boy, Zach, Steven's age; the two were born a few days apart in August. She was a practising Catholic and definitely anti-abortion. I explained that, without a car and needing a babysitter for Steven, I was limited when it came to what job I could take. This one was doable because the bus from the end of my street stopped virtually at her front door. I could then walk a ten-minute walk to the clinic.

Melanie understood, and I really liked her and her home. It felt right, and Melanie and I were to become lifelong close friends. Zach and Steven played together. I told her, as soon as I'd saved enough for a car, I would find some other more suitable job.

That afternoon, the doctor rang and told me, "I would be happy to employ you if you feel 100 per cent comfortable about working with us."

I told him I would be happy to take the job and had found a babysitter that morning. I told him I had taken the pledge to look after all people who needed care, regardless of race, colour, or creed, and I considered this included all women regardless of their choice to have an abortion. I had two weeks before I started, and this made me happy, as I needed that time to see the lawyer.

Legal aid rang me that afternoon and told me my application had been rushed through and was approved. They gave me the name of a lawyer who had funding. I was to give him a call immediately. His name was Paul Grant. As soon as I got off the phone, I gave his rooms a ring and set up an appointment for Thursday. I then rang Melanie to see if she could look after Steven. I would catch a bus to her house and then another on the same route to the city.

Wednesday night came, and Bob came for tea. We had a lovely night. However, Bob was not happy about me working in an abortion clinic. I tried to explain that I needed a job, and it was difficult without a car and with a two-year-old. We made passionate love that night, which was magical. Bob left in the early hours of the morning and said he would take me to see the lawyer the next day.

Bob came the next day and took me to drop Steven at Melanie's and then took me to the lawyer's appointment. He said he would wait for me. I met Paul Grant for what was the beginning of a long legal client relationship.

The first appointment was two hours. He took down all the details of violence, telling me he would be making an application to the courts for an urgent restraining order, which would be for life. He would also make an application for sole custody of Steven, with monthly visitation rights for the weekend. He would also make application for maintenance of forty dollars per week. I found this very draining and upsetting. Bob drove me home. I was so very happy I wasn't catching public transport after that session.

We all had fish and chips for tea that night. After Steven went to bed, Bob and I talked and both agreed it was not the right time for him and me to be getting deeply involved with each other. We had both just broken up with our spouses. We decided to have a six-month break from each other and see each other after that on my birthday in July.

Within a month, the court restraining order was through the courts and granted. It was done as a civil action and was for life. This was early days for domestic violence protection orders. The police had only just started doing them for the courts to process in the last twelve months.

I worked at the abortion clinic three months and caught the bus at the end of my street, getting on and off with a pram. I played a lot of music during this time when home, including INXS with Michael Hutchence. I also played some AC/DC and Cold Chisel both from the '70s. The music helped me cope. Illegal drugs pervaded the world of popular music at this time.

I went to see some movies, *Phar Lap* and T*he Man from Snowy River*. I watched the *Gallipoli* series on television and saw the movie. I took Steven to Lego shows in the city and to visit Nerida with the children often. I got there by bus, and they also came over often.

I had opened an account with Credit Union Australia (CUA), as they had advertised, they had a car-buying service. With three months of regular savings, they would give finance for a car. On the three-month mark, I rang them, and true to their word, they helped me buy a car.

A man from CUA turned up at my lunch hour at the clinic, and I looked at this little green Toyota Corolla. I took it for a test drive, and that was it, I bought it. We filled out the paperwork, including a deposit of $1,000. He said, if my application was successful, he would return in two days after work with the car. And *yes*, he returned in two days with the car.

I then started looking for other jobs. I found one with Queensland Medical Laboratory (QML) at Spring Hill in their main laboratory. I could start in two weeks, as I needed two weeks to give notice at the clinic. So, I gave a little more than two weeks' notice and was sad to move on from the new friends I had made but pleased to move on to doing something I felt happy doing.

The job started in June 1982, and it involved two weeks training—learning how to take blood and all about pathology work. The teacher was Carol Bracewell, and she was so good. I learnt how to take blood, which is a real art. It took me some time to get the hang of it. QML provided uniforms—really nice uniforms—white with royal blue piping.

I bought a pair of royal blue shoes with a little heel. Another really good thing about working for QML was that it was Monday to Friday day work. Cheryl McManus was in charge of all the nurses. In those days you had to be a trained nurse (an RN) to take blood.

I was, after training, initially stationed at head office in Spring Hill doing house calls in company cars. This was good for me, though very difficult, as I had never driven farther than known routes and never in the city. I was absolutely petrified crossing the Story Bridge and driving in the city, but I had to do it. I needed the job to pay the rent and support Steven.

Around this time, I got two cats, Casey and Cleo, as kittens. They were desexed and vaccinated, as I bought them through a pet shop at Carindale. Steven loved the cats. He was happy. His father had him about every second weekend and had taken him to see *Return of The Jedi* and *The Empire Strikes Back*, the second- and third-Star *Wars* movies. Steven began collecting Lego sets, especially the *Star Wars* ones with all the *Star Wars* figurines.

About a month after my training finished in July 1982 the

first case of acquired immune deficiency syndrome (AIDS) in Australia was reported in Sydney. I began researching this, trying to get as much information as I could, as I was working with blood. I found two of the white cells—the T-cell and the B-cell—were at fault.

For my birthday, I bought a microwave, a slow cooker / Crockpot, and a just released sandwich maker. I had the idea of making working and good, nutritious meals for Steven and me possible at the same time. I saw Bob for my birthday, and we decided to go our separate ways.

Doreen and Frank continued to be wonderful neighbours. Doreen gave me delicious recipes for quick meals and the newspaper every evening I got home on the back landing. They loved Steven, and he loved them. On Steven's third birthday, August 2, 1982, I gave him a party in the backyard with a cake. Nerida brought Natalie; Susan; and the new baby, Steven.

At the end of July, I was sent to Inala QML clinic on Biota Street. I had to get very good at taking blood. It was over half an hour from head office to send anyone out to help me, and the nearest clinic to refer a patient to if I was unable to get the blood was fifteen minutes away. I obviously couldn't refer too many people. So, I had to get good at it, which I did.

At Inala, I met Michael and Ruth Bayer who owned a second-hand shop on the corner as you entered the small mall, I was in. I bought some really nice bric-a-brac from their shop to decorate the house. In addition, I bought a gold velvet chaise lounge, which my son now considers a family heirloom. Every Monday to Friday, I drove to Inala in my little green Toyota Corolla, playing the Platters on cassette all the way on.

In the post office, I met Ian Montgomery, who was my age and ever so handsome. I liked everything about him—his mannerisms and the way he talked, looked, and laughed. He asked me out. So, I told him about Steven and how difficult babysitting at night was. Ian came around to my house a couple of nights for tea, but all he talked about was his ex-girlfriend/fiancée. They met every weekend at Celica meetings. They both owned a Toyota Celica. I actually considered Ian to be unavailable, as difficult as that was.

On October 23, 1982, my sister Charlotte (Charlie) married her childhood sweetheart, Allen. Ian came to the wedding with me. It was a small family wedding, and she married in a garden, with flowers in her long blond hair. My brother Jack and his new wife, Maryanne, were there. They had married earlier in the year.

I also went to a wedding with Ian of friends of his. Ian and I went out to meet his family out in the country in his white Celica playing Linda Ronstadt all the way. We also shared New Year 1983 together at a nightclub on the Gold Coast with his sister and her boyfriend.

Christmas Day 1982 was spent at my parents, who had moved to Caloundra (two hours north of Brisbane on the beach). Zach came with me, and they were delighted to see him. He also came with me to visit Auntie Lilly and Uncle Joe, who were also delighted to see him.

I had applied for a transfer from Inala, as I found it difficult working so close to Ian. He really wasn't available, as he was hung up all year on his former girlfriend. This transfer came through January 1983 to Woolloongabba Clinic, Taylor Medical Centre. It was closer to Melanie and home, only fifteen minutes away.

# The rape and near murder of me, 1983 and 1984

I had the first week in January 1983 on annual leave, the third of three weeks' holiday. I reviewed the list I had made out this time last year, and there were items on it I hadn't achieved. So, I made a new list:

- Find a night-time babysitter—advertise
- Join some social groups—the Young Liberals, Parents without Partners, some theatre groups
- Join a health club
- Buy a better car
- Grow some flowers—attend the garden

On the Monday, I placed an advertisement in the position's vacant column of the next Saturday's *Courier-Mail* newspaper: "Wanted: A babysitter in my home at night for a three-year-old boy, mainly Saturdays, weekends, or after 6:00 p.m. weekdays" and included my phone number. In 1983, everything you wanted to know was found in the newspaper. I read that Australia was still gripped by a terrible drought, and there were mice plagues in the farms all over Australia. I saw advertisements for the first IBM personal computer almost eighteen months after its American debut, and it sold for $1,600 in Australia.

On that same Monday, I organised to join some theatre groups—Sunnybank Theatre Group, Queensland Theatre Company, and Australian Postal Institute Theatre Company—with papers coming out in the mail for me to join and yearly subscriptions to pay. I also rang Young Liberals, organising to join them too. I rang the Carindale

Health Club and organised a meeting that afternoon with a view to join.

Dad rang and said he would be coming to stay three or four nights a week from the first week in February. He had found work in Brisbane and planned to cut the commuting down from Caloundra. I had to get furniture for the spare bedroom organised.

That afternoon I went to the health club appointment. I found it was perfect—it had a sauna, spa, tennis courts, and gym equipment and ran a range of classes. I decided that, with the cost of membership, combined with the fact I worked full-time and had Steven, I would pay casually to visit there.

I also went to a furniture shop nearby and bought a bed and wardrobe. While I was there, I saw this solid pine bar which I thought would be perfect for the counter of my shop one day. It was always my dream to have my own beauty therapy business. I bought the bar too and had it all delivered on the Wednesday to our house.

On the Thursday night, I went to a Parents without Partners (PWP) coffee and chat night. I joined up that night. I met Sue Lazarough and Kevin Branch, who had met at PWP and become a couple. Sue lived not from me at Camp Hill—five minutes up the road. She had a son Theo who was deaf and a few years older than Steven. We ended up doing exchange babysitting for each other.

On the weekend, Steven was due to go to his father's. Zach came on the Saturday morning, and there was, as always whenever Zach picked up Steven, yelling and arguing. After they left, I decided to visit the health club. I did an exercise class and then enjoyed the sauna, after which I got in the spa, forgetting I had make-up on.

I had only just gotten in, and I was then joined by a nice-looking man my age. He said, “You have mascara streaming down your face.”

I said, “Have I really?” I was so embarrassed.

He asked me my name and told me his was Derek Molver. He asked me would I like to play tennis the next day. We talked and laughed and decided to book a tennis court for the next day/afternoon at the health club.

I went home and had a rest, as I had a PWP games night to go to that night. I stepped out very cautiously. It was the first Saturday night I had been out by myself. I found the house and really enjoyed myself. I met a lot of nice people and didn’t feel so alone bringing up Steven by myself.

I met Derek the next day, and we enjoyed a game of tennis. I was a bit rusty, but we still had fun. He had the longest eyelashes I’d ever seen on a man. He said he was a scientist who worked for the South East Queensland Electricity Board (SEQEB), now known as Origin. We went for coffee at Zarafaras at Carindale. We got chatting, and I told him about Steven. He asked me if he could call me, so I gave him my home number.

When I got home, there were lots of messages on the answering machine from ladies who had seen my advertisement for a babysitter. I rang people back and scheduled interviews for the following Saturday, which came around in no time. I interviewed five ladies and chose Bonny, a fifty-year-old mother of a twenty-something daughter. She and Steven got on particularly well on the day. She was the one Steven chose.

February rocked around, and Dad came to stay. It wasn’t easy working full-time and getting home just before six at night (I finished at five). I used the Crockpot, and tea was cooked when we got home. I learnt how to cook vegetables in the microwave. Dad treated us to Chinese once a week. We always had the proverbial pot of tea after the evening meal. Dad loved playing with his grandson while I washed up. Derek rang me, but it was difficult talking to him, as the phone was connected to the wall right near where Dad sat.

Work was difficult because my clinic had been designated the clinic to take blood on everybody being tested for T-cell and B-cell studies. I worked out that these were possible AIDS cases and was upset that management hadn't told me. I had to be extra careful taking blood on everybody. Work was quiet otherwise, as it was a new clinic for QML in the building.

There were three floors, and they were all specialist suites on the top two floors. The clinic next door, the opposition, Sullivan and Nicolaides, got all the business in the building. Glenda Ryes worked in there, and she and I became the best of friends.

February was a busy month. I bought a new car using the one I had as a trade. I bought a brand-new Toyota Corolla ordering the sky-blue colour. When the sales representative arrived at my house to deliver it, he turned up in a cherry red one and told me they didn't have blue in stock. I stupidly accepted it. From this, I learnt a lot about assertion, which I was lacking at that time. About a month later, I did a "Responsible Assertion" course through TAFE at South Brisbane. This weekend course changed my life forever.

I had had the car three weeks and was at a Catholic Solo Parent function held in a parish hall at Windsor on Lutwyche Road, the one-way section going inbound. I was parked at the top of the hill with eight cars in front of me—very legally parked.

A car was speeding down the road and hit the outer driver's side at the back of my car, pushing my car into the one in front. It was a nine-car pileup, and my car was the only one that was driveable away from the scene. I was standing out in the rain with police there who would not let any of us shift our cars. It was very upsetting. That night, I met Liz McCaul, who had a son around the same age as Steven, and we became good friends.

My car was only like that for a week, as I had it booked in for repair with insurance. In that week, I was driving to work, and a policeman stopped me. My car really stood out on the road as a brand-new car that had been smashed up. He wanted to ensure the car was legally driveable.

He really upset me by assuming I had caused the damage to the car. He kicked the back tyre where the damage was and said, "It's drivers like you who have no respect for other drivers on the road." After what had happened to me, I felt deeply upset and angry. He let me go, and I said nothing.

My brush with the law didn't end there in February. My application for sole custody of Steven came up for hearing in the Family Law Court. I had to take the witness stand, and the judge asked me all about the violence in the marriage. He asked me if I wanted to deny access to the father, and I said, "No." I was awarded sole custody of Steven due to all the violence and instability. It was extremely rare for one parent to be awarded sole custody. Zach was given access once a month for the weekend. The judge also approved a maintenance order of forty dollars per week to be paid to the clerk of the courts.

My car got fixed in March, with me having a hire car provided by the insurance company. Work continued. It was very quiet, and I wrote letters to Lou and Aaron; Auntie Mescal; my sister Amy in Townsville; and Gail Shepard, who was travelling the world, as well as to Marie Valentine in Paris. In those days, people wrote lots of letters to stay in touch. Derek and I went out to dinner a few times and played tennis.

The weekend before Easter on the Saturday night, Sue (from PWP) had her girl's night out at the Waterloo Hotel. She and Kevin Branch were getting married on Easter Saturday. I wore a really nice outfit, and the venue, the Waterloo, wasn't an upmarket pub. I kind of stood out in the crowd. It was quite busy. We were sitting on long bench seats back-to-back with the people at the table beside us. In the conversation, it came up that my name was Anthea and that I worked for some pathology people opposite the Mater Hospital.

On Good Friday 1983 afternoon, there was a knock at the door. Before I could get there, Steven had let this person in through the screen door. He told me his name was Maxwell Smart, and he worked for a roofing company on the north side of Brisbane, giving me the name of the company.

I said, "I'm renting, and I don't need a roof."

He said he was at the Waterloo Hotel last Saturday sitting behind me and had heard where I worked. He said he had gone there and found a note on the door signed by me (my full name) and saying I was at lunch and would be back soon. He'd then looked me up in the phone book and had found my address. He wouldn't leave. I couldn't get him to go. I cooked tea and put Steven to bed so he would sleep well. While I was putting Steven to bed, the guy went out to his car and got a pile of grey blankets. When I saw the blankets, I asked him, "What are they for?"

He replied, "They are for me to sleep over".

"You can't sleep over," I said. "You have to go. Will you please leave?"

With that, he scooped me up and carried me down to

the main bedroom and threw me on the bed. He threatened me, saying "If your son wakes up and comes in here, I will kill him, adding, "If you make any noise, I will kill you."

I was totally terrified for Steven more than for me. He ripped my clothes off me, and I was naked. My body was not ready to have sexual relations, but he just thrust himself inside me, tearing me to shreds. I was in agony, but he just kept thrusting himself inside me. He then forced oral sex on me, which made me want to vomit. He was finally done, and I just lay on the bed in terrible pain. I was scared Steven would come in, so I pulled the sheet up.

He leant over and whispered, "I am going to have to kill you because you will go to the police."

I realised then I had to make friends with him and convince him I would not go to the police. I curled up beside him and started bargaining for my life. I said I didn't think the police would help me so I wouldn't go to the police. I then explained that, while I'd been brought up to believe the police were good people and who you should go to for help if ever you were lost, that had not been my experience in life.

I told him about the home invasion when I was fifteen and how the police had taken two hours to come and how, when they did arrive, they'd walked in with guns on their hips and had not believed my heavily pregnant mother. I told him about the policeman stopping me on the way to work with my car. I told him about the police on the night of the car accident. I pleaded with him to leave me alive, saying I would not go to the police.

I wanted to go to the toilet, and he followed me in and watched me the whole time. I was bleeding quite heavily. He talked to me about his experiences and finally agreed to let me live. He said he would go and got up to leave.

I felt so dirty and weak. I went in to the shower and took two hours. I couldn't clean myself enough. I washed my hair and blow dried it. I put clean clothes on and got into bed. I was just drifting off, and suddenly I felt someone touch my chain around my neck, shaking it up and down. I opened my eyes, and he was standing above me. He had hidden in the house to see if I would ring the police. He kept shaking my chain as if he was trying to make up his mind whether to strangle me. He said, "I can't seem to kill you. I enjoyed what I had with you."

I said, "A bargain is a bargain, and I won't go to the police."

He then left. I heard the front door shut.

I did not get to Sue's wedding the next day. I spent most of Easter in bed. I did not answer the phone all Easter. On the Tuesday after Easter, I rang the rape crisis centre and was given the name of a doctor at Bardon who saw rape victims, Dr Judith Sperling.

I got an appointment on Tuesday afternoon and left work for two hours to go and see her. I did not say I had been raped but that I was sore.

She examined me and took a step back, exclaiming, "You've been *raped*!" She said I had a stress ulcer, which would take time to heal. She took some swabs and sent them to Sullivan and Nicolaides. She rang the police in front of me. I told her I would not make a complaint—that a bargain for your life is one you ought to keep. She did not understand this. She organised for me to go to police headquarters on the Saturday morning.

I went back to see Dr Sperling on the Friday, as the pathology results were back. They showed I had picked up a new chlamydia infection, a sexually transmitted disease, which was treatable with medication. I went on the medication. On the Saturday, I saw the police and told them I would not make a complaint. They showed me identikit photos of offenders, and I picked him out of the selection. I gave them the details of the roofing company, as they said he was wanted in Western Australia for sexual offences. They said they would find him and extradite him to Western Australia to stand trial for those offences.

He kept ringing me wanting his blankets back. They were obviously to carry me and Steven away dead. I got in touch with Zach and told him what had happened. I know it sounds strange, but after this event, I just wanted Zach. I told Derek what had happened. They said to organise a night to return the blankets, and they would be there to ensure he never came back by giving him a hiding. That's exactly what happened. They beat the living daylights out of him and told him to leave me alone and take his "bloody blankets."

I spent the next four months—May, June, July, and August—deeply depressed. I didn't go anywhere except work and the health club where I saw Derek. We played some tennis, and I did exercise classes.

I turned thirty on July 22, 1983, and felt this was really old. I played music; it was my medicine. The biggest selling album in 1982 was Olivia Newton-John's *Physical*, and in 1983, it was Michael Jackson's *Thriller*. I bought both of these albums and played them a lot.

Steven turned four on August 2, 1983, and once again I gave him a party. Natalie and Susan came, as well as Melanie's Zach. I made him a cake, and his dad came.

In September 1983, the atmosphere in Australia was very happy. Australia had entered the America's Cup with Alan Bond's yacht *Australia II*. There were lots of practise happening at Rhode Island in America. When Australia won the America's Cup that year, the best of seven races, the whole of Australia was triumphant. I watched it on television—after which, it was impossible to feel sad.

In October 1983 my good friends Suzanne and Benedict had their first child, a boy, and called him Clinton Lucas Banning. He would grow up to become a medical scientist.

Life moved on. I was somehow happier. I started seeing Derek on the weekends I didn't have Steven, and we started sleeping together without making love. He wanted to show me I could trust him. He told me he suffered with high blood pressure and some other medical conditions.

I noticed that his laundry was full of beer bottles, and this scared me. Eventually, we began a relationship, and he was just what I needed to restore my confidence. Sexually, we had this amazing chemistry and had the most amazing relationship—the best I had ever had.

We spent Christmas 1983 together, as Steven went to his dads for two weeks. We basically spent the time inside his house at Balmoral like rabbits, spending a lot of time in bed. I would go home every night to feed the cats. New Year 1984 came, and we spent it in his lounge room drinking champagne. It was truly an amazing two weeks. In January, heavy rain came, finally ending the drought.

In 1984, the fax machine came on the market and was seen as the latest in technology. It spread very quickly, with most businesses and all government departments getting one. The fax really took off. In July 1984, the first Apple Macintosh came on the market in Australia.

Steven went to the Stones Corner Kindergarten in 1984, and this was close to my new work. I could quickly pop out and pick him up and take him back to Melanie's.

I spent 1984 working at Taylor Medical Centre and living at Jones Road Carina. I had planted flowers in the garden, and that summer the butterflies came, so I figured it was going to be a good year. I found it difficult to go on living at Jones Road in the house after the event of Good Friday, so I applied for a Housing Commission house. I attached a letter explaining my reasons for wanting to move from where I was, and they were very sympathetic.

In September, I got news that my application with the Housing Commission was successful, and I was offered a lovely little two-bedroom house at 31 Quirinal Crescent, Seven Hills. I accepted it, and we moved there the second week in September 1984.

I immediately put in a request to have it fenced, as people seemed to walk through to the road below. It was high on a hill with two street accesses. I had to buy carpet pieces, as there was bare floor. I also bought curtains for all the windows and made some for the kitchen. I had security grills made for the windows, as I was unable to sleep in an unsecured house after having experienced two home invasions. I took the bar and the chaise lounge, the stereo, and the television for the lounge. I bought Steven double bunks for his room. The place had a bathtub, which I really liked.

In the October, Derek and I broke up. I was at his house one night, and we argued. He threw all my things out on the front lawn one by one. Given the domestic violence I had been through with Zach, I simply couldn't trust Derek after this. I just couldn't be with him anymore. He drove a rusted-out vehicle, and they say you can tell a lot about a man by his car; the way he looks after it is how he looks after his woman. So, I broke up with him.

I applied for a job as a rep with a pharmaceutical company in November, to start January 1985. I was successful with this position and was very excited. It involved two weeks of training in Sydney, held over the last two weeks in January 1985. For this job, I bought some new clothes, as the job entailed going around to doctors' surgeries presenting the companies drugs to the doctors.

We spent our first Christmas at the house, and that year we went to Jack's wife's (Maryanne's) brother's house for Christmas Day. I bought a big tree that got assembled. Steven and I decorated both it and the house.

Casey cat survived the move and happily went in and out through the grills in the windows. We had lost Cleo about six months earlier. She'd simply died, and I wasn't sure of what.

I spent New Year's 1985 at the house and had a few friends over.

## Pharmaceutical repping, Steven starts school, the P&F committee, and making it work in a Housing Commission house

The first two weeks of January 1985 were spent on holiday and in reflection. I had decided that, regardless of all the trauma in my life, I was going to be happy and find this elusive thing called happiness. My list included:

- Work as a "rep" part-time
- Become involved in Steven's school
- Buy a VCR
- Go to the theatre, concerts, and ballet
- Grow a garden
- Practise gratitude every night
- Watch some comedy on television and movies

I decided I would try and think, as well as talk, about positive things with friends and neighbours. Good Friday 1983 remained a closely guarded secret known to only a few.

I found I had very intrusive next-door neighbours who seemed to watch everything I did. But I realised their intentions were good. This was Amy and Ken Niven. At the back, I had a lovely lady, Helen Luckhurst, along with her husband, Kevin, and their children. Her young son, Scott, helped me mow the lawn. On the other side of the house was a devoted elderly couple, the Watsons, who filled their whole backyard with pot plants for sale.

We lived on top of a hill that had bitumen going over the top and a dirt road each side of this road going around the hill. In these two weeks, I wrote a letter to the local Member of Parliament to get the dirt roads bituminised and cement kerbing with guttering done.

The third week in January came, and I put Casey cat into cat accommodation and took Steven to Melanie's on the Sunday afternoon. On the Monday morning, I caught a taxi to the airport and flew out for Sydney. At the airport, I was met at the airport by a Janssen staff member. There was apparently other Brisbane staff who had flown down with me, who I met at Sydney Airport.

We went straight to head office and into the training room. Our bags were delivered to our hotel. We were with the whole Australian team, with staff from all around Australia. I soon found Janssen Pharmaceutical to be a very ethical company that I was proud to work for. In the days that followed, I learnt all about the drugs they sold to pharmacists, particularly a new one being launched on the Australian market at the end of these two weeks—ketoconazole (generic name), sold under the brand name Nizoral.

Nizoral was being launched as a short course oral treatment for vaginal candidiasis (thrush). It had been on the European market for a number of years for long-term use with recalcitrant fungal infections, and this had caused some liver problems. It was, after all, an antifungal and was thought not to have those side effects with short term use for thrush. I found the entire training session very interesting and motivating. I couldn't wait to get out there in the field and start seeing doctors about this new drug on the Australian market for a very common, annoying problem.

I made a heap of new friends from all around Australia but was glad to get back home again. The beginning of the next week brought Steven's first day at school at St. Benedict's Coorparoo. Melanie sent all her children there. Steven was so excited, and so was Zach, his friend. I felt sad about my baby starting school. I had a tear in my eye as Steven said, "Go on, Mum. Go home." He had friends from Stones Corner Kindergarten starting there too, so he was surrounded by friends.

I picked him up at the end of the day, and he said he'd had a great day. I found out ways I could help and be involved at the school. There was tuck shop and reading, as well as the Parents and Friends Committee. Working part-time for Janssen would enable me to do this.

At home I began ringing doctors' surgeries in my territory to make appointments to present them with the company's drugs. I found confining appointments to three days it difficult; you really needed to be available five days a week to get the appointments. I called on some chemists and spoke to them about Nizoral.

I called at Brisbane head office a couple of times a week. I was required to fax my time sheets weekly, including mileage, as I was paid mileage and used my own car.

I found myself feeling sexually harassed by the state manager. I don't think he meant any harm. It was just that he didn't know how to work closely with beautiful young women. There was another young girl in the office, Jayne.

I started dating a doctor who I had met at Taylor Medical Centre. We shared a love of the performing arts and visual arts. Plus, we both had a great passion for medicine/nursing. I told him I did not want to get involved. I thought I had far too many skeletons in the closet and that I just wasn't doctor's wife material. He took me out to the theatre at the SGIO Theatre and other theatre events held at the Hamilton Hall. We went to orchestral concerts at the city hall.

Julie Muller, a girl I'd met at a garden party held for Young Liberals early last year, started ringing and calling frequently. I enjoyed her friendship immensely. We became very close for a number of years. Julie and I would go out on the Friday night that Steven went to his dads. We would go to a bar/discotheque just around the corner from the National Hotel. Sometimes, another friend of Julie's, Glenda Barrow, would come along too. On occasions, we met interesting guys and would all go back to Julie's and party till daybreak.

The album of the year in 1985 was Bruce Springsteen *Born in the USA*. INXS remained popular throughout the whole of the '80s. The 1980s was the era when you sat by your tape deck listening to the radio and waiting for the songs you loved, ready to hit the record button. People would ring up and request songs. This was the beginning of people making their own playlists—their own compilations of music. There was no such thing as Spotify or Apple Music. The dual tape cassette came in mid-1985, making it possible, for the first time, to copy music for your friend.

Steven continued to enjoy school. I continued to work

at Janssen till the end of June 1985, when I resigned; I felt it was impossible to cover a territory for the company on a part-time basis. I was performing work over five days of the week. I truly loved working for them and cherish some of the happy memories I made doing regular trips to the Sydney head office.

In June 1985, my divorce came through. I was kind of happy and kind of sad—a real mixed bag of emotions. I went clothes shopping and bought some acid washed jeans, which were very popular, and some new tops in the popular fluoro colours of pink and green. I had my hair done in the latest style, which was crimped, and bought some velvet scrunchies, which were also popular. I bought a blazer that had the ever-so-'80's shoulder pads. I already had the Adidas white shoes. All of this made me feel better.

I watched *Comedy Company* on television every week. I took Steven to see *Ghostbusters*, and we both laughed and laughed. It became one of my all-time favourite movies. Steven and I watched *Hey Hey It's Saturday* together if we were both home on a Saturday night. I practised gratitude every night, writing in my gratitude journal three things in the day I was grateful for. I wrote in diaries and journals extensively, which has made this book possible. I have always found journaling a very important part of my healing journey.

In June 1985, *E.T.* the Extra-Terrestrial came out, and Steven's dad took him to see it. I'd passed my love of movies on to Steven, so I decided it was time to buy a VCR. I cut out an article from the newspaper that month about VCRs and stuck it in my journal. The article said over half the population owned a VCR. So, time had come for me to buy one. There were video hire shops on every street corner in town. It was just affording everything.

I put in an application with Department of Social Security for sole supporting parent's pension and had this approved. I notified housing of the change to my financial affairs, and my rent dropped considerably, as they took a percentage of my income. I planned to simply have a break and grow a garden.

There was a large, cleared area / housing estate about a ten-minute drive from where we lived, and Steven and I went there almost every afternoon collecting rocks for a garden. They were lovely rocks, and I carried them back in the car. I started spending every day out in the garden, as much as my back would hold up. I dug up an entire section near the fence and a circular section in the corner. I began edging this with rocks, with a big rock in the centre of the circular section.

I got five free native trees from the council that were suitable for our soil. I began planting trees. The garden was something Steven and I did together, and we both loved it. Casey cat came out while I was in the garden, sunning herself. She loved it too. Dad came to visit (behind Mum's and the family's back), and he was very impressed with our garden. They were moving to Townsville.

Other great gardeners we had visit were Doreen and Frank, who came regularly, as well as Auntie Lilly and Uncle Joe, who all bought me cuttings. I was actually happy for the first time in a long time. I had found this elusive thing, like the butterflies, called happiness. I finally felt free of Zach and had to learn to somehow lay all the domestic violence of the past to rest. Not all men commit domestic violence, and not all men are rapists; in fact, most aren't. It was my level of intellect that enabled me to see this.

In spring 1985, September, Julie and I were in town one Friday night at a piano bar in an upmarket hotel at the top of George Street. We met a group of professional guys, two of whom were Christian White and his friend Jack. Christian and I got talking and realised I had actually met his father and sister years earlier in 1980, when I'd stayed with Suzanne at the Grange in her flat. They, his father and sister Janet, were in the real estate office. He played in a band, Quick Exit. And as it turned out, I had been to a number of his gigs and had seen him playing guitar.

He asked me for my number and asked if he could call me. He was fairly good-looking, about five foot eleven and of medium build, with a clear shaved complexion and brown hair with a slightly receding hairline. Christian had unusual shaped eyes. He said he had Chinese somewhere back in his genes, but they were definitely Australian eyes.

Christian did call me the next day and a couple of times the next week. We enjoyed chatting and laughing together. His friend Jack lived near Steven's school a few doors down. Christian invited me to watch his band play on a Sunday afternoon, and I went along a few Sundays, after which he came back to my house, and we had tea with Steven. He took a positive interest in Steven, who really liked him.

He asked me out to dinner one Saturday night when I didn't have Steven and came and picked me up in his little yellow car. We drove to a Mexican restaurant, Montezuma's, on the north side of town not far from where he lived at the Grange. I wore a blue, above-the-knee dress with a black belt, shoes, and bag. I went to a lot of trouble with my blonde hair this night and also my make-up. I was very nervous, like a kid on a first date.

After dinner, we went back to his house. He made me a cup of tea and then we went and sat in the lounge room. Before long, we made love on his lounge room floor. It just happened so naturally after we started kissing. I couldn't walk afterwards, and he carried me to his bed, where we just lay arm in arm. It was all so beautiful.

Christian and I continued to see each other all year, working around his engagements with the band. If he was playing one Saturday night, I would simply sit up and wait for him. He would drive to my house with all his music gear in the car and stay the night at my house. Steven came to really love him. Christian had training in computing—a degree in information technology, and Steven wanted a computer.

Steven loved his television. Some of the shows we watched together included *The A-Team*, *Cheers*", *Webster*, *Who's the Boss?* and *The Cosby Show*. An interesting current affair show started called *60 Minutes*, and I watched this every Sunday night. I had a miniature, gold velvet-covered lounge chair for Steven to watch television in. I got it from Bayer's Second Hand on Biota Street, Inala, from Ruth and Michael, who I kept in touch with.

In October 1985, my good friends Suzanne and Benedict had a second baby boy and called him Lincoln Wesley Banning.

I continued to write lots of letters and, when Christmas came, sent heaps of cards to people all over Australia who I kept in touch with. We spent Christmas Day 1985 at Christian's sister Janet's place.

All the children were playing together, and Steven suddenly collapsed and went blue. Christian quickly put us in his car and rushed us to the Royal Children's Hospital, which, at that time, was at Herston, a ten-minute drive. I handed Steven directly to medical staff, who resuscitated him. He is asthmatic and had an anaphylactic reaction to all the different colours in the lollies. He stayed in hospital overnight and was fine the next day.

On the eve of New Year 1986, Christian's band had a gig, and I spent the night at home until he came home. I spent a quiet week following—once again having my New Year reflection time. I decided to keep on keeping on with my life the way it was—to continue to find humour in my life and to practise gratitude, as well as to grow my garden.

At the first meeting of the Parents and Friends Committee (P&F) at Steven's school, I was elected secretary. I knew nothing about secretarial skills, but I soon learnt. It was a voluntary/honorary role but a huge learning curve for me. I met Janice and Ron Flanagan, who was president of the P&F, and Noela McCormack, who helped me a lot. These people were all good friends of Melanie and her husband, Laurie Bernardo.

In 1986, Australia was forging its own new identity, firstly, with the worldwide success of the film *Crocodile Dundee.* Paul Hogan was brilliant in the movie. Secondly, Australia was also experiencing widespread success overseas with the series *Neighbours*, with Jason Donovan and Kylie Minogue. Kylie was also belting out her solo albums. *Neighbours*, about a suburban beach town in Australia, was successful first in Australia and then in the United Kingdom and then Europe. Both of these successes helped to forge that new identity of Australia. Meanwhile, back at home in Australia, we had well and truly become a multicultural nation.

The biggest-selling album in 1986 was Whitney Houston's album of the same name. Christian had introduced me to some new music including Crowded House, U2, Jack Garrett, and Midnight Oil. There was also Eric Clapton on guitar and Tommy Emanuel on piano. Christian made cassette tapes for me of all this music. He was very popular in our house; even Casey cat smooched up to him.

In July 1986m Steven and I travelled by train, "The Sunlander," to Townsville to visit Mum and Dad and Amy and Tony. (They had moved.) The relationship with my mother was very strained, but everybody else was happy to see us. We took lots of photos down on Pallarenda beach. We also went to Magnetic Island for the day.

A week went by quickly, and Steven was back to school, his grade two, when we got back. I was also back to being the secretary for the P&F. This involved getting a lot of notices out and writing the minutes of meetings, as well as helping with fundraising. I convened a plant stall for their fete and organised an art show.

In the springtime, September, Christian decided to take us away to Caloundra to Kings Beach, one of my favourite places on earth, to celebrate our first year together. His other sister, Brenda had a unit there. So, we booked Casey cat into a five-star cat accommodation, and off we went for a whole seven days. We flew a kite, played cricket on the beach, built sandcastles, and generally had a wonderful time.

Steven decided when we got back that he wanted a Nintendo entertainment system, which had just been released on the market for playing games using the television as a monitor. I told him, if he could earn half of the cost through delivery of the local paper, I would put in the other half. So, he took on a weekly paper run of the *South-East Advertiser*, the local free paper. I set it all up in his name and helped him with the run, which was close by to where we lived. It was good exercise for me, and Steven went delivering on his bike.

At the end of the year, I decided I would pull out of the property settlement proceedings from my marriage. I had simply had enough and couldn't take any more. This was a decision I would regret for ever more.

Christmas came around fast, and we put our big tree up, decorating it with some decorations Steven had made at school. We had a tradition that, every Christmas, we bought two new quality decorations for the tree. I sent lots of Christmas cards as usual, and we spent the day at my brother Jack's house with his wife, Maryanne, and my niece Amber and nephew, Kannon.

Before long, it was New Year 1987.

## Beauty therapy training, May 1987 to May 1989

In early 1987, an advertisement appeared in a Saturday newspaper (*The Courier-Mail*) asking for applications to commence beauty therapy training at Kangaroo Point Technical College in May. It had been my dream to have my own beauty therapy practise on a shop front since I'd visited a beauty therapist in Darwin in 1974 to have my eyelashes tinted. I knew that was what I wanted to do. I put an application in as soon as I could.

You needed grade twelve to do the course, as it was an undergraduate university degree—an associate diploma in applied science. I had grade twelve. I was called up for an interview and was very nervous. I was eventually selected to take part in the course. I applied for Austudy with Centrelink and was accepted. I also applied with Marg Downes to work part-time for a pathology company called Renbond, which had been set up to supply clinic staff to both main companies. The pathology world was in strife, and this was a cartel set up to keep them afloat.

May came quickly, and I got to the college. I had to supply my own textbooks and pay a small fee each semester; the rest was paid for by the government. This was only the second time the course had run. Up until now, the only beauty therapy training available had been exorbitantly priced private beauty schools. There were about twenty-five girls in the class.

Subjects covered included but weren't limited to facials, manicures, pedicures, hair removal, waxing, make-up, skin, anatomy and physiology, business principles, first aid, life skills, and work experience.

I met Gail Last another student in her thirties. Incredibly enough, her husband cut Christian's hair, as she and her husband had a salon in the city. I met Gail's friend Karlyn and also Jenny Latter, as well as all the other girls. Suzanne came to the college as my client to practise on.

Christian and I continued to date all year, working around his band nights. He had built a sound studio at his house for band practise. Steven continued all year at St. Benedict's School; he was doing year three. I studied hard all year. Steven continued his paper run and, in September, bought an Atari game console. In addition, we bought a computer that ran off the television as a monitor and had lots of interesting software. We bought this from a second-hand shop run by Betty and Bill, a couple we got to know. We visited their shop often at Norman Park.

The top-selling album for 1987 was Bon Jovi's *Slippery When Wet*. I continued to listen to heaps of music. Jimmy Barnes from Cold Chisel was forging out a solo career, and so was Daryl Braithwaite from Sherbet. Christian was four years younger than me and introduced me to heaps of new music. Music was something that bonded us. He would often pick up my guitar and play and sing. Both Steven and I loved this. Christian was incredibly supportive of me with Steven. The years rolled by very quickly. I seem to be always working on an assignment.

On the Saturday before the Australia Day holiday, we came home at 1:00 p.m. after my work to find our beautiful dog, Bella, had been baited and was dead. She was a white labradoodle, and Steven really loved her. We were both very upset. A friend came over to bury her for us.

On January 26, 1988, Australia had its bicentenary—two hundred years since Captain Cook landed on the east coast of Australia. To celebrate. Princess Diana and Prince Charles came to Sydney. It was marred with protesters proclaiming Australia was aboriginal land. There were celebrations all around the country.

At the end of April 1988, World Expo opened to the public, running for six months, until the end of October, with forty-one countries participating.[11] An area of land covering forty hectares (ninety-nine acres) on the south side of the river near the city was converted from shipyards to parklands, including a subtropical beach with real sand.

The museum, becoming the new museum, was shifted to an area at the end of the grounds, which also housed the new performing arts centre that had three theatres. The library was shifted from in town to this area, becoming the new state library. Expo changed Brisbane from a sleepy country town to a world-class city. The slogan was "Together, We'll Show the World." The motto was "Leisure in an Age of Technology."

The carnival attracted more than 15 million visitors to the area now known as Southbank, which is a must see for anybody coming to Brisbane. You can access it from Southbank bus station or South Brisbane train station.

I studied hard all year, getting up to go to the college. I worked every Saturday morning at either Capalaba clinic with Margaret Southern or at Carindale clinic with Gay Poll. I took Steven with me, and he enjoyed shopping while

I was working. In those days, the shops closed at midday on Saturday.

Johnny Farnham's album *Whispering Jack* sold millions of copies in 1988, and he was named Australian of the Year that year.

I continued to practise gratitude, keeping a yearly journal, among other journals. I continued to ensure humour was in my life. I watched *Mother and Son* with Gary McDonald and Ruth Cracknell. I also continued to watch *Comedy Company*, which ran from February 1998 to November 1990.

In no time, it was 1989, and I did work experience with Jane's Beauty Therapy at Camp Hill, owned by Jane Boule. She held a party at her house in February, and I was invited. I went, along with Julie Matthews.

At the party, a man, a psychologist, named Dennis propositioned me, and I told him I wasn't interested. Julie and I left the party together.

Following this, Dennis kept asking Jane for my number, and I got tired of telling Jane not to give it to him. After this, he kept turning up at the Kangaroo Point TAFE canteen when we were on morning tea. Basically, he was stalking me. He came over to talk to me and gave me his number and said to give him a ring. I said, "I will think about it and give you an answer by after Easter," which was a month away. He still continued to bother Jane.

I told Christian what was going on, and he didn't have an answer. After Easter, I phoned Dennis and gave him my number to stop him ringing Jane. I told him I did not want to go out with him. April 5, 1989, came, and it was my graduation from beauty therapy. Christian and I went together. It was a dinner on board a floating restaurant.

## Dennis and getting engaged and moving to Majestic Outlook, 1989

In mid-May, Dennis rang me. I told him I was unavailable. I was going to the Villanova Art Show. I stupidly agreed to go to the art show with him. He bought me some lovely things at the art show, including a long, pink, knitted outer jumper. I told him I had difficulty with the cold. The next time I saw him at my favourite coffee shop, La Dolce Vita, he had bought me thermal underwear top and pants in orange and green. When I said I didn't like the colours, he changed them for pink and blue.

I found myself falling for him. He was stunningly handsome, with black hair and fair skin and beautiful eyes, a little taller than me, and of medium build. I told him about my relationship with Christian, and he threatened to harm him if I wouldn't go out with him. So, I agreed to go out with him.

The next time I saw him, we went out to dinner at a romantic restaurant, after which we came back to my house and cuddled and kissed. I felt guilty because of my relationship with Christian, and I told him this. I stopped seeing Christian.

In June, I was ill with the flu and went on antibiotics. Dennis said he would come around and keep me company, which he did. We ended up having sexual relations. This continued throughout June.

In July, I was two weeks overdue for my period and saw the doctor at Coorparoo. I was on the pill, but the antibiotics must have affected it. She examined me and said my uterus looked pregnant and gave me a form to have a pathology pregnancy test done. I did a test you buy from the chemist, and I was pregnant. At this stage, I didn't say anything to Dennis.

For my birthday, July 22, 1989, Dennis asked me to marry him and presented me with a very expensive baguette diamond ring. I said I would have to think about it. He left the ring on the dining room table. Steven got up in the morning and was so happy. He wanted me to get married and told the whole neighbourhood, "Mummy is getting married." I really felt my whole life was flying out of control, and I was still in love with Christian. I accepted the ring.

In September, I spontaneously miscarried the baby at ten weeks pregnant. It was horrible. I desperately wanted another child. I spoke to Dennis about children, and he said he wanted children. I had stopped taking the pill but would probably start again with my next period, due to my state of mind. I did not get another period. In December, I found myself pregnant again.

In the meantime, some real estate agents had come around door to door canvassing a property down the road at Majestic Outlook. Dennis was with me when they came, and we went to have a look at the property. We loved it and decided to buy it. Dennis put his property, a unit at Nundah, on the market, and I borrowed $5,000 from Credit Union Australia. I guess I wanted marriage, more children, and a house. And I wasn't getting that from Christian.

We moved to 96 Majestic Outlook in October 1989. I couldn't part with Quirinal Crescent and tried to take it all with me, digging up the entire garden.

The house at Majestic Outlook was chokers full of stuff. All of Dennis's things filled the spare bedroom, and all the things I had purchased to run a business filled the lounge room. The carport was full of the garden from Quirinal Crescent. It was utterly ridiculous. The downstairs area where I was going to run a business flooded, so I couldn't do it.

Dennis's mother interfered in our relationship. She rang every night when we were having the evening meal, upsetting it. Dennis would rip the sheets off the bed every week, saying she was going to wash them, which was an utter invasion of privacy. She rang me and said many upsetting things. Dennis tried to get me to give Steven up to his father and said he had changed his mind; he didn't want children. I simply, once again, didn't tell him about the pregnancy. I was suddenly deeply unhappy.

Steven was riding his bike and came off it and broke his arm. It was twenty-four hours before I took him to the hospital, as I didn't know what to do. It was a greenstick fracture, where the bone isn't actually broken but, rather, is bent. Dennis was ignoring Steven and this some how was connected to the twenty-four-hour delay getting medical assistance as Dennis didn't believe there was anything wrong with Steven.

I continued to work in pathology Monday to Friday in October. Dennis just wanted me working. He didn't really care whether I was happy doing it or not. He followed me into the shower, watching me take a shower. He lay directly on top of me in bed. It just wasn't working.

Christmas 1989, Dennis went to his mother's house, and I went to my sister Charlie's house. My mum and dad and other family were there, including my sister Amy and niece Christina. Charlie was studying psychology, and her boss (she also worked in the department) was Dennis's best friend. Mum and Dad did not look at me or speak to me the whole time I was there. Dad played a game where, in front of Mum and the family, he pretended he hated me too. It hurt like hell.

New Year 1990 came, and we spent it at the house at Majestic Outlook.

# CHAPTER 7

# The "Dark Years" (1990 to 1995)

## The assault, 1990

In the first weeks of January 1990, things were very tense at home. I was working full-time at a pathology clinic for Renbond. In the mornings, I was experiencing morning sickness and would arrive to work vomiting. I felt unwell most of the day. It was horrible.

I hadn't told anybody about the pregnancy other than Steven. Secretly, we wanted a girl and had planned to call her Eloise. Steven was worried about me. He knew something was wrong.

On the night of January 21, 1990, Dennis came home late. He had been at his mother's place for tea. It was just before midnight when he came in the front door and went into the kitchen.

He came down to the bedroom and stood with his head on the side of the door. I was putting my face creams on looking in the mirror of the dressing table, which stood beside the door. I walked around the bed behind me to my side of the bed. I sat there for a while writing my to-do list.

I have always been unable to remember the events clearly that occurred following this. It is a blur in my mind. I know he spoke to me. About what, I can't remember. He touched me inappropriately and my hand got broken. All of that is a blur, but I remember what happened after that.

I got up to go to the bathroom and escape. As I got to the end of the bed opposite the wardrobe, he punched me hard with a clenched fist in the top of my stomach. I fell backward into the open clothes cupboard into a pile of jumpers. I was winded. I couldn't get my breath. My uterus started contracting so hard, and I was in agony.

I yelled out to Steven, "Help, help me, Steven." I tried to escape by running up the hall. Steven came out of his room next door and saw everything. As I ran up the hall, Dennis chased after me, punching me in the breasts all the way. My breasts were sore from being pregnant.

I was yelling out, "Call the police! You're not going to get away with this!"

I picked up the phone (connected to the wall in those days) and dialled 000. He continued punching me in the stomach and breasts. Though the phone became disconnected from the wall, I kept clutching it to my left ear.

I eventually fell to the ground and was lying on my back near the china cabinet in excruciating agony, with my uterus cramping hard and my breasts aching. He came and stood on me. I tried to get up and push him out the door. Steven was screaming, "Stop! *Stop*! Stop hurting my mother."

He was in the front doorway, and I was kneeling in the doorway. He had his hands around my throat, and I really believed I was going to die. My whole life flashed before me. Apparently, what came out in court is I must have bitten him on the lower legs, but I have no recollection of doing this. I was fighting for my life. He finally left after I'd passed out in the doorway; perhaps he thought I was dead.

Steven woke me up, and I made a rush for the toilet. I was in terrible pain. I passed a lot of blood and tissue into the toilet. I knew I had miscarried. I got sanitary protection, heaps of it, organised and changed my nightie, as the old one had blood on it and was ripped. I rang Christian and asked him to come and help me. I went and sat on the gold chaise lounge, and there I stayed. I knew if I got up, I would collapse or bleed heavily or something.

The police arrived late, just as they had after the home invasion, when all the action was all over. Dennis came back without his shirt, brandishing scratches I must have put on him. But I didn't do it deliberately; nor do I have memory of scratching him. I didn't find out he had scratches until I was on the witness stand in court.

He told the police he was a psychologist, a professional person and made me out to be the aggressor. I did not see him properly when he came back, and I later realised he was showing off his scratches. I wondered why he didn't have his shirt on.

He left, and the police officers spoke to me. I simply don't remember this—I only recall feeling they didn't believe me, just like they didn't believe my mother the night of the home invasion. My PTSD came well and truly out of its box that night. It had been in remission.

The police officers rang an ambulance, and I was taken to hospital. Not long before the ambulance arrived, Christian arrived, and I guess it looked to the police like I had a lover and that I was the aggressor. At the hospital, I was attended to. Apparently, my blood pressure was dangerously low. The doctors spent three hours getting it up to an acceptable level. Due to the sudden changes in pressure in my eyes I lost 60 per cent of the vision in my left eye.

I was taken to a ward, and I refused a vaginal examination. I was embarrassed and ashamed of what had happened, though it wasn't my fault; it was an unprovoked attack.

I had pain in my left hand and couldn't use it. I had terrible pain in my chest, and I ached all over. I somehow knew I wasn't pregnant anymore.

The police came the next day to see me and spoke to the

doctors, who told them there was nothing wrong with me. The pain in my chest was indigestion. I believe the doctors didn't want to get involved because it was domestic violence. So, what were the police to do when the doctors behaved like this? They could only assume I hadn't been assaulted.

A system is only as good as its weakest link. The police and the courts were doing all they could to address the domestic violence problem. But while the doctors took the stance they didn't want to get involved and didn't investigate properly or report properly, they were effectively perverting the course of justice. For domestic violence to be addressed properly, the doctors had to take some responsibility and investigate and report accurately.

I was discharged from hospital. I saw a lady doctor (who shall not be named), whose husband works as a surgeon at the hospital I was admitted to. I asked her for more X-rays, but she wouldn't do them. Now you can't bite the hand that feeds you, can you? She examined me and said I had widespread soft tissue injury, which wouldn't show up on X-ray. She ordered blood tests, and when my liver enzymes were elevated, she said, "You are an alcoholic!"

That was it. I might have been to hell and back again, but I was no alcoholic. So, I changed doctors.

I went to a lady doctor who I thought, from reading her pathology requests, would be a really good doctor. I was to see her for the next twenty years. She ordered a bone scan. It showed two broken bones in my hand and a fractured rib over the heart, with all of the ribs except the last dislocated and removed from the breastplate. I had deep bruising, with bruises taking weeks to come out. New bruises would appear on my chest and abdomen every day for a month. The deeper the bruise, the longer it takes to come out.

This doctor really didn't want to get involved either. She

referred me to a psychiatrist for my state of mind; the PTSD was bad. I was hypervigilant. I couldn't sleep at night. And I was having flashbacks of all the trauma I'd experienced in my life, along with nightmares.

I saw Dr Bronwyn Beacham, an amazing psychiatrist who really helped me. I told her about the baby. I saw her almost every week for about three years for hourly sessions. She put me on a medication for anxiety, which was temporary, and diagnosed me with complex post-traumatic stress disorder, which began after the birth of Steven. Complex relates to the many traumas that followed.

Christian helped me quite a bit too. On discharge from hospital, I went to his house. I couldn't go back to the house at Majestic Outlook. I was at Christian's for three days, and Dennis came there, knocking loudly on the front door for fifteen minutes. He came two days in a row. I knew I had to leave.

On Saturday, January 27, 1990, I looked at a house I saw in the newspaper, 60 Leura Avenue, Hawthorne. It was a house divided into two, with a flat on the side. I rented the house section—a spacious and a lovely old house a two-minute walk to the Brisbane River.

Melanie's family, the Bernardos, brought their van and helped me move. So did Christian and other friends. I saw a solicitor who was known to me. I took the dishwasher from Majestic Outlook. I saw a real estate agent about putting that house on the market; after what had happened there, I couldn't go back. I brought Casey cat to Leura Avenue; she had been neglected and was not in good shape. I applied for the sole supporting parent's pension once again.

What followed from 1990 to 1995 were the darkest and worst years of my life. All the boxes remained unpacked at the house for six months. I cut myself off from Zach, Steven's father. I couldn't take all the contention when he came to pick up Steven anymore. Christian took Steven to his dads on access and picked him up again. I got a new telephone number and cut a lot of people out. I couldn't face my world. I took a major interest in world affairs beyond me and will list some that interested me in this chapter.

Nelson Mandela was someone who always inspired me. I admired him for his perseverance after having been wrongly imprisoned in South Africa and spending long spells in solitary confinement. In 1990, he was released from prison. From 1990 to 1994, apartheid was disassembled in South Africa.

Tim Berners-Lee published a formal proposal for the World Wide Web in 1990. In the same year, East and West Germany were reunited after the collapse of the Soviet Union. In addition, Margaret Thatcher resigned her position as prime minister of the United Kingdom.

I continued to see police officers and gave a statement, telling them I wanted lawful justice; I wanted Dennis charged. I'd never gotten justice after the 1983 rape, and I'd never gotten justice after all the domestic violence of my marriage. This time, I wanted this thing called lawful justice, and I wanted it badly. The fact that I had been entitled to it in the past and had never gotten it was what was driving me to get it this time.

In June 1990, the matter was coming up for mention in the magistrates' court. I found out from my solicitor that Dennis had been told by the police not to worry about turning up, and the police weren't intending on showing up. In this situation, the case would have been dismissed.

The day before, I went to the court and lodged a letter to be read by the judge on the day. Nobody showed up. My letter was read. And the case was set down for committal in the district court in September.

At the committal, I was required to take the witness stand and was questioned by Dennis's barrister and my barrister, a barrister working as a Crown prosecutor. The case was set down for trial in the district court in February or March of the following year, 1991.

## The court case, 1991

The year, 1991, began with us having spent Christmas and New Year at home. I had a dreadful flu and spent Christmas in bed. My entire family, other than Charlie, had come to visit. They walked in, inspected the house, and walked out again. They didn't stay for a cup of tea or anything, which only reinforced how much they did not love me. I knew Dad loved me behind Mum and the family's back. Steven spent a lot of time in the pool next door, where a young girl lived.

I spent every night unable to sleep, sitting up and watching the gulf war on television. Iraq was given until January 15 to get out of Kuwait and didn't. So on January 17, an army of coalition forces from thirty-five countries went in, led by the United States. Australia sent troops. I watched the whole thing; on February 28, Kuwait was liberated. I was really afraid there was going to be another world war.

An interesting thing happened with music in the early '90s. I stopped listening to modern music, and Steven started listening to modern music. He listened to Pearl Jam and a Guns and Roses album *Use your Illusion*. He also listened to an Irish band I had introduced him to, U2, and loved their *Rattle and Hum* album from 1988.

I stopped listening because there was grunge, hip hop,

and punk, and I was not interested in any of these genres. Also, the lyrics changed around this time. No longer were songs about the love between a man and a woman because society was changing how it saw couples. Same-sex couples were now gaining acceptance. Babies were now being conceived differently. My sister Charlie was going through the IVF programme and trying to have a baby at this time.

Steven did introduce me to Chrissy Amphlett and the Divinyls, thinking I would like the music, and I loved it. Freddie Mercury, who was lead singer of the band Queen, died of AIDS. He was homosexual. Acceptance of LGBT people in society was happening.

Society was certainly changing. My court case was only the second held as a closed court for domestic violence cases. Women were only just starting to seek court action for violent acts. The fact was a closed court afforded me privacy and protection but gave the perpetrator anonymity so didn't really work, particularly if the sentence was only nominal if he were found guilty.

The day in March came for the court case, and Christian drove me into the city and parked the car. We walked to the district court, getting there early. I talked to Greg McGuire, the Crown prosecutor acting for me. The selection of the jury took place first. That was nerve-racking.

I then had to take the witness stand and take the oath. I was on the witness stand for eight hours with two breaks. I was sitting close to the jury, and I found this frightening; at times, they scared me. Dennis stood in the dock.

The barrister for the defence, for Dennis, cross-examined me, asking a lot of questions, which enlightened me. He had obviously told the police and his barrister that I had attacked him. I was, up till that time, not aware he had bite marks or scratches on him. It explained why he'd come back in without his shirt. I'd stayed right away from him when he'd come back that night. I was shocked that he'd told them all this.

I was asked about my work in pathology, which I thought was irrelevant. I kept talking too quickly for the lady taking all the transcripts in shorthand that day. The judge kept slowing me down. The defence barrister kept trying to trip me up on my account of what happened. He ran through everything that occurred and then said, "Did I leave anything out?"

I had to really think, and I then said, "Yes. He stood on me." He must have denied this.

There was little medical evidence provided to show I had been assaulted, other than the bone scan and an ultrasound showing a torn tendon in my left shoulder. The hospital refused to provide proper notes and supplied a few random pages, saying they would have the doctor come and take the stand on the day.

This doctor flew out to London the day before the court case so was unavailable. Neither of the lady doctors I saw wanted to provide statements. Without extensive medical reports, it was difficult to prove I was assaulted to the extent I was assaulted. There was no charge possible for death of an unborn child at that time, so I kept this out of court. I was very embarrassed about this happening to me and wanted privacy. This did come into force as against the law twelve months after this court case, as did stalking laws. I always believed it was what happened to me that caused these to become law.

The next day, Dennis took the stand, and due to a very clever and talented Crown prosecutor, the truth came out. Dennis admitted assaulting me and said it was something he deeply regretted. He admitted everything.

The jury took one hour that afternoon to find him guilty of indecent assault and of common assault (unprovoked assault).

The following day, the sentence was handed down. This was a $5,000 fine with six months to pay or six months imprisonment, which was paltry in relation to what he earned as a psychologist. He had presented all these references so got off almost scot-free.

I had gone through all that for nothing; though I had won, I had really lost—so much. Because it was a closed court there is virtually no record of the trial ever happening if you were to do a search. I can't print his name here because it was a closed court. The closed court only served to protect him from that day onwards.

He went on practising as a psychologist. I contacted the psychologist registration board at the time, writing them a letter, but they were not going to take any action. After all, it was only his fiancée who he had assaulted ... It was just a domestic matter. For domestic violence outcomes to change, we as a whole society had to change our attitude towards domestic violence.

This thing called "lawful justice" that I had so hotly pursued does not exist, for law is something you find in a very big, black textbook, and justice is something handed down in the courts. They don't coexist. Like happiness, lawful justice is a very elusive thing. So, I had really lost—my self-esteem, my pride, and so much mentally and emotionally—by going through this trial. A piece of me was lost forever. I had lost so much time out of my life. The court just re-offended me.

The only consolation for me was I felt much better about having not gotten lawful justice in the past. I now knew I had done the right thing. The way our system was currently set up, not going through any court cases in the past was best for me.

Things have to change. We began as a nation of convicts, where the guilty were guilty and had to prove their innocence. We are now a nation where the guilty in a court don't have to prove anything. It is the innocent who have to prove the accused is guilty. The pendulum has fully swung the other way.

Don't get me wrong I have the utmost respect for law and order. I believe a civilised society is defined by law and order and by how we look after the frail, ill, and aged. I grew up in Penang, where there was little law and order; it wasn't a civilised country at that time. I am thankful for the law and order we have in this country. It's all we have and, without it, we would not be a civilised society.

The police actually have an extraordinary difficult job to do. I can understand why they did not believe me. With doctors not wanting to get involved in court matters, how are they to do their job? With courts handing down lenient sentences, sometimes their work is all in vain. Regardless of how police officers in my life have treated me, I have the utmost respect for each and every one of them. I am able to see the bigger picture.

After the trial, I sank into the beautiful old lounge suite, a Chesterfield (like a Genoa), that Christian had bought me late last year and watched world affairs, cuddled up to Casey cat. Boris Yeltsin became Russia's first elected president with the collapse of the Soviet Union. Somehow, I couldn't face my world, and I had to look at the world beyond me out there.

The internet first became available for unrestricted commercial use this year, 1991. I thought, *I must do a computer course.* And I started making enquiries. I bought our first real computer from Betty and Bill at the second-hand shop. It was new. Bill bought a whole heap of them at an amazing price at an auction and passed the saving on to his customers.

I thought, *I must snap myself out of this state of mind.* I was deeply depressed. I decided I would like to do some voluntary work, as well as take a computer course. Computing kept Steven, Christian, and me connected

I kept humour in my life. Christian, Steven, and I would all sit down and watch *Fast Forward* religiously once a week and laugh out loud the whole time. We just loved the show. I would tape it and watch it again and again. Steven watched *South Park* and often laughed out loud at this.

Christian knew it was my dream to have my own beauty therapy business, which would have been possible from the house. I had Steven's room divided off with shelving for a business, and this led on to another room that had its own entrance. Steven's room was huge. Christian and I began living together after the trial. It was totally normal and acceptable for couples to live together outside of marriage, unlike in 1953 when I began this story.

Christian began making me furniture for a business. It was an absolutely beautiful and unique couch he made me—with pull-out tables for massage and manicure, as well as pedicure, all laminated in peach laminate. I adapted the foam from an old lounge for the mattress, which, when covered, was like a waterbed. He made me a manicure table out of a desk with peach laminate and edges painted black. I wanted my salon done in peach and black. He was amazing—a multiskilled person.

The police kept in touch with me for after the trial. They realised I was telling the truth. I developed a friend in the Women's Safety Unit and told her I wanted to do voluntary work. She offered for me to come and help at the unit, doing shopping centre displays and stalls, and I accept an honorary position on the steering committee of the South East Brisbane Safety Audits Committee.

This kept me busy and involved, and I felt something I hadn't felt for a long time—a sense of purpose.

Safety audits are about identifying areas in the physical community environment that are either unsafe or could do with improvement and fixing them. This could mean adding more street lights or cutting back bushes, for example. This voluntary work helped me regain my confidence through getting out with other people and performing tasks.

Meanwhile, the director for Public Prosecutions had been in touch with me about criminal compensation. I felt I couldn't go through any more court cases, and I declined the offer to process compensation for me—something I regret. It was just that, at the trial, I had been re-offended by the procedure. I had lost so much time and had endured such emotional upheaval going through the court case that I didn't want to go through it again. I didn't want to be re-offended once more and lose more time.

The Majestic Outlook house sold and the proceeds of sale were held up in Dennis's solicitors trust account. He just wouldn't settle them.

I found out about a course called Commercial and Office Fundamentals starting at Seven Hills College of TAFE in February next year, 1992. The course would full-time and would take six months. I applied for a spot and went for the interview. I was successful and was so excited. The course included word processing, data base, spreadsheets; DOS for computers, typing, microfiche, fax, and business principles.

Towards the end of 1991, Charlie gave birth to a boy and named him Dennis's surname, which was also a boy's first name. I felt this was an act of contempt, so I never spoke to her again after this. I hadn't spoken to her much before this. Mum had well and truly brainwashed her and my younger brother to believe I was a horrible person.

Christmas and New Year were very quiet that year, 1991, because Christian and I broke up just before Christmas. It was entirely my fault. I asked him to move out; I just couldn't cope any more. I was too drained after the trial.

We had tried to make a baby, and I just didn't fall pregnant. Christian had problems making love to me, which I can't write about for his privacy. I think it was everything that happened. We were both over it all. I regret asking him to move out and wish I had tried harder to make it work.

## Getting motivated again, 1992, and meeting Richard

January 1992 was spent in reflection, looking over my whole life. I realised I'd stopped practising gratitude, and I needed to start doing this again. I also needed to practise positive affirmations and learn how to meditate. In 1991, I had written a lot of poetry, and I desired to have an anthology of my poetry published one day.

January 1992 was also when I first felt a desire to write a book about my life one day. I prepared myself for study with the course starting in February. I continued to see Dr Beacham, the psychiatrist. I was unable to sleep at night and sat up watching world news on ABC and SBS. There was trouble in Bosnia.

I watched the Gay Mardi Gras held every year in Sydney on the television set. There were often protests by LGBT people for their civil rights in cities around Australia throughout the '90s.

Steven started high school the last week in January at Villanova College and found himself being rejected by Zach Bernardo (Melanie's son), his friend of the last ten years. Zach was calling us "povos," short for poverty. This was a Catholic private school that, from my experience, hadn't adjusted to divorce or women bringing up children on their own.

The rest of society had changed, and there was no longer a stigma attached to bringing up a child on your own. In fact, many couples were opting to live together, and divorce was now common. Blended families, where two divorced parents had remarried with family, were starting to become common. There were even sitcom television shows about this.

I was deeply wounded, as I had always paid Zach's mother well above award rates for looking after Steven. I had bought the whole family gifts at birthday and Christmas (a big family). I had taken Zach and his new brother, Nathaniel, to the theatre with Steven several times and paid for their tickets, as well as a zoo. There is no question that I contributed to his family's wealth. My psychiatrist told me this was absolutely the worst age for my son to be coping with rejection.

Steven's father helped with the private fees, and he would ring the school, undermining me and saying the most malicious, untrue things about me. He had been doing this with friends for many years. He had used Steven as human ammunition, turning him against me. This was revealed in a discussion about Steven's "love/hate" relationship he had with me. Steven quickly slipped into a depression

February 1992 came, and I started the Commercial and Office Fundamentals course. On the first day, I met many new people and made a new friend, Kay Jacqt. It was exciting to sit behind one of the portable computers, about the size of a four-in-one printer today or a little bigger. I learnt how to log in to the college portal and start my file and to save everything too. On this day, we started learning typing, which I'd always been hopeless at. The college had a canteen where we had our breaks.

I was worried about Steven but didn't know how to help him. He was also upset about Christian and I breaking up, as Christian had been so good to him. Steven started spending long spells in the neighbourhood telling anyone who would listen how he was a neglected and abused child, coming home very late, and being very difficult to manage.

I continued at my course. I struggled a lot to concentrate and to focus but I was determined to complete this certificate. Most days, I turned up at college after taking Steven to school. But there were days when I went home to bed afterwards.

The course continued, and it was really great learning computer software like Word Perfect, which eventually became Word and spreadsheets, which eventually became Excel, as well as Data Base. DOS (disc operating systems), which operates all computers today, was amazing, and I am so glad I learnt it.

Music and computing connected us at home. Steven listened to popular music. He listened to Nirvana, with Kurt Cobain, and their *Nevermind* album. He also listened to REM's *Automatic for the People*, which he introduced me to, and I loved it as well. We played the song "Everybody Cries" over and over, as it seemed to help us both. Music started to help Steven like it had helped me. My taste in music completely changed early nineties. I could no longer listen to the lyrics of my old music about women and men in love. I turned to alternative music—relaxation music to calm me. I also liked orchestral music, any piano, guitar, or harp or a combination of all three.

About this time, Eric Clapton's four-year-old son walked out of an open window of a high-rise building in New York and died instantly. The window was being cleaned Eric Clapton, a famous guitarist, was one of Christian's heroes. Eric wrote "Tears in Heaven" after this for his son, and we often played it too.

I continued my voluntary work with the Queensland Police Service. In April 1992, I was presented with a Certificate of Appreciation for services assisting officers in their work by the then commissioner of police at a police function. I consider this to be one of my lifetime achievements. I was totally surprised; I didn't expect anything. They told me that day I had done enough, and it was now time for me to move on with my life.

In May 1992, I completed my computing course and was presented with a certificate that represented to me that I did have the ability to apply myself and achieve.

In June 1992, I answered an advertisement in the personal column:

> Wanted: A lady who probably lives in a big old house and likely has a cat; loves being in nature, at home in a rainforest; appreciates art and music; has a good sense of humour; 35 to 38 years of age. For a permanent relationship, apply. PO Box 123, Brisbane City.

I wrote a letter, as the woman the ad described just sounded like me. What started was an exchange of letters with a "Richard" that went on till October. I couldn't wait to get his letters and the correspondence was all I could cope with.

In July, my birthday came, and I turned thirty-nine—approaching forty. I somehow was fighting depression again after doing so well all year. My complex PTSD was particularly bad, and I struggled with it.

The situation with Steven was getting me down. He was spending a lot of time at friends' houses and was being difficult when he was at home. His birthday came, August 2, 1992, and he turned thirteen. I made him a carrot and walnut cake, which was traditional in our house at birthday time.

Everything was not going well at Villanova, and Steven wanted to leave. I left a teacher/parent interview at the school in tears. Villanova had offered to have Steven free of fees. I decided to send him to the local state high school, Balmoral High School. This was a mistake. He fell in with the wrong crowd and began being truant from school, going to this boy's house to smoke pot.

One afternoon in August, there was a knock at my front door, and when I answered it was people from the Department of Family Services Child Protection Unit. They had received a number of complaints that I was abusing Steven, and I was under investigation. It was all based on what Steven had said in the community.

They interviewed me and Steven several times over a month. I tried to explain my son had a love/hate relationship with me as a result of his father turning him against me. They interviewed people who had complained. They inspected our house and Steven's room.

They spoke to both Villanova and Balmoral High. After six weeks, they reached the conclusion Steven was a thirteen-year-old who had gone off the rails and that I was doing everything I could to look after him—that, in fact, there was no abuse. It was a very upsetting six weeks.

I was unable to sleep at night with the PTSD and sat up till all hours watching world news. The European Union was created when the Maastricht Treaty was signed. Bill Clinton had been elected as president of the United States. The mall of America opened in Minnesota. Euro Disney opened in France. Bosnia and Herzegovina declared independence. The Bosnian violence had become a full-blown war in April, with thousands of men and boys executed. Australia started accepting refugees from Bosnia in July.

I wrote a letter to Dennis, begging him to settle the proceeds from the sale of the Majestic Outlook property, which were held up in trust for months. He settled it, leaving me about $4,000 after the credit union was paid back, providing that I never claimed criminal compensation.

With some of the money, I decided to buy a new sound system as they are now called—no longer "the stereo." All music was converting to CDs, no longer records/vinyl, with compact speakers, and I wanted something that would play CDs. This involved selling my old stereo with great big carved wooden speakers. It was very difficult to part with. It was a furniture piece that had been around since 1975.

I also decided to buy Steven a great big four-foot bay window fish tank, which cost $1,000 fully fitted out. It was also a furniture piece. He was keeping fish in two washtubs in the backyard. Keeping fish in a beautiful tank became a shared passion of ours, something that connected us like computing.

I watched old movies, as there was a lot of sci-fi at the movies. The genre didn't interest me, so I hired movies. I got *When Harry Met Sally*, a brilliant romance/comedy from 1985. I also got my very favourite movie *Out of Africa*, a romance/drama from 1989. Then there was the 1984 *Ghostbusters*, an American supernatural comedy. Lastly, I got my other favourite, a 1960 drama/comedy called *La Dolce Vita*. Movies helped me a lot, and none of the movies at the cinema interested me. Life was changing. Steven started going to the cinema and enjoying the movies. Was I getting old?

On October 28, 1992, Richard and I met for the first time. This was the start of a lifelong friendship. We went to a coffee shop at Dockside on the river. It was a lovely meeting, which closed with Richard saying, "Are there any ferries at the bottom of the garden?" I thought he meant fairies, so I laughed. It was established that he meant ferries. After this, we went for a romantic ride around the Brisbane River on a City Cat.

We continued to see each other and went out for dinner three times. We began sleeping together just before Christmas.

Christmas 1992 rolled around again, and we spent it at home together. We put the great big tree up and decorated it together. I have photos from this year with a bike for Steven under the tree at midnight.

I made rum balls as well as white Christmas and got Steven to deliver them around to the neighbours on decorated Christmas paper plates with sweets and a card. I stopped sending heaps of cards, as I had cut myself off from so many people.

New Year 1993 came, and I drank champagne at midnight. I drank very little alcohol through these years.

## Struggling with PTSD, 1993 to 1995

In January 1993, Dad came to visit. I told him about all the problems I was having with Steven, and he offered to take Steven for a few weeks of the holidays. I discussed it with Steven and rang home as Dad requested, asking if Steven could Steven come for holidays. In a few days, Dad came and got Steven and took him up to Helidon, where Mum and Dad lived.

Dad took Steven for a driving lesson. This did not go so well and ended with Steven driving into a fence on their property of some acres. Steven had difficulty with Mum. He said Mum said a lot of horrible things about me and tried to turn him against me. Consequently, Steven ended the holiday after five days, asking to come home, and he did not want to go back.

Steven got home and listened to his music, Nirvana and Smashing Pumpkins and U2. He went to the movies and saw his favourite movie of all time, *True Romance*, starring Brad Pitt in his first movie. It was directed by Quentin Tarantino on a shoestring budget. There were a lot of movies in the early nineties being produced on shoestring budgets with actors and directors who later became household names.

Steven was being very difficult. He would run away and ring me at all hours of the night to come and pick him up from all different addresses. I found life very stressful.

Richard came to visit often. He was an administrator at Labrador High School on the Gold Coast and drove down and back every day in his little blue bubble car with a mobile phone in it. Richard had a bachelor's of business and was doing a part-time graduate course. He sometimes stayed over.

Life was difficult with Richard's mother. She would

wait every night to have dinner with him. Richard had never had a relationship with a woman, and he would turn thirty-seven in March. His father had died, and his mother kept him to look after her and the house in her old age. She had convinced him he was ugly, and no one would want to be with him. Richard's nose was a little out of proportion on the big side.

I told Richard I loved him just the way he was, but he insisted on going and having a cosmetic rhinoplasty done to reduce the size of his nose. Just before Easter 1993, Richard went into a private hospital and had his operation. As it turned out, the surgeon said it had been broken and not mended properly. After this surgery, he stopped getting colds all the time.

His mother was making it very difficult for us to see each other. So was Steven, who fought against me seeing Richard. We, Richard and I, had joined a number of theatre subscriptions at the beginning of the year and went to the theatre often. Steven had stopped going to his father's. He simply refused to go, and I couldn't make him.

Richard and I went out the country to Kingaroy to visit his brother Howard and Howard's wife, Rosa, and their children. We stayed in a nice cottage inn. We also went down to northern New South Wales to Bellingen to meet his brother Paul and Paul's wife, Robyn, as well as the children. His other brother Gordon lived in the Johnson family home.

In July, I turned forty, and Richard brought me some beautiful red roses and took me out to a romantic restaurant on the water of the Brisbane River. August 2 was Steven's birthday, and the third was Richard's mother's birthday, so we all had dinner at my place, along with his Auntie Margaret who was once a trained nurse. I met his Auntie Janet and his cousin Ravind after this.

So, I had met all his lovely family. There was difficulty meeting mine, as I was not close to them anymore, and my mother despised me, making it difficult for me to visit. Despite this, we went up to Helidon to try and visit. Richard was shocked by the way my family carried on. Mum spoke to me in an awful "smart" tone of voice and did not speak with love at all. Dad virtually ignored us the whole time we were there.

On getting home, I tried to explain, but describing what had happened over a whole lifetime was difficult. Richard came from a loving home and found it hard to believe my mother had never loved me. He left, and that night, I sunk back into world news, which I hadn't watched all year. Intel introduced the first Pentium microprocessor, and the first web browser was launched. Computing connected Steven, Richard, and me.

My dearly beloved Auntie Lilly died after going back and forth from hospital having a series of mini-strokes. I saw her the week before she died. Uncle Joe was devastated.

Around this time, Steven was assaulted by a bully at Balmoral High School with a whole lot of boys gathered around yelling, "Kill him! Kill him!"

The police got involved, and they did nothing. The school did nothing. Steven had a big egg on his head and a CT scan showed concussion. Steven and I were really very upset. Steven became truant more often after this.

On the anniversary of our first meeting, October 28, 1993, Richard asked me to marry him as we passed under the Story Bridge on a City Cat on the water. It was very romantic. Not long after, we went to Wallace Bishops and chose the most elegant and beautiful diamond ring, also putting a wedding ring with diamonds in it on lay-by.

We went to St. Mary's Anglican church at Kangaroo

Point on the cliffs and signed the intention to marry, organising a ceremony. This was our favourite church. We had gone to some orchestral concerts here. We began a pre-marriage course. A lot came out in this course, and it concluded just before Christmas with the priest refusing to marry us, saying to me, "Anthea, I cannot marry you to this man." For everyone's privacy, there's a lot I cannot say here.

We did not know what to do. I was happy to accept Richard. He was 100 per cent truthful with me about his life, and I was 100 per cent truthful about mine. We spent that Christmas Day with his family at his mother's house, and it was a lovely day. His niece Emily got a bike. I have beautiful photographs of the Christmas Day with the big tree, which Richard and his brother Gordon decorated.

In 1994, my heart condition that had caused me to have a heart attack when I'd had Steven became unstable. It was the protracted period of stress with the assault, the court case, breaking up with Richard, and then Steven's continual truancy and running away. Stress going on for so long caused the Prinzmetal angina to become unstable, with bouts of severe cramping pain in my heart that lasted from a few minutes to ten minutes.

I couldn't look after Steven any more. I sent him to live with his father, who was now living in Adelaide. One night when I was alone, I got severe pain that was not relieved by the spray I'd been given to use, so I called an ambulance.

I was in hospital five days. Whilst there, I had coronary angiograms done. Passing a catheter with a camera on it into my heart via a major blood vessel in the groin, my doctors found my coronary arteries to be clear of cholesterol. That meant I would be less likely to have a heart attack, as there was no blockage. The arteries with Prinzmetal angina would go into spasm when under extreme stress or at rest.

The first half of 1994, I was terribly unwell. I had constant heart problems. My back was giving me a lot of trouble. The torn tendon in my shoulder had become supraspinatus tendinitis with calcium deposits, causing severe pain in my upper left arm. I had to try and get well.

Richard said he couldn't marry into a strange family like mine, and as he said this, it felt like someone had placed a dagger in my heart. He wanted us to go on seeing each other as normal, just not get married. So, I agreed. We went on seeing each other, actually taking a trip to Sydney to see *Phantom of the Opera* and going to Taronga Park Zoo.

The online shopping warehouse Amazon was founded, and I longed for the day we would have internet to explore it.

Throughout these years, 1990 to 1995, I would go for walks whenever I could to the Bulimba shops past all the houses with gardens, and I would, from time to time, catch a glimpse of some butterflies. It was around this time when I was feeling better. I remember taking a walk to the Bulimba shops. I practised positive affirmations every morning and also read positive motivational books when I could throughout the day. I had learnt how to meditate, and this helped me a lot.

By mid-year, I felt much better, with the stress of Steven taken off me. I applied for a job I felt I had commitment to. This was with Merck Sharpe and Dohme as one of Queensland's heart care nurses. I was successful with the position and consider this one of my career achievements.

The job involved going out to doctors' surgeries and seeing patients who the doctors believed would benefit from the programme. I was required to use a Reflotron machine and measure patient cholesterol, as well take base observations and ask lifestyle questions. We talked to patients about making lifestyle changes they wanted to make.

Richard and I were actually very happy during the second half of 1994 while I worked this job and did not have all the worry of Steven. My medical conditions settled down. Richard wanted "his own place"—to move out from his mother's.

I found him a nice, affordable apartment on Redfern Street, Morningside, and helped him move into it and set it up. He had already collected many things for it, and it was ten minutes from me. We continued to see each other as we always had. The friendship grew stronger. We went to see a Spielberg movie *Schindler's List* about the Second World War in Europe.

During this time, Steven had rung me twice sounding very distraught. He said his father was assaulting him and had broken a statue over his head. On the third time he rang me, he sounded totally gutted, so I told him I would get him back. I had sole custody of Steven, so I rang the federal police, who organised for him to be sent back to me.

I will never forget getting him off the plane in December. He vowed he would be good for me and said, "Oh, Mum. Now I know why you left him. I don't blame you anymore."

The relationship between Steven and his father was never the same after this. Steven went to see *Pulp Fiction* that December and really enjoyed living so close to the movie cinema and that I'd encouraged a love of movies.

Steven went back to high school at Balmoral High to do grade eleven the following year, 1995. He answered the phone really rudely when my boss had called in January 1995, and the company cancelled my contract to commence in February that year. Steven continued to spend a lot of time in the neighbourhood at friends' houses, including Dennis Brubech's house.

Richard bought a mobile phone, which was very

expensive. Everyday people were now just starting to buy mobile phones, which had their infancy in the late '80s. In the first half of the '90s, only doctors or important people owned mobile phones.

In 1995, the online auction site eBay was founded, and Java programming language was released. The World Trade Organisation (WTO) was created. Steven got *Friday* out on VHS and watched it and really enjoyed it. He also went to see *Heat and Casino.*

I would say that the first six months of 1995 were the lowest point in my life ever. I would go up to the river to a spot I could park my car and just look at the river and play music loudly because no one could hear. I felt trapped.

In June 1995, I made the decision I had to change my life. So, I wrote a list with a plan for how I would dramatically change my life. It read:

- Go back to nursing in aged care at night
- Look for a shop New Year for a beauty therapy business
- Move within walking distance to the shop and transport
- Sell my car to help fund the shop
- Set Steven up in a unit with tax cheque
- Continue to go out with Richard
- Stop watching world and local news
- Read Saturday's newspaper every Saturday

So, now I had a plan. I was very decisive. My mind was made up. The next day, I saw an advertisement in the local paper that read, "Wanted: A registered nurse three nights a week for aged care at Annerley Nursing Centre." I applied and got the position. I started in July 1995, just before my birthday. Going back to aged care nursing was really hard, but I did it because it was part of my plan.

Steven turned fifteen in August. I was no longer eligible for the sole parent pension, and he was old enough to leave school.

The rest of 1995 sailed by with me at least feeling I was helping people at night and had some purpose. I keenly searched real estate options, looking at vacant shops in the hope of finding something suitable, as well as affordable.

Richard enrolled Steven in a photographic course and took him to classes every week, picking Steven up afterwards. Photography was something Steven was interested in.

In November 1995, shortly after Princess Diana separated from Prince Charles, she went on television in an interview with Martin Bashir. Millions across the world sat riveted as she opened her heart. She spoke about the strain of being a member of the royal family, her depression and bulimia, her husband's lack of compassion towards her, and his ongoing relationship with Camilla Parker Bowles. I no longer felt I came from such a strange family and saw that everybody had their problems.

Christmas came, and Steven and I spent Christmas at home with our great big tree.

# CHAPTER 8

# The Realisation of a Dream: Beautiful Solutions

## Building Beautiful Solutions

The next year, 1996, began with me working three nights a week in aged care. I had worked New Year at the home. Steven started back at school at the end of January doing grade twelve. His friend Dennis Brubech had run away from home and started living with us. I bought all the uniforms and textbooks for both of them to start school.

Richard discussed with me that now he didn't want children. He had changed his mind. He said we would find a shop and build a business and that the shop would be our baby.

On February 14, 1996, Valentine's Day, Richard was at the Laundromat doing his washing, and he rang me on his mobile phone. There was a shop opposite advertised for rent, and he asked me to come up and have a look at it. I quickly dropped everything and drove up. We looked at it together.

It was at 682 Wynnum Road, Morningside. Looking in, I felt it looked like the black hole of Calcutta. But believe it or not, I believed I could set my business up in there. It was long and narrow and could be divided into three rooms and was like a blank canvas, I could do anything with it I liked.

We took the number on the sign, which was home-made, and after Richard finished his washing, we went back to his place and rang the number. Richard and I both spoke with a Chinese couple, Mr and Mrs Yip, who were impossible to understand. They eventually got their daughter, who spoke English, and arrangements were made to meet at the shop in a few hours at 2:00 p.m. We went to the shop on time and met with the Yips.

Through their daughter, we agreed to negotiate a lease on the shop, paying a deposit of $500, which was the first month's rent. This was something I could afford in the long term. Richard paid the first $500 deposit as a Valentine's Day gift. I was very excited. I would start working on the plans for the council to get approval for the licence, which was required.

We put a block of land which we'd bought a few years earlier up at Mt Glorious on the market. Richard said we would put the proceeds of the sale into building the shop. The land, acreage, sold quickly for a profit, and the proceeds were available in May when building commenced.

I started looking for accommodation close to the shop. Richard already lived walking distance to the shop on Redfern Street. I could move from Leura Avenue. The noise at that time staying there was phenomenal. The council was having ten City Cats built nearby at Bulimba, and the noise would go on all year.

I found a unit, Unit 2, 37 Moore Street, owned by George. I moved to the unit. Steven had dropped out of school and started working at a restaurant in the kitchen. He eventually wanted to become a chef and thought this was a start. Richard moved to live with me at Moore Street, and Steven, with his friend Dennis Brubech, moved to Redfern Street. The units we lived in were a few minutes walking distance to each other. I spent a tax cheque of nearly $2,000 setting Steven up in the unit.

It was just after we moved that Casey cat passed away.

I had taken her to the vet, and she had kidney failure. She did not survive the move and kept threatening to die, and I would plead with her to stay alive. She finally passed on.

It rained heavily all March and April that year, making building of the shop difficult, and we didn't have a signed lease anyway. Meanwhile, I was trying to negotiate a suitable lease through lawyers and the landlords' lawyers. This was difficult because of the language barrier. The lease had relocation clauses in it, which meant I could easily be moved.

I didn't want to spend a lot of money setting it up only to be moved. Eventually, Mr and Mrs Yip and I met in the backyard of the shop, and they said they really wanted me as a tenant and would have the relocation clauses removed. On May 1, 1996, the lease was finally signed by everybody.

I had already found a builder, Trevor, who was wonderful. I had already submitted applications for a licence to the council, which were successful. I had bought the remaining furniture and equipment I needed and, so, had the measurements of everything. Richard's mother had paid for a multi milo machine, which was several pieces of equipment in one worth several thousand dollars. I picked it up for $1,500 from a beauty therapist closing down, who gave me heaps of things and ideas. The multi milo was compact, taking up little floor space. It was a tight squeeze, but everything had a place, and it all fitted. I could very much imagine running this shop/salon.

Time had come for me to sell my car, so I took it to a car yard and simply sold it for $5,000. I needed to get work I could catch public transport to and that paid better. I applied to work as an occupational health nurse at Treasury Casino Brisbane, which had opened in April 1995, the previous year.

The position meant working four ten-hour shifts Friday, Saturday, Sunday, and Monday nights, which were the Casinos busiest nights. I was successful and absolutely loved this job, working with the dealers and pit bosses. The job involved providing health care to staff, not the public, and working closely with security. The headquarters were underground under the casino.

The shop started being built on May 5, 1996, by Trevor, who had ordered in all the materials once I gave him the go-ahead and the rain had finally stopped. Two walls were constructed to divide the shop into three rooms. The front wall had lattice at the top to allow the air conditioning from the front to flow through.

The shop had its own toilet for a client, which was essential for a beauty therapy salon. A one-way glass window was placed in the front wall so you could see into the front room of the shop. The back wall had a sliding door, which went into the back room. The middle room was the treatment room. The back room already had a kitchen sink. I put the hot water on.

The landlord for the Redfern Street unit was a cabinetmaker and was making all the cabinets up to my drawings and specifications in peach laminate that matched the manicure table Christian had made for me. Trevor project-managed the operation, and I couldn't have done it without him. I had to go and buy a sink unit for the treatment room and a sink unit for the front room. I had to go and choose lights. I had to choose the paint colours with the local Bristol's store helping me.

Trevor found me a plumber, Brad, who I trusted to do a good job. I was horrified when I saw the finished job. There were pipes going up the wall everywhere. I had to modify the design of the shop and install the cupboards so they covered all these pipes and pay to have the cabinets modified to fit over the pipes. I chose not to pay the plumber.

The electricians came in and did a wonderful job of installing downlights and beautiful overhead contemporary chandeliers. I paid them a bonus. The painters came in and also did an amazing job. I had them take my bar away, as well as the couch and a counter and paint them all to match. I got a glass artist to build all the glass shelves in back by mirror in the front of the shop. I got glass especially cut to fit the bar / front counter.

Betty and Bill, who had the second-hand shop, helped by sourcing me all these beautiful things to decorate the shop with. They found French antique mirrors and a lovely comfortable client chair, which went back and up and down. Trevor had recommended I go with brass fittings throughout, and I did.

After the shop was built, there was signage to be done. I got the local sign people at the end of the street to do the front windows, and they did a great job making me a shingle as well.

I spent the whole time angry in the back of my mind that I would not have another baby. And though I was very focused on not having a child, the shop had turned out zooms better than my dreams. It was absolutely, unbelievably beautiful and professional. I now had to organise stationary and write a price list. The latter was quite difficult. Richard did the price list using Microsoft publisher software. He also made gift vouchers and signs for the shop. This was a first for him using publisher. I saw ladies only.

I got a professional company to do the business cards, and they did the ladies lips in red instead of peach, so I took them to court and won. My motto was "For professional beauty solutions," and I had a stunning figure of a lady as my logo. She appeared on the front window, the shingle, and below the front counter.

In August Steven's birthday came. He and Dennis moved out of the flat. The landlords were heavily into religion and tried to push this onto the boys. The evening Steven and Dennis left the landlady was going to do an exorcism on Dennis to flush out all his demons. He had just been diagnosed with schizophrenia from all the marijuana smoking. Steven had met a girl, Carol, who visited next door, and he moved out to live in a flat with her

Prince Charles and Princess Diana got divorced.

. In the September, it was time to open. I had employed a receptionist. I put the two billboards out and a Ficus tree I bought from Bunning's. This tree became a landmark; if it was out, I was available or consulting in the salon. Betty from the second-hand shop was my first client. She came for a manicure. I wasn't good at waxing to start with, but in time, my weakness became my strength.

Facials became my favourite. I just loved to give a lady a beautiful facial and improve her skin. Eyebrow waxing in those days was seen as a small, insignificant service but became something I loved to do. It was an artistic exercise for me, and I believe that, in my time, I contributed greatly to putting eyebrows on the map, making them an important treatment. Eyelash and eyebrow tinting also became my speciality; getting just the right colour for a person was very important to me.

Business was slow to start with, but that was how I wanted it. Almost everybody who came come back, and this was a good sign to me.

I didn't know what hit me the first Christmas, during the pre-Christmas lead-up to the day. It was suddenly extremely busy, with people wanting gift vouchers and last-minute gifts. I had time off from the shop between Christmas and New Year and just worked at the casino.

## Ill health and running the shop, 1997 to 1999

In 1997 Steven began working for the cinemas at Bulimba and Hawthorne, eventually running their cafés. He loved movies and got to see lots of them. He was working toward his certificate in hospitality.

One Friday night shift at the casino in early January, I had severe throbbing pain in my left pelvic region all night. The next Saturday morning, I was waiting on the doorstep of a doctor's surgery in Morningside to see a doctor. When the doctor's surgery opened, I saw Ingrid Tall, who sent me for an ultrasound, which I went and had that morning. On the Monday, I went and saw her for the results. She told me I had a suspicious solid mass on my left ovary and sent me for a CT scan. I was so upset. I knew solid meant cancer.

I shall never forget walking back to the shop that day up Wynnum Road, crying my eyes out. I had just established a shop for ladies for beauty therapy, and here I was, about to lose all my feminine parts. Somehow, life seemed so unfair at that moment.

I had the CT scan done on the Wednesday and went back to see Dr Tall Friday. She told me it could be cancer. I went back to see the lady doctor who I routinely saw, and she gave me a referral to see a surgeon. I made an appointment to see the surgeon the following week. When I saw the surgeon, he said I would have to have a full pelvic clearance—my uterus, ovaries, everything. I was deeply upset and distraught. I couldn't cope with a diagnosis of cancer. He booked me in for operation the end of February, which was three weeks away.

I continued to work at the casino and at the shop. I notified the casino's administration, and they let me know they only wanted healthy staff working in the health centre. They asked me to resign, which I did. Due to the diagnosis, I did not put the receptionist who I had employed back on after Christmas in January.

I spent a lot of time thinking and decided, if I was going to die, then I would rather die with all my pieces and parts. I also decided I'd rather work and pay back my debt of overdraft to build the shop. The day of the operation came, and I didn't turn up—just didn't turn up.

A week went by, and the surgeon rang me at my shop. "Where are you?" he asked.

"At my shop," I told him.

He replied, "You have been at the top of my basket all week."

I explained how I felt.

"Can't we just take the tumour and the ovary?" he asked.

I agreed with this, and he booked me in at the end of one of his lists on March 15, 1997, at the Mater Hospital in Brisbane.

The day came. It was Richard's birthday, and I went in a taxi to the hospital. I signed the consent form for just the tumour ovary and tube. I was wheeled into the operating theatre believing I had cancer. When I woke up, I had been cut from my outer right side to my outer left side, and it felt like I had been cut in half. I was in agony and had a drip with pain relief in my arm, with a button I could press for pain relief. The staff complained I pressed it too much.

A doctor who assisted with the operation came and told

me the mass was benign. She said they could tell by looking at it. I wanted pathology results to confirm. Apparently, it was a corpus luteum, an unfertilised egg that doesn't dissolve but grows and grows and contains teeth, hair, and nails.

Absolutely fascinating that I had spent a whole year angry and focused on my ovaries and the fact that I would not have any more children, and one of my eggs refused to die and tried to make a baby by itself. I ended up with an ovarian tumour. Cancer or not, I had gone through all the emotions one goes through with cancer prior to the surgery. I was relieved it was benign.

Recovering from this surgery was difficult. I was very sore and also developed an infection in the wound, which resolved after antibiotics and drainage. I tried to go back to the shop after four weeks to do a manicure for Betty but couldn't sit in one spot for more than ten minutes. I waited the six weeks as advised. My mother rang when I was recovering, and this was the last time, I spoke to her.

I bought a laser machine and an electrolysis machine from Elsher Lander, whose products I sold. I booked in to do an electrolysis course with Beauty Skills Academy in the second half of the year. Elsher showed me how to operate the laser, and I did a laser safety officers course. I did a lot of research into use of the laser.

Richard and my clients were talking about the internet and email a lot. Richard had an email account. So, I decided to enrol in a course on the internet and email through TAFE one night a week for six weeks.

The presser being operated in the dry-cleaner next door had been a problem since I'd opened. Debra seemed to enjoy really slamming it, which wasn't conducive to a peaceful environment for beauty therapy treatments. I first contacted the landlord of my shop and their shop, and when I got nowhere, I rang the council. Then I wrote to the council, who came out and heard it. They then did help me.

In 1997, the first Harry Potter book was published by J. K. Rowling. Steven came to see me and was excited about this. He told me some of the movies he'd been to see at the cinema, including *Good Will Hunting* with Matt Damon and *Devil's Advocate* with Al Pacino, as well as *Fifth Element* with Bruce Willis. He loved the job at the cinemas and was happy living with Carol.

I started doing agency nursing and relief pool work at Mt. Olivet Hospital (now St. Vincent's) on the weekends. I continued to work the shop during the week. A patient with a tracheotomy (tube in the throat) coughed sputum on my face one night at work. Following this, I got mycoplasma pneumonia and was very ill in July and August when it was quiet in the shop. I took eight weeks off trying to recover.

On August 31, 1997, Princess Diana was killed in a tunnel in Paris after being chased by the paparazzi. The whole world was in mourning, with possibly the biggest outpouring of grief the world had ever known.

With my savings and more overdrafts, I bought a little red Laser car. The council wrote to the dry-cleaner next door, and they have to get rid of the presser.

Eventually, in September, I started operating the shop again, and it got busy. Christmas came, and I took a complete break between Christmas and New Year.

In 1998, the shop got very busy; it really took off. I was working every second Saturday night on a relief pool at Mt. Olivet or doing agency in nursing. In hindsight, I should have let go of nursing. But I couldn't; it was part of my identity, part of me, and I enjoyed it very much.

In June, I developed a lump in my left breast, which seemed quite large and was mobile. I went to the lady doctor

I regularly saw, and she sent me for an ultrasound. The results showed the lump was just fatty tissue and nothing to worry about. The doctor examined me and said it was nothing to worry about based on the ultrasound results.

In August, Steven and Carol came to see me and told me Carol was pregnant with my first grandchild, due next February. I was very happy. Steven told me they had just been to see a comedy, *Something about Mary*, and that he had gotten out *Fear and Loathing in Les Vegas* with Johnny Depp on VHS. He was really enjoying his job at the cinemas and seeing lots of free movies. He saw *The Wedding Singer* and *The Waterboy*, as well as *The Truman Show* with Jim Carey.

The search engine, Google, was founded. There were also other search engines founded, but Google was the most popular. Apple computers revealed the first iMac computer. The United States had a budget surplus for the first time in thirty years. Stem cell research from the human embryo began.

At the end of 1998, my shop, Beautiful Solutions, was very busy and doing really well.

Christmas came, and I was very happy. Steven spent Christmas with Carol and her family. Richard spent Christmas with his family. And I worked it at Mt. Olivet, and it was actually very beautiful to work a Christmas.

In 1999, I told one of the girls I worked with, Leonie, about the lump in my breast, and she looked at it. She told me I had to get a second opinion. She said the best way to find out in a day whether the lump was malignant was to go to the Wesley Breast Clinic. So, I made an appointment at the clinic for the next week.

I then had to get a referral. So, I went to the doctor's surgery in Morningside and got a referral. I went to the clinic on the due day and had to change into a gown for, firstly, a mammogram and then an ultrasound of both breasts.

I waited to see the doctor for the results. She said the area on my left breast was highly suspicious, and consequently, they wanted to do a fine needle aspiration of the area. I waited about an hour and then had this procedure. It was frightfully painful, but I endured it.

She said she'd never been surer prior to an open excision of a lump that mine was malignant. She said they would send it off to pathology, and she would ring me at 5:00 p.m. I left the clinic with Richard with tears streaming down my face. Richard drove me home, and I cried the whole way. On getting home, I put ice on the wound to relieve the pain and swelling.

At 5:00 p.m., the doctor rang and told me the lump was malignant. I said I would go back to my regular doctor for a referral to a breast surgeon. Once again, I was in tears. Richard and I just hugged each other and rocked back and forth. I went to see my regular lady doctor, and she was surprised, having received a copy of the results from the breast clinic.

She referred me to Dr Neil Wetzig. I made an appointment to see him privately in a week's time. When I saw him, he said I had to have a full gland clearance under my left arm, and this would permanently affect arm movement. He also said the lump had to come out urgently, as it had been there for seven months now and was highly suspicious. He put me on one of his lists for a week's time at a public hospital he also worked at. But to do that, I had to go to the outpatient's and see him there at the breast clinic.

I was having a lumpectomy and full gland clearance with radiation following. In order to keep the bills paid on the shop I applied to have my superannuation paid out, as I had been diagnosed with a terminal illness. I turned up at the hospital on February 8, 1999, for operation the following morning. On February 9, 1999, when I was to go to theatre at 6:00 a.m., Carol had gone into labour to have the baby. One driving force in my mind to get through the surgery was that I wanted to see my granddaughter grow up.

Richard waited at the hospital the whole day for me. I didn't come back to the ward until 5:00 p.m. that night. He was worried I had died. When I woke up in the ward, I didn't remember anything. Apparently, they couldn't wake me up because my blood pressure had slipped down very low, and they'd had trouble getting it up. At least I did not have all the pain I'd had after the abdominal surgery. I was just sore, with a drain going into a bottle from under my arm. I was only in hospital two days. I wanted to get out and see the baby. She would be called Eloise.

I was going back to the breast clinic every few days with the drain. Eventually, after ten days, the drain came out, and I developed a seroma (a collection of serum fluid), which had to be drained with a needle a couple of times. I had all these physiotherapy exercises to do to get the movement back in my left arm. I already had the tendinitis in the left shoulder. I did all the exercises as instructed. The wound healed nicely.

The radiation began a month later in early March. Richard took me every day and brought me home five days a week for twenty-five treatments. Around this time, I started back at the shop. I closed the doors and operated by appointment only, doing only those treatments I felt I could manage. The doctors told me I could never do massage again, but I started very slowly a little every day and found this actually helped me get the movement back in my arm.

Around this time, I started doing laser facials and laser treatments. These treatments paid well, and I could manage with my arm. I did not at this stage put them on a price list. I chose my clients, choosing those who I believed were suitable and would benefit from the treatment. I had enormous success with the laser, and word travelled fast. I was the first in Brisbane to do a laser light facial; it was really my idea.

Steven came over often to see me and lived with me for a short period. He was really worried about me. He was so excited the next movie in the Star Wars series, *Phantom Menace*, had come out. He explained that the last one, *Return of the Jedi*, had come out in 1984, following *The Empire Strikes Back* in 1980, so it was a long time coming.

Richard and I did not resume sexual relations after the breast cancer. It changed both of us. I felt my femininity had been attacked. I just didn't feel the same. It took a lot out of me, and I had to keep working at the shop. I started working a lot of evenings at the shop and finishing late—too late to walk home—and I started staying overnight at the shop. I started buying tasty healthy takeaways for tea and having birdbaths. I dreamed of living in a unit behind the shop and living alone. I couldn't handle intimacy anymore.

In November, that unit I dreamed of moving to came up for rent. I told Richard I wanted to move out and live by myself at the back of the shop. I rented the unit, 1/55 Burrai Street, Morningside.

The move wasn't easy. I left a lot of stuff with Richard. I thought I'd better get a secure part-time job in nursing to pay all the rents. I started work at Nimbin Nursing Home, which became Treetops RSL New Farm, two nights a week, Friday and Saturday nights, just before Y2K at Christmastime. Everybody was talking about the Millennium bug.

In December 1999, my girlfriend Nerida Doss died of

a heart attack on Hayman Island. She and Maurie had gone for a holiday there. She'd collapsed and had been flown to the mainland but had died in hospital.

## Y2K and GST

As New Year 2000 approached, the world was hyped up. There was widespread talk of all the computers failing at twelve midnight. There was also widespread talk of all the electricity shutting down, along with all kinds of other things, as though the world would stop at midnight, a new century. At the nursing home where I had started work, I was working New Year's Eve, and I had to learn how to start a generator in case the electricity failed.

In January 2000, I bought my first mobile phone. It was a very small Motorola, and I loved it. Texting had only just started, but I wasn't texting yet. At this stage, just about everybody owned a mobile phone. Cameras were starting to appear in phones around this time. It was the technology of the phones that advanced rapidly in the next fifteen years. With nearly three million users of the internet by the year 2000 and mobile phones, globalisation was happening, increasing world trade and causing media, including both world and local news, to become easily available.[12]

GST (goods and services tax) in Australia was all over the news, both those for it and those against it, causing much confusion for business owners and the public. The Howard Government brought it in on July 1, 2000. I had to go through all my stock front of shop and take sales and import tax off and add GST of 10 per cent on. It was a nightmare.

It meant my French skincare products, Algologie, sold for less, and the Australian, Elsher Lander, sold for more. I didn't know whether or not I had to register for GST, but I did. I didn't know whether or not I had to put in quarterly statements. I think the rest of Australia was just as confused.

With all my ill health, the books had not been done, and that was a weight on my mind. Richard was to keep the books for me. I had kept all the source documents—bank statements, invoices, receipts, and other records—so they could be done.

I bought a laptop from Dell. The company helped me design it to suit my needs. It had a new at the time DVD drive and lots of USB ports for the portable flash drives that were becoming popular. I was very excited when it arrived.

Working at the nursing home put some perspective into my life. Being a committed registered nurse, all these years almost made me feel guilty in the shop looking after the outer sixteenth of an inch of people and the whole emphasis being on image. Nursing was about looking after the whole person, regardless of race, colour, or creed, and it didn't matter what they looked like.

At the nursing home, there was a male registered nurse, Kevin, who I worked alongside all year. We were strongly attracted to each other, but I didn't think it wise to get involved with someone I worked with, and I was unable to cope with intimacy anymore. We remained friends all year.

## Battling the tax department, 2001 to 2005

January 2001 brought Kevin and me together at a chance meeting at New Farm in the street where the shops were. We decided to go for coffee and go out for dinner during the week. We decided to go away together up the north coast to Mooloolaba Beach for a few weeks. We went to Underwater

Sea World and had a lovely time. He worked the same nights I worked, and it made work more enjoyable.

My brother Tony and his wife, Tania, come down from Townsville to visit. They brought my nephew Joshua, born January 5, 2000, the year before. They brought me news that Dad and Mum weren't well.

On March 8, 2001, my second granddaughter was born. She was called Bella. I was there just after she was born and fed Bella her first bottle. She was born hungry. Steven and Carol were very happy, and I was happy too.

In late May, my mother died, but I did not get news of this till days after the funeral, when my sister Amy rang me in early June. I was devastated. I had waited and waited all my life for her to love me, and now there was no chance she ever would. There were many things left unsaid—just so much I wanted to say to her. And now all opportunity was lost. After my mother died, I couldn't function for about six weeks. Richard was a great support to me.

Kevin was so upset to see the change in me that he went right off the rails. I went up to visit him at Ipswich, and he was shooting up with some kind of drug. He was also putting alcohol in a water bottle and drinking it at work. I promptly broke it off with him, as I did not want to be a part of these scenes. I continued to work at the nursing home for the rest of 2001.

I started to receive letters from the tax department about my taxes, which had not been submitted, giving me dates that I was to have them submitted.

On September 11, 2001, terrorists highjacked three planes and flew two into the World Trade Center's Twin Towers, bombing them and killing and injuring thousands of people. The day was eerie. I remember it well. There was nobody on the streets. I walked to my shop and walked home again after a few hours. I watched in horror on a television I had only just bought.

The United States declared a war on terror. This incident changed the world forever. Never would it be the same at airports or, in fact, anywhere. Security was stepped up.

In 2002, I stopped working at the nursing home and had a break from nursing for a few months. I was worried that the books weren't done and asked Richard if he could start doing them. He came to the shop regularly, and we started doing the books. It was a mammoth task.

Kevin started stalking me at the shop, and it got difficult to leave an open sign up with the door open.

I had some really lovely clients who were very loyal, and I very much enjoyed seeing them. There was Kay Kohler, who had cerebral palsy, and she and I get on so well. Kay was one of many who really appreciated me. I loved doing Belinda's eyebrows, as she had the most amazing eyebrows. There was Georgie, who called me her waxing lady. There was Georgina and also Cheryl, with her husband, Lorenzo, and so many others. I simply couldn't mention everyone, but I couldn't forget Raelene and her sister Phillipa.

In mid-August 2002, Carol disappeared. She left a note that she'd gone to New Zealand. She'd apparently had an online love affair through a dating site. We didn't know where the girls were. Steven got home from work at the cinema to discover this and rang me. He was devastated. I went over and helped him pack everything up, and it was transported the next day to my garage. Steven came to live with me for about six weeks. We found out the girls were with a friend of Carol's on Russell Island.

Steven found a vacant unit next to Richard in the same complex and rented it from George in October. Steven and I struggled to cope with what had transpired.

I continued to get letters from the tax department. They were now threatening to throw me in jail. I submitted doctor's letters, showing I'd been seriously ill, and this was what had put the books behind. They were patient and waited. I got a case manager who was very understanding.

Christmas that year, the girls and Steven came to my unit, and I cooked a nice dinner. Steven finished his cheffing course.

In 2003, Richard took a redundancy package with the Education Department and started helping me every day, Monday to Friday, to get the books done and up to date. I saw my accountant and started submitting taxes. On July 22, I turned fifty. Richard gave me a spa unit insert for the bath. I went away to Caloundra, my favourite beach, for a week and stayed at Rolling Surf.

On my birthday, Kevin died surrounded by alcohol bottles. The autopsy showed a dangerously high level of alcohol in his blood. I knew he was once a very beautiful person, but alcohol and drugs changed him.

The 3G network for smart phones was introduced, connecting the phone to the internet. The new phones that came out were slim and sleek, unlike their predecessors. They were very expensive.

In 2003, Steven started a year-long full-time certificate program in information technology and computing, his other passion along with cooking. This got his mind off Carol, and he started dating Jesse, who was a hairdresser on Oxford Street, Bulimba, where the cinemas were.

Richard and I continued to work on the books at the shop. I also continued to see clients at the shop and just loved providing services to them. My sheer enjoyment when doing a nice facial only deepened, and I got really expert at shaping eyebrows. My weakness when I opened, waxing, became my strength. I felt I was really helping many ladies in the shop. I was able to have full movement of my arm and had no problem performing full-body massage.

In 2003, my Auntie Mabel died. She'd spent a few years in a nursing home following a stroke, after which she was unable to talk. She had the stroke after returning from a holiday with my Mum and Dad. During the holiday, she'd had a major falling out with Mum, who was very mean to her.

In 2004, I took a career position as night manager/supervisor for a site in Brisbane that had three hostels and several independent units. I worked three nights a fortnight—Saturday and Sunday one week and Sunday the next week. I immensely enjoyed this job.

In hindsight, taking it on was ridiculous. I was one registered nurse for three hostels with about eighty residents in each and only one nurse in each hostel. Walking around between the hostels with security was a challenge.

In 2004 and up until September 2005, I did this job and also worked at my shop. I continued to work on the books with Richard. The friendship between Richard and I strengthened after I moved out. Slowly, month by month, it got deeper. We were going to the theatre throughout 2003 to 2005 through the week.

Richard told me about this social media site founded in 2004 called Facebook. I thought one day I might explore it.

I was going swimming in the mornings, getting up at 5:30 a.m. and getting there at 6:00 a.m. from 2003 till 2005.

## The sentinel event in nursing, September 5, 2005

I went to work as usual on September 4, 2005, the Saturday night before Father's Day 2005. It was a long drive from my unit at Morningside across town to the western suburbs in my little red Laser. I arrived at the first hostel where the night started from at 9:45 p.m. and got handover.

Then I went on a brisk seven-minute walk to the second hostel, where I took handover. There was a lady who was dying in this hostel and on regular morphine.

I then went to the third hostel, walking all the way in the night air with security. The third hostel was very busy, and I had an inexperienced nurse on duty. At this hostel, there was a lot of tension in the air. I took the handover and stayed to help, making me back late to the first hostel.

It was a very busy night. I barely got a break walking around between the three hostels doing what I could to help. The two-way radio was busy all night, and so were security staff. I had a new staff member on at the first hostel, who was a reliever and normally worked day and evening. This girl, Toni, kept disappearing throughout the night, which was not helpful.

I was supposed to give dangerous drugs out between 5:15 a.m. and 5:30 a.m. at the first hostel to stay on schedule. This nurse was nowhere to be found at that time and reappeared at 5:40 a.m. We quickly got the medications ready (it was required by law to have someone check with you) and were on our way out to administer the first one when a call came over the radio for urgent help at the third hostel.

I told the third hostel staff to call an ambulance. I quickly gave the medications out correctly and got over to the third hostel but was delayed on the way by a psychotic patient having an episode that involved running into everyone's rooms and upsetting people. I very quickly got her a "when necessary" medication and asked the nurse to sit with her until the medication took effect.

I arrived at the third hostel to find two ambulances

outside. On walking in, I found the first patient on the floor with her foot nearly severed and blood everywhere. She had gone to get up, which she was allowed to do, and had slipped on a bedspread on the floor. The nurse told me that the resident in room 27 had tried to commit suicide and asked if I could go there, also saying the resident in room 42 had fallen out of bed. I went to the resident in room 27. He was a diabetic on an overnight "no check list."

On entering his room, I saw blood smeared all over the walls and furniture. He was covered in fine cuts all over his body. There was a suicide note on the locker beside him. I got the blood sugar equipment and took his blood sugar, which was low. I gave him a sweet drink.

Over the radio for hostel two, the nurse requested I attend to give the morphia to the dying patient, as it was overdue, and the patient was restless. I radioed that day staff would be on duty in a matter of minutes, but I had the keys. I calmed the suicidal patient and an ambulance person came in and took over. A third ambulance had arrived.

I went to room 42 and found an elderly demented patient on the floor and distressed. I made her comfortable with a pillow and blanket and checked for breakage/dislocation. I found it was highly likely she had broken the upper bone in her thigh to her hip. I calmed her with my voice and by stroking her forehead. I got the ambulance personnel to her. I went to the office and started preparing the three charts for transfer to hospital. I rang the nurse manager for the hostel and informed her of what had gone on.

I then went to the second hostel to give the morphia and handover and then back to the first hostel to give handover.

I stayed at the third hostel to talk with the nurse manager who had arrived. I stayed for three hours overtime, for which I was never paid, doing necessary reports. I was not responsible in any way for what happened. I am not Houdini and cannot be in three hostels at the same time or in several different places within the same hostel at the same time. I had one inexperienced new nurse in the third hostel to support me, plus a relieving day nurse in another and one regular night nurse in the other for all these residents/patients.

I was exhausted emotionally, mentally, and physically after this night. I got home at 10:00 a.m. and slept from twelve midday to 7:00 a.m. the next morning, nineteen hours. I missed the meeting at 9:00 a.m. that Monday morning. I just couldn't drive forty-five minutes to get there. In my absence, those present tried to blame me. The fault was clearly with management for not providing enough experienced staff and registered staff per patient/resident.

On the Tuesday, there was a knock on my door. A courier from the site delivered a notice to me. They had stood me down on full pay. I had not caused anything that had happened to happen but had done my best. I rang the union, who said they would represent me.

At the time this was all happening, I had to move out of my unit on Burrai Street because it sold. I was moving in a week to another unit at the back of the building. I found all this very unsettling and disturbing. I was deeply upset and felt traumatised as a result of the events of that night. I felt unable to operate my shop and cancelled the next fortnight's appointments. In beauty therapy, you give a lot to your clients, and there was none of me to give after this.

I wrote letters in the next two weeks to management of the site. Phone calls took place with the union and with managers at the site.

In the second week after this happened, I moved to the unit at the back. I found moving soul destroying. The landlords of the back unit had simply stopped renovating it when they knew they had a tenant, sending the wooden shutters back. The windows had no treatments at all. The unit was smaller than the one I was in, and my furniture didn't fit.

My doctor referred me to a psychologist, Stan Steindl, who was wonderful and really helped me a great deal. My complex post-traumatic stress disorder came out of remission. I couldn't sleep, and when I did, I had nightmares. I was hypervigilant and really affected by stress. I cancelled more appointments at my shop and didn't make any new ones.

I found out through the Catholic Community there was a night RN job going at Penola Nursing Home for two nights a week. This was a place for retired nuns, a forty-bed nursing home, which sounded very doable after the site where I'd previously worked. I went for an interview the day before Melbourne Cup Day on November 5, 2005, and started that week.

The week after I moved to the unit, my car was stolen. It was found after a month, needing repair, in the eleventh hour just before the insurance company was going to pay out on it.

Richard drove me to a meeting out at work with the union present. I was invited to come back.

"Is anything going to change?" I asked. "Will there be more staff?"

"No," I was told. "Nothing is going to change."

So, I said, "No then. I won't come back."

Dad visited early November, and I told him I wanted to change my surname after the sentinel event. I told him I was considering Bryant, and he was horrified. Bryant was his biological father's name, and he'd never accepted Dad.

Dad told me Tony was suing him for $2.5 million. Dad

also told me Tanya (Tony's wife) had taken money from the till from their joint business in the Daintree, and I offered Dad an explanation. I said perhaps they felt they were not being paid properly, as they were working seven days a week. All in all, Dad left and was very angry with me. I never saw him again.

Christmas 2005 was difficult. I felt unable to run my shop and struggled to do the two nights a week. I felt shattered after that night at work and then moving house. Steven came quickly on Christmas morning and collected his presents and left. He was spending the day with Jesse and her parents.

## Getting out of the Wynnum Road premises, January 2006 to May 1, 2006

January 2006 came, and it was one of those low points in my life like after the rape of 1983 and in June 1995. These are times when I have deeply revaluated my life and thought up a plan to get back on my feet. I saw an advertisement for a registered nurse refresher course to go back into hospital work in *The Courier-Mail* newspaper. I rang up and got all the paperwork, twenty-five pages long, and submitted it to Princess Alexandra Hospital (PAH). I went for an interview in February and got a place in the course. I negotiated—at the end of it I would work in gynaecology and plastics, which fitted with beauty therapy.

I thought I would do a Plan for my "comeback."

- Do refresher RN course at PAH commencing May 15, 2006
- Get out of Wynnum Rd. shop premises at end of lease

- Find another bigger premises for the shop
- Shift the business to bigger premises
- Employ a manageress for the shop
- Work at PAH part-time in gynae and plastics
- Still see my regular clients at the new shop

So, I had a plan, which had always worked for me in the past. May 1 came quickly, and Darren, a builder and my god-daughter's boyfriend, was booked to take the entire infrastructure of the shop apart. It was going into storage with the furniture. It was the day before the lease ended.

I had spent the previous months cleaning out the shop. All in all, ten black bins of rubbish went. Natalie, my god-daughter had helped me pack the smaller stuff up into boxes. Richard had helped me with the rent throughout these months.

I had found a bigger shop to rent on the way to Bulimba, on Hawthorne Road, about five minutes away and had been negotiating a lease on the premises. It was a very tall building, once a warehouse, and I planned to put in a platform to make two floors. I had found a manageress, Phillipa, and was drawing up a contract with solicitors.

Pulling my beautiful shop to pieces was heartbreaking, but I just kept imagining the beautiful shop we would be going to. Everything was in place. The six-week long, full-time course would start on Monday, May 15, 2006, and I would sign the lease on the new shop at 4:30 p.m. that afternoon.

# CHAPTER 9

# The Fire and the Aftermath (2006 and 2007)

## The fire (May 13, 2006) and two weeks following

Steven rang on the Friday night, May 12, 2006, and said he and Jesse wanted to come over for Mother's Day, as they were busy on Mother's Day Sunday, with Jesse having a daughter, Angel, and with Jesse's mother. I said the house was a mess, and I would rather see them quickly on Sunday. That night, early in the morning, I heard fire trucks and ambulance screaming by very close.

I awoke in the morning, about 9:00 a.m. to loud knocking on my door. On answering the front door, I saw it was the police. There had been a fire at my son's townhouse. Jesse had died in it, and they were still looking for Angel. I told them Angel was not there. She was at Jesse's mum's place. Steven had been taken to Royal Brisbane Hospital (RBH) intensive care unit. I was cold and stunned. I could barely move or breathe. I was in shock. The phone rang. It was a friend who'd seen the fire on TV, with Steven on the roof jumping out of the building and then trying to get back in to get Jesse.

I drove a few minutes around to the townhouse and met Richard, who lived next door. I saw Steven's unit completely gutted. Forensic people were taking bags of ashes out of the premises. I was in absolute shock, upset to the core of my soul. Richard told me he saw Trent, Steven's flatmate, jump out of the window near the bathroom. He said the fireman knocked his door down with an axe and that his unit (which had a common wall) had nearly gone up in flames too.

He said Trent had gone downstairs and found the whole downstairs alight and then woken Steven and Jesse, giving them about three seconds to get out. Richard told me they had found Jess behind the bathroom door all curled up and burnt.

I was shaking and cold and having trouble breathing. It took me a few hours to get myself together to drive up to RBH. I ended up catching a taxi. The hospital phoned and asked why his family wasn't there. I finally got to the Intensive Care Ward at 3:00 p.m. Steven was in an induced coma, and his lips were all black and burned.

I washed all the soot off his lips and talked to him as though he could hear me. He had a big, blue cold air device around his left leg, pumping constant cold air. They told me he had shattered many of the bones in his foot and leg jumping down one floor on to cement pavement to escape the fire. I stayed till about 9:00 p.m.

The next day was the May 14, 2006, Mother's Day, and I got up to the hospital about 10:00 a.m. Steven was still in a coma. He later told me he was deciding whether to live or die, and it was only me there talking to him that made him decide to live.

Natalie and Darren visited. I stayed till 3:00 p.m. in the afternoon, telling staff about my course starting the next day at PAH (Princess Alexandra Hospital) and that I didn't think I could do it now.

On getting home, I rang my sister Amy and Dad's sisters, Auntie Vera and Auntie Mescal. I spent the evening in tears. I couldn't believe what had happened. It was all so surreal, like something out of a fiction novel.

The whole hospital was upset about Steven being in the fire and now intensive care, for this was the hospital that he worked in and was known well around. He was employed in the information technology department, installing new computers and equipment, as well as software, and fixing computer problems. Nobody could believe what had happened.

I was to start the course the next day and sign the lease. How could I go on as planned? Charles Lennon said, "Life is something that happens while you're making other plans." Well, the next day Monday, I slept in. I just never showed up, ringing them at 11:00 a.m. The RBH had already rung them and told them about Steven. They offered to do the course for me at a later date one on one, which was incredibly generous of them. My mind was completely focused on Steven. I could think of nothing else.

I got to the hospital about 3:00 p.m. that day, Monday. Steven had been transferred to the special needs unit. He was out of his coma and breathing on his own. The staff had told him about Jess, and he was devastated. On top of this, the doctors had told him he would never walk again and that he would never wear shoes again.

He said to me, "Mum, the doctors said I will never walk again."

I replied, "Steven you're my son, and you *will* walk again, even if I have to teach you."

At that point, the doctors came in and repeated this news to us. They said they were recommending a below-knee amputation because there were so many broken bones it was inoperable. Neither Steven nor I would sign the consent.

At 4:30 p.m., I forgot that I had an appointment to sign the lease. Steven was talking about Jesse's funeral on Friday and how he wanted to be there. It was planned I would hire a fold up wheelchair. He wanted me to go and buy him an outfit to attend. That would be the hardest shopping expedition I had ever been on.

The hospital arranged physiotherapy for Steven on Tuesday, Wednesday, and Thursday to try getting him to walk on crutches. Standing up proved to be the hardest thing. He kept falling backwards.

Friday came, and Jesse's funeral was held. It was a very sad but beautiful occasion. I met Jesse's parents and younger brother. Steven stood up and spoke at the funeral. The wake was held at the yacht club at Bulimba, and there were a lot of people there. Jess was a well-known hairdresser on Oxford Street, Bulimba, and Steven was well-known too from his days in the cinema café on Oxford Street.

I took Steven back to the hospital after the funeral. He was exhausted. He had a pass to attend the funeral. It was a major thing for him to do so soon after the fire.

On this night, Steven told me that Jess was walking back and forth between him at the back bedroom window and Trent at the front windows when a huge fireball came up the internal stairs and blew him out the window. He was suffering such anguish saying, "Why me? Why did I live and not Jess?"

On the day after the funeral, Steven was transferred to the burn unit. He had burns on his back from sliding down the hot tin roof. He spent a week there and was discharged but had to come back every day for dressings. His lungs had been burned from breathing in the fire, and he suffered breathing difficulties. He was walking on crutches short distances but with great pain.

## The aftermath, June 2006 to June 2007

After Steven was discharged from hospital, he stayed with Natalie and Darren, as I did not have the space at my place. There was still stuff everywhere from moving. He stayed there for two weeks, after which a group of friends leased a house where there would always be someone around to help him. The house was in Norman Park.

I visited all the op shops and got him a suitcase full of clothes, which were actually really nice. Steven was faced with the dilemma of getting new ID, and this proved very difficult, including getting a new copy of his birth certificate from Perth registrar for births, deaths, and marriages.

A friend bought him a phone. There were people leaving things on my doorstep for weeks. The generosity of the community was overwhelming. Within three months, Steven had everything to furnish a house, new ID, and new bank cards, but it was Jess who was irreplaceable.

A lot was lost in the fire. My hopes and dreams for the future of my career and business went up in smoke that night. Steven lost his mobility; eventually, his career; the love of his life; and everything he owned. And he wasn't insured. It was a life-defining event for both Steven and me.

I temporarily went back to Penola Nursing Home for a few weeks after Steven got out of hospital but couldn't cope. I went on a sickness benefit, and I lived on plastic (credit cards). I simply couldn't function; just attending daily living tasks was a terrible effort. I was paying the rent late, not knowing what day of the week it was. The landlords asked me to move out, giving me ten days to find somewhere else.

I found a heritage listed property, a beautiful cottage at Norman Park, walking distance to Steven and moved within eight days. It was soul-destroying (if my soul wasn't already destroyed). I started seeing the psychologist, Stan Steindl, regularly once again. He was an amazing support.

I shall never forget August exhibition holiday—the day after I moved there sitting on the lounge with my stuff all dumped around me. Steven had just gone back to work. They found him a desk job. He went back to work too early and was not suited to a desk job.

The television aerial needed repair, so I called a tech from the local paper. Martin Board, a very kind, generous family man who was Scottish, turned up at my house. He fixed my TV aerial, and that began a lifelong friendship; he remained a support in my life.

I paid $1,000 in the next few months in carpentry fees to have this house fully set up with wall hangings, shelving, and wall-mounted units in the kitchen. It looked so homey and beautiful. In November 2006, three months into the lease, the owners told me they were putting the property on the market, and I had first option to buy.

I wrote to my father and asked him for a loan to buy the house to put a roof over Steven's and my head after the fire. I saw a solicitor about having a loan agreement drawn up in such a manner that my father could not lose even if I died. My father took absolute objection to this letter, telling the whole family and extended family I had written to him asking for a handout, not mentioning the fire.

Auntie Mescal did come over from Western Australia and did provide emotional and moral support. It was very nice to see her. Uncle Mike her brother did provide Steven with some financial assistance and came to see us.

My sister Amy had rung me earlier in the year just after I moved to this house, telling me she needed a bone marrow transplant to save her life and was looking for a donor. I said I couldn't be her donor because I'd had cancer. My brother

Tony ended up being a donor for her. She had spent most of the year in the oncology unit at RBH. Amy had gotten this letter to Dad for me and was the only one who showed any concern after the fire.

Steven came for Christmas lunch that year, bringing a girl, Emma Foote, who became a lifelong friend of his. The cottage looked beautiful that Christmas.

The house sold in February just after the lease was up, and I had a month to move. I moved again at the end of March, early April 2007. I moved to 3/65 Grosvenor Street, Coorparoo, and I craved stability. I was determined to stay at this unit for many, many years or as long as I could. I spent April and May unpacking and setting up. I telephoned Martin, who came and set my television and stereo equipment up. He also helped hang some paintings for a small fee. The landlord also hung paintings for no fee. I was exhausted but my complex PTSD was in remission.

## Pulling myself together, June 2007

In June 2007, I decided I had to pull myself together. I rang Penola Nursing Home about going back there on night shift and was told a few free nights were available. So I started back the following week. There was a nursing home walking distance to me, Coorparoo Nursing Centre, that was advertising for a night RN, so I applied. It was three nights a week, and between the two, I would work five nights a week.

My whole shop was in storage, and I felt after all that had happened, I couldn't do a business on a shop front again. I would keep enough to do a room from home and sell the rest. I sent a lot to auction and sold many items, reducing my debt and putting an end to storage fees. Parting with these things was heartbreaking. It was the death of dreams, and I felt sad.

I enjoyed my work in nursing but didn't want to spend the rest of my life working in nursing homes. I enjoyed night work. No matter how busy you got, it was a peaceful time, and I always got time to sit outside and just think.

I badly wanted a cat but couldn't have one in the unit. I did, on two occasions, get a cat but ended up giving them back after a week with a friend saying to me "You'll get sprung". The landlords, Mr and Mrs Saunders, were the landlords from hell. But I was determined to stay no matter what. They would do inspections and inspect my property—how I had set the unit up, not their property. They wouldn't fix things. For example, the letter box was faulty, and the tap in the bathroom dripped. Mr Saunders was clearly suffering with dementia; as an aged care RN, I could identify this.

I joined a friendship group, Judy's Making Friends, as I had the weekends off, and started going to dinner dances. I made a number of new friends, including Roy Kettle, who remained a friend for many years. He lived about an hour away from me, but we enjoyed chats on the phone. I went to the movies and some orchestral concerts at the Performing Arts Centre.

In late July 2007, Amy died of leukaemia. The bone marrow transplant had been successful, but she died from the drugs used to prevent rejection. She phoned me three days before she died, and we had a nice conversation. She was very tired and got exhausted easily. I was really saddened by her death. She was my younger sister. I took a week off work following her passing.

Steven was struggling to come to grips with everything.

To our knowledge there had not been an inquest. The police put the fire down to a cigarette, despite the photos showing the fire had indisputably started in the kitchen. Steven did not receive any compensation or insurance, and he was not insured. It all seemed so unfair and so unjust. We just had to keep on keeping on, as we had no choice. Steven tried very hard to go back to work and went back too early.

I couldn't believe that none of my family helped or cared after the fire. Steven's father sent him a few hundred, as if that was really going to help. I was really trying hard to pull myself together. But at night I had to go to work because I didn't sleep. The only way I could sleep was when I was exhausted after night shift.

I started a potted plant collection for the small balcony, just anything that fed my soul. I bought a garden seat for the small, private grassed area outside our unit to sit in the sunshine. I started enjoying nature—sunshine, rain, storms, the moon, the birds, and going for walks among trees and plants. I searched for butterflies, but there weren't any. I hadn't seen any for a long time and didn't know where they had all gone.

I began listening to music again—piano, harp, and/or guitar. I played REM's "Everybody Cries" a lot, and it would make me cry, which is healing for the soul. I played Charles Azanavour's "You Have Got to Learn" and certain other songs to heal my soul. Music that was peaceful and relaxing helped me heaps. I bought a water fountain and had the sound of running water in my lounge room.

I saw Stan regularly for hourly counselling sessions. I met with Melanie once a month for coffee and regularly met with Mavis, the manageress of the dry-cleaning shop next to my business on Wynnum Road. Suzanne lived on the other side of town, and we had regular phone chats. I also wrote some letters to other people.

On the night of the fire, Carol, Steven's former partner and the mother of his girls, arrived back in Brisbane from New Zealand. I had seen the girls at his house when they were visiting. They all came for Christmas 2007, and we had lunch together at the Grosvenor Street unit. It was a really lovely day and so nice to spend some quality time with my granddaughters.

# CHAPTER 10

# Conceding Bankruptcy (2008 to 2010)

## Going bankrupt, 2008

New Year 2008, I sat down and took a long hard look at my life. I certainly was, amazingly, together again but had a lot of debt from a business that was suddenly aborted and from living on plastic in 2007. I made a stupid decision to work seven nights a week to try and pay it off. No more would I be going to dinner dances or meeting up with friends. I was working seven nights a week without a dream. It was horrible.

I rang some financial advisors and saw my accountant. Everybody I spoke to advised me to go bankrupt, but I kept working. I calculated it would take me five years of working seven nights a week to pay everything off with interest. They said I had nothing to lose. I didn't own a house; my car was worth less than $5,000; and I didn't own anything valued at more than $1,000 and was living in stable long-term accommodation. It would be my excellent credit rating I would lose.

I was of two minds, I ummed and ahhed and just kept working, meanwhile paying all the money to debts. I sometimes didn't have enough food in the fridge. The financial advisors I spoke to helped me to know how to put everything in place so I could declare bankruptcy. My accountant assisted me to know how to fill out the debtor's petition and told me where to get all the paperwork from.

In July 2008, I took a two-week holiday and booked to

go to Caloundra. I was on route to go there and broke down out in the middle of nowhere on the highway in the pouring rain. It was difficult. I didn't have a location to give the roadside assistance people, and the rain just kept belting down. I eventually got help and got towed back to Brisbane with a car packed full for a holiday. A friend also came. I transferred all my stuff into his car, and my car went to the mechanic's.

The significance of this night is that, after getting home, I became ill with a respiratory infection. I didn't get back to work for some time. I was diagnosed with pneumonia end of July and was terribly ill. I notified creditors I was ill and needed to go on some hardship programme or use up credit in accounts. I spent all of August in bed; at times, I felt I couldn't breathe and should have gone to hospital but managed at home on antibiotics from my doctor.

Early September came, and I decided to declare bankruptcy. The last six weeks had created a situation which would fit with declaring bankruptcy. I began filling out the forty-page document. It took me days, along with collecting supporting documents. On September 10, 2008, I got a taxi into the trustee insolvency office—Insolvency and Trustee Service Australia (ITSA)—in Brisbane City and lodged my completed debtor's petition.

I was declared bankrupt the following day, September 11, 2008. It felt like an enormous weight had been lifted off my head.

## Life after bankruptcy, from September 11, 2008, to 2009

I immediately cut my working hours back to four nights a week—two nights in each home, Coorparoo Nursing

Centre and Penola. I would enjoy two nights in each home, especially the feeling of connection I had in each home. I was now working to live, not living to work.

I could now start going to dinner dances again. I could start meeting up with friends again. I could start again to deliberately spend time with nature and listen to music, instead of work, work, working. I would read books and go to the movies. I could start to live again. I booked some dance lessons and found these to be sheer joy.

In 2009, I started art courses at Brisbane Institute of Art, beginning with oil painting and then drawing. I did an art appreciation course mid-year, which involved going out to different galleries and learning how to look at and value art. We also learnt all about the art industry and how different galleries are run.

Steven came to live with me early 2009 till late 2009, and he was still suffering badly. I did find this a terrible strain on me. The house share arrangement he had had broken up. He moved back out to house share with a girl called Jo to a house on Bennett's Road, Norman Park. Steven had gotten his driver's licence while he was living with me and bought a car, a white Holden Commodore, from a friend he'd once worked with at the hospital.

## The work events 2010: End of my nursing career

As 2010 started, the world was in economic recession. I thought it would be a good year for me. In January, an earthquake in Haiti killed millions, and I was once again taking interest in the world outside mine.

On June 24, 2010, Australia's first female prime

minister, Julia Gillard, was sworn into office as Australia's twenty-seventh PM. She was elected unopposed by the Parliamentary Labour Party.

I continued working at the two nursing homes. In early April, I turned up at Coorparoo Nursing Home for a night shift and received an instruction from the director of nursing that I was to send a male worker home when he arrived, citing a problem with his police check. When he came on duty, I carefully did this without problem.

I turned up the next night to be told by one of the personal carers that Maria, another personal carer, had heard that I had "dismissed" him. As a result, she intended on coming to my home and entering and doing harm to me.

I was never the same after this night. The threat triggered memories of the home invasion I'd endured when I was fifteen. I started having nightmares. It also triggered memories of the man who entered my house on Good Friday 1983 and would not leave, raping me.

I saw Stan, my psychologist, who explained Maria's comments were like someone piercing a hole in my psyche with a sharp instrument, and the complex PTSD had started to leak out. And leak out it did, until fully unpacked at the end of the year, 2010.

I had about a month off work on workers' compensation after this night.

On the night before the exhibition holiday in August, I turned up to do a night shift at Coorparoo Nursing Centre to find a pool alarm going off next door, which was keeping everyone awake and unsettling the dementia patients. There had been a storm, and this had caused the alarm to go off. On arrival, the sunroom was flooding, and we had to mop all that up.

Following this, three male patients were assaulting each

other, and I had to break it up and medicate them. Everybody was awake because of the constant alarm sounding. At one stage part of the building lost power, and it was out till the morning.

A nurse had locked three patients in a room to stop them wandering, and this had upset me, triggering memories from my childhood. This same nurse had put a patient back to bed who had fallen out of bed and didn't bother to get me. I discovered that this had happened when I checked on the lady and found that her foot was very red. Another nurse told me what had happened.

All in all, it was a very disturbing night. Even the resident possum had come inside looking for shelter and had hidden in the linen cupboard. This night shift triggered all kinds of memories for me, including the sentinel event. Even being locked in my room in Penang came back to me. This was when I'd had chicken pox, and my mother was pregnant with my sister. The men assaulting each other brought back the assault on me in 1990.

On August 21, 2010, I turned up to do a night shift at Penola Nursing Home. I have little memory of this night. I know it was a dreadful shift. I relieved an RN who I had known for years. She was three hours behind in her work due to the workload, which made it very difficult for me to start my shift. She was making comments putting me down and bullying me. I left in the morning and knew that was the last shift in nursing I would ever do. I never wanted to go back, ever.

I saw my regular doctor, and she filled out workers' compensation forms for me based on a recurrence of the PTSD. Going through workers compensation was dreadful. I decided to change doctors and go to Dr Egerton, who I'd seen a half a dozen times at the doctors' surgery Morningside.

It was early December when the approval finally came through for the workers' compensation. They back paid me to August 21, 2010.

On December 11, 2010, I saw a psychiatrist for workers; comp whose job it seemed was to get my compensation claim cancelled. He assessed me as suffering with complex PTSD, saying this had nothing to do with work. Just after Christmas, the claim was cancelled. I appealed it but lost the appeal.

# CHAPTER 11

# After I Finished Work (2011 to 2013)

## The floods and 2011

The next year, 2011, began with rain. As a result, I had an ant invasion in my unit. Ants seeking higher ground is always a sign to me that lots of heavy rain is on the way. I promptly put in an application for unemployment with doctors' certificates, so I went on the sick list. I also put in an application for income protection insurance through my superannuation. I was told it would take months to come through, and when it did, Centrelink would be paid back.

In January 2011, just before the rain started, Uncle Joe O'Sullivan died in Caloundra Hospital. He was totally demented when he died and did not even recognise me. He died of heart failure. He had remarried, and his new wife received his entire estate.

The rain came, and it never stopped. I lost power at one stage for thirty-six hours and had a full fridge and freezer. The landlord was fairly prompt in fixing the problem for me, as it was only my unit and not the area. The rain came in the garage, damaging stored items in there.

The picture of the railway bridge at Grantham cast all around the world was right near my grandfather's property entrance and near my cousin's place. My grandfather had passed on many years ago. Grantham was my mother's hometown, and it was the worst hit. I was concerned that my mother's ashes had been washed away, as they had been scattered on top of her father's grave at Ma Ma Creek Cemetery.

Uncle Henry and Auntie Jenny lived at Withcott, a town outside of Grantham that was in the path of the water. They were flooded but were OK once the water subsided.

Brisbane and outer lying towns were all flooded, as well as towns up the coast of Queensland. It was reminiscent of the 1974 floods. Brisbane was built around a river, and that river broke its banks. This flood cost the insurance companies millions. Insurance on houses in low-lying areas or along the river would never be the same again.

The income protection insurance was eventually approved in April, and they back paid me to January 1, 2011. Centrelink got paid back first. I had to put in a claim every month for the income protection insurance, seeing the GP for this. It was painstaking, but I did it, and so did Dr Egerton, for which I am most grateful.

On April 29, 2011, Prince William married Catherine Middleton, making her Duchess of Cambridge. She wore a stunning dress, and it was a wonderful family affair at Westminster Abbey. I watched it on my computer.

Dr Egerton referred me to see a psychiatrist, and I saw Dr Allison McColl for sessions weekly. It was very expensive, but I had health insurance to help. She said the complex PTSD would not go back into remission now and that I had to learn to accept that all this trauma had happened to me.

She said I had to learn ways to manage the triggers and the catastrophic thinking. She suggested I do a cognitive behavioural therapy course (CBT) held at the hospital. She also suggested I go on a drug to help with PTSD and sleeping, to be taken at night. I initially resisted everything. I was fighting suicide, but I didn't tell anyone.

I did regularly meet with my girlfriend Suzanne. We would sit for hours talking over lunch, and this was particularly helpful. We met at Vinnie's Café at Newmarket.

Christmas 2011 came. Steven came to my house/unit, and we had a lovely day. It was Steven keeping me alive. I couldn't desert him and leave him in the world alone. I thought how strange it was that it was me who'd kept him alive in the hospital after the fire.

## Steven coming to live with me and 2012

In early 2012, I was really suicidal, though again I told nobody other than Dr Egerton and Stan Steindl. Both guided me to take the medication Dr McColl wanted to put me on. By Easter, my mind had thought up a plan and a time frame to commit suicide. I was scared. I knew I didn't really want to die. I saw Dr McColl and went on the medication, which took a month to build up to the desired dose and be effective. It took all the suicidal thoughts away, thank God.

Auntie Mescal came to visit from Western Australia, sensing something was wrong with me. It was that kind of family support that I really appreciated. It was her seventieth birthday in February.

In order to help myself, I agreed to do the cognitive behavioural therapy course (CBT) at Belmont Private Hospital where I saw the psychiatrist. The only problem was it started at 9:00 a.m. every morning Monday to Friday for three weeks. I knew with the chronic insomnia I suffered; I couldn't make a morning appointment. So, I went into hospital for the three weeks to do the course, which was covered by health insurance.

Belmont Hospital is a world-class mental health hospital

at Carindale in Brisbane. The CBT course was absolutely amazing. It changed my thinking and changed my life. CBT gave me a way of coping with catastrophic thinking (imagining the very worst is going to happen). It gave me a way of coping with triggered memories. It caused me to stop being so hypervigilant and gave me ways of coping with anxiety.

The course caused me to realise I held immense sadness, anger, and grief and gave me ways both to address and to cope with these emotions. My life would be permanently better after doing the CBT course. It gave me tools for my coping toolbox. I just had to get used to a new way of thinking and remember to keep it up.

In July 2012, my brother Jack died of a heart problem. He had not long been diagnosed with atrial fibrillation, a condition in which the heart flutters instead of beating properly. He lay in a morgue for unclaimed people for three weeks because we had to get the public trustee to release funds from his bank account for a funeral first.

I notified my brother Tony about Jack's death (though he doesn't remember this) and he told Charlie my sister. Charlie took over and organised the whole funeral without really asking input from anybody. The eulogy at the funeral upset me. She said things that were not true; even people in the audience disagreed with some things she said.

I was deeply affected by my brother's death. My heart condition, Prinzmetal angina, became unstable, and I was having sporadic chest pain. After the funeral in August, Steven came to live with me. I paid him to buy and set up a new laptop for me, as I had been hacked with the old one due to old hardware.

Steven filled my garage with his furniture and effects. I gave him my queen bed and bought a single bed for my room. I had to clear the spare room out for him and put some cupboards in my room. I created a great space in my room with a false wall from the cupboards and a bed covering above my bed. It all looked very pretty.

In September, October, and November, I attended the CBT follow-up course one night a week. These sessions were about processing grief, sadness, anger, and more. I also did the Art for Therapy" course one morning a week. It was great, introducing me to portrait drawing, which I had a natural flair for. These sessions involved having a meal in the dining room, and the food was great. I soon got to know heaps of people at the hospital.

December came, and Steven and I had a lovely Christmas. We had the girls on Christmas Day.

## Granddaughters staying, 2013

In 2013, Bella, my second granddaughter, started high school. She looked absolutely beautiful on her first day with her long blond hair pulled back in a ponytail. She had her nails done and looked so perfect, like she was trying really hard. Steven picked the girls up on this morning and got them McDonald's for breakfast and then took them to school, giving them money for lunch. This became a regular thing, as Carol would send them without breakfast or lunch. She would let them stay home if Steven didn't pick them up.

There were a lot of problems at their home, with arguments with the mother and each other, so much that one of them always seemed to be staying with us on a fold-down bed in the lounge room. I found this extremely difficult. Steven was always running over to their house at Carina and picking one or both of them up. Eloise was thirteen in February and already had a boyfriend. Bella was twelve in March and had already started to go off the rails.

I made them birthday cakes on their birthdays and cooked a special dinner, which they appreciated. They didn't seem to get fed at home and always were hungry and would eat huge meals at our house.

In early 2013m from February through May, I did the Acceptance and Commitment Therapy programme (ACT) at Belmont Private Hospital, which was held one afternoon a week for eight weeks. The course was amazing. Like CBT, it taught a different way of viewing one's thoughts and further changed my thinking, giving me more tools for my coping toolbox.

I also attended the CBT follow-up one evening a week. My mental health was improving in leaps and bounds. I did a programme called Towards Better Sleep, four evenings over four weeks, with Stan's practise, Psychology Consultants at Morningside, in June 2013.

In June, I took another art course on drawing. Plus, I did a holiday workshop on acrylic painting. I set up an art area at home in the study area of the house. Though it was small, I managed to draw there. I tended my potted plants on the balcony and went for walks. I was always looking for butterflies, but they are very elusive and hard to find if you go looking.

It seemed one of the girls was always staying with us, and though I found this very difficult, I was thankful for the quality time I got to spend with each one of them. It was cramped in my bedroom with a single bed and all the cupboards in there, but I was grateful to have my son with me. In 2013, I kept a gratitude journal and wrote in it every night, finding three things in each day to be grateful for. It really helped lift my level of happiness. I watched some Mr

Bean DVDs. He never failed to make me laugh, no matter how many times I had seen the DVD.

Christmas came, and Steven and I managed to find a small space for a small-fold down Christmas tree and decorated it with the traditional decorations.

At the end of the year, I was ever so grateful for the income protection insurance, which enabled me to afford Health insurance to pay for all the courses I did at Belmont. I was certainly feeling much, much better because of both not working and all the courses I had done. I was looking forward to a new year, 2014, and planning to start writing this book.

# CHAPTER 12

# Back to the Beginning (2014 and Beyond to 2021)

## Back to the beginning, 2014, and then a drug raid

On the eve of Australia Day 2014 (January 25, 2014), I began writing this book. And as it so happens, that is where I am now up to in writing this book—2014. It has taken me over seven years to get here to this point; it is now June 2021 as I write.

It has been a mammoth task—reliving my life, especially all the trauma—but I have found acceptance that it all happened. It wasn't right or just or fair, but it all happened. With acceptance, there is inner peace and release of the trauma from me—an inner peace I have searched for all my life.

I began with Eloise and Steven bursting in with McDonald's as I was starting to write. Well, that hasn't changed. They still love their McDonald's. The storms over Brisbane in January still happen, but I am not still living in that unit on Grosvenor Street, Coorparoo. I am now living in a huge, old rambling house in Coorparoo, which does allow cats! I have lived here since early April 2014, just after I started writing this book. Let me tell you about why we had to move and the house.

In February 2014, there was a knock at the front door. I answered it and found two detectives and four uniformed police officers, as well as two dogs. They said they had a search warrant and showed it to me. I let them into our small unit. They made me sit still on the lounge. Two of them went into Steven's room. They emerged with a very small packet with half a teaspoon of stale marijuana in it.

They searched the whole premises, turning everything upside down and inside out. This search concluded with them saying Steven would be charged with possession of an illicit drug. They told us somebody had tipped them off that Steven was a drug user and a dealer. They could see he clearly wasn't either, other than the odd bit of pot. We worked out that it was highly likely to have been Carol to have done this. She was forever telling the girls their father was a drug dealer.

A few weeks following this, I received a notice to leave the premises, giving me two months to go. A neighbour had obviously told the landlords what had gone on and we were apparently listed on some police site as being in possession of drugs.

We spent March looking for a suitable premise. I had a list, and this house at Coventry Street ticked all the boxes, as well as having ducted air conditioning.

I wrote out my "list for a new home":

- Must be able to have a cat
- Spacious room for Steven and the girls
- Bathtub
- Lock-up garage or storage space
- Coorparoo
- Good security
- Air-conditioned area
- Area for a garden
- No big lawn to mow

We moved April 3, 2014, and it was a massive move. I had been at the unit at Grosvenor Street for seven years. I put the new house in both Steven's and my name. It was just around the corner, about seven streets away, and a better location, as it was walking distance to everything, including a park, and on a bus route.

## The house at Coventry Street, 2014 and 2015

The house is a very big either five-bedroom or three-bedroom house, with a study and a sunroom. The underneath is a big lock-up area with a garage and laundry. There is a very small footpath out front to mow and an area out front under the stairs where I can grow a small garden. There is an area at the side stairwell where I can keep potted plants.

The house has fully ducted air conditioning, with a state-of-the-art system. The kitchen is huge, and the lounge/dining is huge too. There is one bathroom. We were paying about seventy-five dollars too much rent at Grosvenor Street, so increase to live here is just thirty-five dollars. The "drug" tip was a blessing in disguise. We moved to a better location within Coorparoo.

After moving, which took three weeks, we spent time unpacking and setting the house up. I needed to buy big floor rugs for the expansive polished floors. I had to buy a pantry cupboard. Martin helped with this, coming to the store with me and transporting the flat pack home and then assembling it.

We planned to get indoor cats and had permission for two on the lease. I started monthly as I could afford it, getting cat-proof mesh security screens on the windows to be opened, as well as a security door for the side with a cat door. Adrian from M & L Security made them up for me each month. I didn't need to buy new curtains, as I already had some. There were frosted windows at the front letting lots of light in.

Martin installed a TV aerial on the roof, and the owner paid for it. Martin installed TV sockets in most rooms. He helped put wall hangings up—paintings, clocks, shelves, and hooks and rails. He charged me mate's rates. He was really great.

By the end of September, I wanted to get our cats. I went online to the Little Paws Cat Rescue site and fell in love with this little girl—a black-and-white tuxedo kitten with big eyes. We made arrangements to go down to Burleigh Heads on the South Coast to meet her. The morning we were leaving, I rang the foster mother, and she told me this little girl had two brothers the colouring Steven was looking for.

We drove down and met these little kittens and decided to put an application in to take all three. They were a month old, born September 1, 2014. We would call them Lucy, Felix, and Tiger. They would be ready in a fortnight after vaccination and desexing. We drove down in a fortnight to pick them up; our application was successful.

A lot of people were interested and put in applications. Because Lucy was so pretty, many people wanted her. Steven bought the cat-scratching palace for them, and we got them the best litter system, woodchip, which turns to sawdust and absorbs all the ammonia/smell in the process. We took our babies home and cuddled them. Steven and I were very glad to have a cat again after losing Casey cat. The kittens were very playful. We had a cat canopy to keep them in to start with, as the house was huge and they were so tiny.

Christmas came again, and Steven and I spent Christmas together. The girls visited after Christmas Day. Steven and I had gone to the nine o'clock Mass together on Christmas Eve at Lady of Mt. Carmel Church.

## 2015

The cats were very playful and wanted to play every night. Things didn't work out with Steven and me sharing, and he moved out to live with Darren. (Natalie and Darren had split up.) I had a big empty house and, at first, didn't know what to do. Steven had occupied the huge main bedroom.

I began getting this room ready to rent out. The wardrobe cupboard doors were all peeling and needed painting, so I got them painted. I furnished the room with a queen bed and a fridge and microwave, building a kitchenette into it. I had shelves put in and a television on an entertainment unit.

My income protection insurance was coming to an end in August after five years. I put in an application for permanent and total disability, and this was paid out in August—$50,000. I put an application in with Centrelink for a disability pension. This was after the time the cutbacks had happened for people being approved for disability pension. It would take eight months before being approved and would be back paid if it was approved. It was finally approved two weeks before I left to go overseas in late April 2016.

I had to pay the rent on my own and needed someone to house share to pay the rent. I advertised in Saturday's *Courier-Mail* in August and got two suitable replies. I interviewed both women. I had no experience choosing tenants or house sharing.

I chose Helen Saunders, a social worker, who worked out perfectly but eventually moved out to live with her boyfriend. She kept in touch for years after. From then on till end of 2018, I chose some wrong tenants. They either smoked or had pets. Or they worked shift work or wanted my company regularly. I learnt from experience how to share and how to choose tenants, who eventually went on my lease as an approved tenant and who would work out for the house.

I paid for and did all the training to become a marriage, funeral, and civil celebrant. This was always my dream.

I booked and paid for a holiday to Europe, including a Mediterranean cruise for the following year, leaving just before the anniversary of the fire on May 12, 2016. It was a lifelong dream of mine to see Europe, especially France and Italy. So, the trip was perfect.

I spent money and time transforming the back study into a beauty therapy room. Martin helped me. I thought, if I could just do three to six hours a week, it would be a pleasure and bring me into contact with people I loved to see.

I badly needed a new phone and bought my first smartphone. Just about everybody had a smart phone from about 2010 onward. It took me some time to learn how to use it.

Christmas came, and Steven brought a friend, Dave, for Christmas lunch. Eloise came too. We had a great meal, and everybody took home dessert—seconds, plum pudding. It was good to see Steven again, as I had hardly seen him all year. We'd had a little falling out over his moving out.

## The European holiday, 2016

There was a lot to do before going overseas. I had to buy a suitcase and a cabin bag, and many things I wanted to take "just in case". I had to get foreign money, Swiss and Euros, to have cash. I got my hair done at Red Fox on Cavendish Road with Siaka the day before I departed.

On that Tuesday night, I stayed up and packed. We would be leaving at five o'clock the following morning, May 11, 2016, meaning I had to be at the airport an hour earlier. Helen was living in the house in my absence to look after everything and the cats. My knee had been quite sore for a couple of weeks, and I could hardly walk on it. Martin called in and brought a fold-up walking stick for me.

Richard was taking me to the airport. I had a panic attack on the way there, the first and only one I've ever had. I was actually terrified of leaving Australia alone and being met by a stranger at 8:00 p.m. at the airport in Rome. It was a trip-a-deal organised tour with mostly Australians and a few New Zealanders. We would all meet up in Rome.

There was a two-hour stopover in Dubai from around 1:00 p.m. to 3:00 p.m. I had three seats to myself all of the way and spent most of it sleeping. I had my arm that had been operated on during my bout with cancer all done up in a pressure sleeve and was wearing my special flight stockings and a pressure sleeve on my knee. I was the walking wounded but determined to do this trip—the fulfilment of a lifelong dream.

At the airport in Rome, I walked around and around with my suitcase, unable to find this person meeting "us." I found a group of Australian-looking people and asked them, and it just so happened they were the group waiting to be met like me.

Eventually our tour guide surfaced. He ushered us out into two waiting buses. We had to follow him briskly with our luggage. We were driven to our hotel and told to help ourselves to breakfast the next morning.

The next day was Thursday, May 12, 2016, and it was a free day in Rome. I simply caught a taxi and went to the Trevi fountain and made a wish. I saw the Coliseum from the outside and walked around Rome. I had a famous cup of coffee at a small coffee shop and had to pay to use the toilet, as you do in Rome. You very quickly pick up the language, as no one speaks English.

The following day (the anniversary of the fire), we were taken by buses leaving at 10:00 a.m. to the Port of Civitavecchia, an interesting forty-minute drive through the country to the ocean. We boarded *The Jewel of the Sea* for a ten-night Royal Caribbean Mediterranean cruise. The ship departed at 5:00 p.m., and I felt so happy. I went to a piano bar and had a glass of champagne. Our luggage was delivered to our cabin. I went up at 7:00 p.m. for dinner and had a delicious meal.

The next day was spent sailing at sea. So, I checked out the swimming pool and just enjoyed being at sea. I love cruises. The sunsets and sunrises were amazing. I had paid extra to have a balcony cabin, and I loved spending time out on my balcony.

The following day, Sunday, we docked at Marseilles, Provence, on the coast in the South of France. I did a day trip in an open-air bus, touring all the amazing buildings so old and built of sandstone. The history stunned me. I just couldn't believe the beauty of this area of France. We set sail at 6:00 p.m.

The ship docked in Barcelona, Spain, at seven the next morning, Monday, and we spent Monday and Tuesday in

Barcelona. All the activity in this city was unbelievable, as were the hundreds of beautiful boats and yachts moored in the harbour. We departed at 6:00 p.m. and arrived on the island of Palma de Mallorca at 7:00 a.m. Wednesday morning, spending the day there, where Christopher Skase hides out. We saw a famous church that is forever being built, with several steeples.

Thursday was another peaceful day at sea. The following day, Friday, we arrived in Valletta, Malta. I was taken with this island; all the buildings are sandstone. It has to be seen to be believed.

On Saturday, we arrived in Messina, Sicily. What I found amazing is that these two islands are so close but so different. I did day trips on all the stopovers.

Sunday was another day at sea. And on Monday, we arrived back at the port in Italy at 5:00 a.m. and disembarked at 8:30 a.m.

We were met by buses and taken to our hotel, which stored our luggage, and we went off on a tour of the Colosseum, which dates back thousands of years. It was stunning to imagine what went on here all those years ago, with slaves fighting and lions all in an arena. The next day, we were taken to the Vatican, the centre of the Catholic religion where the Pope lives. And on this Tuesday afternoon, we travelled to Florence to begin a ten-day bus tour of Italy, France, Switzerland, Germany, and Monaco.

I saw the Leaning Tower of Pisa and the beautiful city of Venice, going for a ride in a Venetian vessel called a gondola with a man paddling it. I saw the Eiffel Tower by night with all the lights and Paris by day and night. I visited a perfume factory in France and saw the famous Louvre art gallery, as well as glass-blowing in Murano, Italy. I stood on the steps at Cannes, where the red carpet is put out for the Oscars every year.

Most of all, I loved Switzerland, with snow melting on the mountaintops and running in waterfalls down the slopes. The colours of this country were unbelievable—the blue skies, green grass, and blue lakes contrasting with the snow. I was taken with how clean it was and with its wide streets. I went to Europe to see Paris but loved Switzerland.

It was time to leave Italy, and I had become ill; I wasn't up to all this touring. I could barely walk with a stick my knee was so sore, and I had caught a super-bug in Rome, as did a number of other people on the trip. On Tuesday, May 31, 2016, we flew out of Rome at 3:25 p.m. and stopped over in Dubai at 11:25 p.m. for a few hours.

I nearly fell out of the plane disembarking in Dubai, hurting my frail left arm when I fell into a wall.

We boarded once again at 2:15 a.m. for a 2:45 departure. The cabin crew identified that I wasn't well. I could barely walk, had trouble breathing, and could hardly talk.

They deemed me unfit to fly and told me they were off loading me. I had no choice. An ambulance was waiting outside. I was taken to a Saudi Arabian hospital, where I stayed overnight. The nurses there dressed my arm and gave me drugs to help me breathe. They treated me well. I was wheeled down to the airport the next morning in a wheelchair.

The airport staff tried to get me to pay another fare home, and it was not till they talked to a male person in Australia, Richard, that I got a seat on a plane coming home to Australia. I spent two hours in that airport being wheeled around from place to place, trying to convince the airline staff I was fit enough to fly. It was horrible. I eventually boarded a packed plane and tucked my head in the whole way and didn't say a word to anyone.

I finally arrived in Brisbane and was wheeled off the plane first, straight through customs to the cafeteria at the front, collecting my luggage on the way. Richard arrived about ten minutes later, and I was very glad to see him. He drove me home. I first cuddled my cat, Lucy, and then took to my bed after giving Helen a gift I had bought for her.

Helen stayed on in the house for a couple of weeks to take care of me, cooking her famous chicken soup. After she left, I slept night and day for three weeks. I organised Meals on Wheels, as I couldn't cook, shop, or clean up.

I recognised I needed help so rang up a government agency and got assessed for cleaning and someone to do the shopping. Both, along with transport and personal care, were approved. I spent the rest of the year in bed with difficulty getting up to go to the toilet and answer the door for Meals on Wheels. The trip may have nearly killed me, but I was very glad I did it. It was the trip of a life time—and yes, I did it. Good memories I will have forever.

In December, Suzanne and Benedict moved to Tasmania. I w0uld miss Suzanne dearly.

I couldn't do Christmas that year, 2016. Steven got cold meats and salads and, we had a nice lunch. The girls visited, and I sent some texts and Facebook messages.

## Ill Health, 2017 to 2020

### *2017*

New Year 2017 came, and I knew I had "to pull myself together." But the last time I'd done this, before the fire, it hadn't all gone to plan, so I dared not do another plan. I knew I had to get back into exercise slowly and gently, as well as art and writing. I needed to stay connected to friends and nature. My knee settled down, and at least I was able to walk again.

I would get up as many mornings as I could and slowly exercise to jazz ballet music from decades ago. On the mornings I couldn't get up, I would lie on my bed and do slow gentle exercises from there. It is amazing how much exercise you can do lying on your bed. I aimed to exercise five mornings a week.

I slowly got back into art again. Sometimes, I would just draw or colour, something I could lose myself in and give my mind a break. Other times, a painting would take a couple of weeks to finish. My mental and emotional health seemed to be in good order. It was just my body that was falling apart, starting with my back.

In April 2017, Mavis, my friend from the dry-cleaning business next door to my shop, died from breast cancer. It had spread to her liver. Her death made me very sad, as did my Uncle Henry passing away the same month.

I continued to do positive affirmations, practise meditation and gratitude, and do gentle exercise.

By November, I was feeling strong enough to do a small number of hours in my beauty studio I had created. I thought I would do this in the new year so started preparing. I rang the tax department and activated my ABN. I organised and paid business insurance. I contacted a few beauty supply companies about buying some products to do facials.

On December 9, 2017, the Australian Parliament passed an act that allowed same-sex marriage. This officially changed the face of the family unit in society.

In December, just before Christmas, I was diagnosed with breast cancer again—the same breast, the left one. I cancelled the business insurance and got my money back. I attended appointments at the Princess Alexandra Hospital especially made for me, and surgery was scheduled for January 25, 2018, to have a mastectomy (breast removal).

## *2018*

I prepared myself and my life for the surgery and chemotherapy following. I bought a wig, which looked quite real and some nice turbans. I went to the dentist and had a scale and clean, important before having chemo. I bought two post-surgical bras.

I went to the hospital as requested on the morning of January 25, 2018. The surgery was booked for the afternoon. Steven and Eloise were there before I went into the theatre about 2:00 p.m. Inside, I was crying; on the outside, I showed a brave face. I really couldn't get my head around losing a breast. But if it meant survival, I would do it.

I came back to the ward about 7:00 p.m., and Steven and Eloise were there for me. I don't remember a thing about what happened. Pain levels were managed well, and I did not have pain. I had a drain going into a bag from under my left arm.

I don't think I could have done it without Steven and Eloise being there for me. I had some sandwiches for tea, and staff changed me into a fresh gown. I settled down to sleep the night and awoke in the morning with some discomfort, for which I was given pain relief.

The pathology came back. It was a Grade 3 highly aggressive triple-negative cancer. I had been very lucky it was caught early on a routine mammogram with ultrasound. This was a different cancer to the first, an oestrogen receptor cancer—making it two primary cancers I'd had.

After three days, I went home with the Hospital in the Home nurses visiting daily for about ten days till the drain came out. Again, I took to my bed for these days, getting up for longer each day. My exercise programme stopped, and so did my art. I was just so tired; all I could do was sleep.

I commenced chemotherapy in mid-March six weeks after the surgery. This was difficult for me, as I didn't believe in toxic chemicals. It was firstly, the heavy-duty stuff, one bout every three weeks for three months and then a lighter chemo, but damaging to the body, one bout weekly for three months.

I had steroids during and after each treatment to help my body cope, which caused me to put on weight. I also had anti-nausea tablets following for four days to help with the nausea.

Natalie, my god-daughter, married Theo Mandrakis. They already had a daughter together, Angelina. Theo was from Greece, and they moved to Greece. I was happy for Natalie but would really miss her.

On April 16, 2018, my lifelong friend Melanie died. She was at their holiday house and just dropped dead of a heart issue. This was a tremendous blow to me. I was deeply saddened. I had last seen Melanie on her birthday the day my chemo started and was so glad I had taken the time that day.

After three weeks, my hair all fell out, and I found waking up in the morning with hair all over the pillow upsetting. I had my head shaved so it couldn't fall out anymore

The chemo left me exhausted. All I wanted to do was rest with the cats.

In July, I started on the lighter treatment, which caused peripheral necrosis of the nerves (death of most or all of the nerve cells in the fingers and toes). I had simply had enough and couldn't take anymore. So, I stopped the chemo just before my sixty-fifth birthday.

My scalp had broken out in all these itchy carbuncles, so I saw a skin cancer doctor at Coorparoo. For about eight weeks, I went for weekly sessions to have all these eruptions removed with liquid nitrogen. It was ever so painful. I would come home and take strong pain relief and go to bed.

On May 19, 2018, Prince Harry Duke of Sussex married Meghan Markle, making her Duchess of Sussex. She wore a very simple, plain dress, and it was sad her father would not walk her down the aisle. So, Prince Charles did. Only her mother was present; no other family members attended.

In August, I started nanny work, looking after two boys before school, Harrison and Jacob, for their father, David, every second week. I enjoyed the work, especially walking them to school. They were amazing boys. Harrison suffered with ADHD.

In September, I looked at other places to rent. I was fed up with sharing. For the last year, I'd had a forty-year-old chef, Scott, who had his girlfriend, Charlotte, move in. He was a really nice bloke but came home at midnight, showering with her in the room beside me. He went in and out all night, sitting up and smoking and keeping me awake. They stayed up nearly all night. It just didn't work for me.

I decided to stay in the house and ask Scott and Charlotte to leave. I move within the house. I would move down to the main bedroom, having the big bedroom instead of occupying two rooms. I would then rent the two bedrooms out. I would have all my things in one room and have the kitchenette and the bathroom basin for myself.

I would move my computer desk and office down to the sunroom/art room, which was next to the main bedroom, and move the chaise lounge from the art room down to end of the dining room, where my office was set up. I got removalists to do this, swapping my two bedrooms over with the existing main bedroom were huge. Taking furniture out of the second bedroom and turning it into a room for rent was also a big job. This all happened in October. It was like moving, just in the same house. I had to go through all my clothes and belongings and send a lot to St. Vincent De Paul's Society.

In November, my old room was finally ready to rent out, and I advertised it on flatmates.com.au. The third person to look at it, James Roa, took it, and he is still with me. He is a sixty-four-year-old window cleaner with a thirty-year-old business and a farm and wife down in Kyogle (northern New South Wales). The other room would take some months to get ready for rent, with Christmas and New Year approaching.

Steven helped me with this move and painted the wardrobe doors in my old room to rent it. He came for Christmas, and we had a nice Christmas. We went to the nine o'clock Mass at Lady of Mt. Carmel church with Eloise. New Year I had champagne and watched the fireworks in Sydney on TV.

Natalie and Angelina had come home for Christmas. Her Theo had died in an accident earlier in the year. They were now going to live in Brisbane.

## *2019*

On January 25, 2019, my father passed away after a year-long battle with brain cancer on the Sunshine Coast. I had become estranged from him in the last fourteen years but had spent the last year emotionally preparing for him to die. I still felt very sad and experienced real grief on his passing.

My sister Charlie had taken over everything and did not send me any updates. Though my cousin Paul maintains he sent me and my brother Tony regular updates, he sent us nothing. It was all very upsetting and distressing.

At my father's funeral, Charlie dominated and took over the whole ceremony. She did not even allow Tony to have input, maintaining she knew what Dad wanted. Eloise and Steven came to the funeral with me, and Eloise drove us to Caloundra on the Sunshine Coast where they all live and where Dad had lived. The funeral was a really lovely family affair.

In February, I gave up nanny work. David, the boy's father, had moved to live with his girlfriend, and it just wasn't the same anymore. I guess life is forever changing and evolving; very little stays the same. I wanted to get back into art and writing this book. I did get back into practising positive affirmations and meditation, as well as gratitude.

I saw Dr Egerton and Stan Steindl regularly throughout the year. I was tired and lethargic after the cancer journey and spent much of the time resting with the cats. I spoke so much to Lucy she started talking back to me, and I am sure she understands a lot of English.

I had to re-home Felix, as he wanted to be an only cat. A lovely lady, Georgina, gave him a fur-ever home and fed him gourmet food and bought him a sheepskin mat.

I eventually rented the other bedroom out and had a number of different people come and go, eventually finding Craig, who also has PTSD and helps me with the small garden we have and the potted plants.

In March, April, and May, I saw a number of clients in the beauty room. This was with great difficulty. I was unable to sit on the beauty stool for very long at all to do eye rows, tinting, or facials because of my back, which had deteriorated even further after chemo. I would break out in a cold sweat doing waxing and facial work and had much trouble with my back when waxing.

In July, Steven was fed up living in the state housing town house he was in and desperately needed accommodation without stairs. This town house backed on to the yard of the town house that had burnt down so wasn't good for his PTSD. It was cruel of state housing to have given him no choice and housed him there.

I had finally reached a point of acceptance; I would not run the room for beauty. I just couldn't do it anymore. So, I started converting the studio into a guest room for him to stay until a transfer came through for him. Parting with my beauty therapy things was heartbreaking, but it had to happen I really couldn't do it anymore. It was the death of a dream.

In October and November, fires started all around Australia, fuelled by heat and high winds.

By November, I had the room ready, and Steven went into hospital, having problems with his eyes and his stomach and the PTSD. He got out of hospital mid-December and came to live with me. At Christmastime, Natalie joined us for Christmas tea, and the girls, Eloise and Bella, came between Christmas and New Year.

By Christmas, the fire situation in Australia was dreadful, with nearly all of Australia alight.

## *2020*

In January, all the fires had joined up, and Australia was alight. We lost millions of our wildlife. Countries all around the world sent us firefighters, and people from all around the world donated money.

In early January, I got the news that the cancer was back in a lymph gland under my left arm. This showed up on a routine mammogram. It was a recurrence of the aggressive triple-negative cancer.

The Breast Clinic at Princess Alexandra acted quickly. I was booked in for surgery in a fortnight, mid-January. I had the affected lymph node and 120 other lymph nodes removed, going right up into my shoulder. I was to start chemotherapy end of February but opted out due to the global Covid pandemic. I didn't think it was a good thing to do given the worldwide epidemic.

In early March, just before I was to commence radiation, I fell down the back stairs, breaking my left arm. The arm was to be held up during the treatment. The hospital made me a shaped beanbag by putting me in the desired position and then removing all the air from the beanbag, making a firm impression of where my arm was to go.

I had twenty-five treatments over seven weeks, going Monday to Friday days. Steven took me to everyone, driving me and waiting in the car till I was finished. The radiation was to my left neck and upper chest, as the oncologist said this was the next place the cancer would be likely to reoccur. After most sessions, Steven bought us McDonald's soft serve. I kinda needed it as my reward. I put on weight. I do just love McDonald's ice cream.

By May, I had completed the course of radiation. I was very tired and had a persistent cough. The radiation had gotten my throat. Steven and I celebrated with scotch whisky, just a couple each, and Domino's pizza. Auntie Mescal came from Western Australia to see me after I'd gotten through cancer once again.

In August, Steven got word that suitable accommodation for a disabled person had come up. We went to look at it—in Murarrie, fifteen minutes from me. It was a spacious unit only a few years old on the second floor with a lift up to the unit. He took it and began moving a week later.

This proved epic, as it took till the end of September for him to get out of his old unit. We then put air conditioning in his new unit, which he needed for his lungs. Both Richard and I contributed to the cost.

I bought him some lovely new things that he needed—a designer toaster, a kettle, and a microwave; fans; a gorgeous blue dinner set, and a smart TV for the bedroom. He threw his old lounge out, and I gave him an antique lounge/daybed. I got all his rugs and the mattress shampooed. Martin put up his paintings and kitchen curtain and a few other things.

By Christmas, he was all set up, with boxes still left to sort. We had a quiet Christmas. Steven's eyes were still not well. He was diagnosed with shingles in his eyes. Eloise called in before Christmas with my two great-granddaughters. Manaya and Ariana, her two daughters, and I gave her $250 to buy Christmas presents.

Eloise now lives with Karn, her boyfriend since she was twelve. Living together is totally acceptable in today's society and has been since the '90s.

I gave Steven cash this year too, as well as the traditional chocolate and scratches. I just couldn't shop with Covid and the pandemic.

## Finding Happiness

*2021*

The most significant thing to happen in 2021 was the global roll-out of the Covid vaccination. I will have mine soon. Significantly within our family, Steven was approved for the NDIS (National Disability Insurance Scheme), and our family doctor, Roger Egerton, retired on June 30, 2021.

On the world front, on January 8, 2021, Prince Harry and Meghan Markle announced they would be stepping down from the Royal family and moving to Canada.

I've contested my father's will. He had his will changed in 2016 and left it all to Charlie. That will be heard in a trial later in the second half of the year. It has been dragging on for a few years now.

The other event in 2021 was the finishing of this book. I set a goal at the beginning of the year to have the book finished in 2021. It is now June, so that is achievable. In 2022 will be the professional editing and publishing of the book with Balboa Press, a wonderful publishing house, backing me all the way.

Writing this book has been incredibly therapeutic—in fact, cathartic—bringing all my repressed emotions out. As I wrote, I felt so many emotions coming out—emotions that had buried themselves inside me during difficult experiences, particularly the fire and the rape. The book has enabled me to release my emotions into the universe, allowing them to leave me. This has brought about an acceptance that it all happened.

Acceptance is an amazing thing. It releases you from all you hold onto that makes you unhappy and leaves you happier. All the trauma and ill health is certainly not fair or right or just. But now, after writing this book, I accept it all happened. I don't have to remember it anymore—it's all in this book and out there forever.

I had regrets before writing this book, which I have expressed in these pages. Incredibly having finished, they are gone from me. It has something to do with acceptance. I accept it all happened the way it did. I made the best decisions at the time with the information I had at the time—like when I broke up with my first boyfriend, Barry, or when I didn't get a property settlement from my former husband.

These regrets have left me. They are gone. They are in the book. Holding on to regret only holds you in the past—holds you to things that make you unhappy. Letting them go makes you happier.

I have found forgiveness for others and myself. I kinda forgive my mother for the way she treated me—not fully yet; it is still a work in progress.

I forgive myself for going all dressed up to Sue's girl's night out, so I stood out in the crowd and that rapist picked me. I forgive myself for not having a security door on the front door the afternoon he came to our house. I put a security door on the front door of every house thereafter. I forgive myself for pursuing lawful justice after the assault and going through with a trial, even if I feel I really lost a great deal in doing so. I forgive the police for never getting it right about me.

Forgiveness for yourself and others is an incredibly powerful tool. It is not easy to find; often, forgiveness for others is about understanding the situation from their perspective. You really have to search your soul to find forgiveness. But the rewards are worth it. Again, it is about releasing from you some piece or pieces of the past that you're holding onto. Writing this book has enabled me to find some forgiveness, but I need to work on finding a lot more.

If you are having trouble finding forgiveness, Stan Steindl has written an amazing book, *The Gifts of Compassion*, available on Amazon.

Gratitude, a grateful attitude, is essential to finding happiness. It is impossible when feeling gratitude to feel unhappy. I recommend a daily dose of gratitude for everybody, particularly at night before sleeping. I use a gratitude journal from www.givingthanks.com.au.

I feel gratitude for all the wonderful people who came into my life, like Richard Johnson, who has always believed in me and helped me, and Martin Board, who has been a wonderful friend and an incredible support. I'm grateful for Melanie, who looked after Steven; without her helping me, I couldn't have managed.

I am also grateful for my Auntie Mescal, who has always been there for me, and my friend Suzanne Banning, who has forever been a friend to me since the birthday party for my turning twenty. I am deeply grateful for other friendships I have had, with Peta Tall in the '70s and Julie Matthews in the '80s and Christian White, who was ever so kind and helpful to me.

I am ever so grateful for the professional support I have had in my life, particularly from my psychologist, Stan Steindl, who I have seen since 2005. I am grateful for some amazing GPs I've been lucky to have care for me, among them Dr Roger Egerton, from 2010 to 2021. I am also grateful for Dr Bronwyn Beacham, who I saw from 1990 after the assault till 1994 and whose help was invaluable.

Consider the importance of a good relationship with a GP. Also consider how counselling could help you if you are going through a rough patch. Don't be afraid to get counselling.

My gratitude list goes on forever. I'm grateful I've been on four cruises, that I lived among a culture different from my own as a child, and that I have seen so much of this beautiful country. I'm grateful I finished all the education I did and got all the jobs I had and to have seen all the live theatre and movies I've been too. I'm grateful I had a child; that I've had two beautiful cats, Casey cat and Lucy; and that I can now afford rent in a beautiful house by sharing with others. How could I possibly feel sad about my life when there is so much to be grateful for?

Gratitude brings me to attitude. They can take everything off me, but one thing they can't take from me is my attitude. Nelson Mandela, all those years he spent in prison, taught me this. It doesn't matter what happens to you in this life; it is how you deal with it that counts. You can choose your attitude, which is why it's important not to say things or react in the height of conflict. Instead, withdraw; go away and think about it.

I have called this book *The Elusive Butterfly of Happiness* because happiness, like butterflies, is elusive. And just as butterflies come and go and are impossible to catch, so too with happiness. That brings me to my question: Is happiness something you go searching for? Or is it something that lives inside you? Before writing this book, I thought it was something I could go looking for and that I would find it. I now believe it is something inside me, and I can engage in activities to increase it.

I have already spoken about mental and emotional activities like acceptance, forgiveness, and gratitude.

By the way, I saw a butterfly this morning in the

garden—the first I have seen in years—the day I finish the book! How zat?

There are external activities you can engage in, which I have spoken about throughout this book—like actively keeping humour in your life. This is vital to overall happiness. I get my old movies out and watch them over and over. Favourites include *One Flew over the Cuckoo's Nest*, *When Harry Met Sally*, *Mr Bean*, and *Ghostbusters*.

There is also music, which is food for the soul. It is important to listen to *your* music—the music that brings you relief, release, and/or relaxation. I can get the same relief from anxiety from certain music that I get taking a dose of a sedative.

I managed to keep up with modern music till the mid-'90s. I didn't become stuck in a groove of the '70s or '60s.

Also, there is connection to nature and the earth. I believe it is important to spend time with nature and honour the seasons. I purposely listen to storms and the rain, as well as birds in the morning and evening. I will deliberately sit in the sunshine (with sun protection if sitting for too long) or somewhere where I can see the sunshine.

To go for walks and look at the gardens and trees is to connect with nature. To spend time bushwalking or in a rainforest if you can be is incredibly beneficial. To go for a drive to the beach or a rainforest ignites the soul. I am fortunate to live near a park and have a kitchen from which I can watch the sun rise every morning.

Connection to life is surely important. To make sure you connect with whatever family you have and to connect with friends, make the time; make the effort. Keep the memories of those who have passed alive by lighting a candle and thinking about them—about the good things.

Connect with neighbours and the community in whatever way you can. Voluntary work, for example, with organisations like Meals on Wheels, could achieve this. Connection with the world by keeping an eye on world news can also be valuable; it can also be distressing and depressing. I carefully filter out whatever will trigger bad memories for me and have breaks from it.

Happiness is surely connected to a state of good physical and mental well-being. Taking care of oneself is important. Having regular checks has kept me alive for longer than would have been had I not gotten checked.

Reward yourself for little and big goals achieved.

Exercise will increase happiness, as it releases endorphins— "the feel-good hormones."

So, what is happiness? I again ask. Is it a balance of brain chemicals? Endorphins, the hormone released when you do something that makes you feel good about yourself, certainly influence brain chemicals.

Endorphins are released when you exercise or laugh or listen to music that feeds your soul; when you do voluntary work, have a massage, or give or receive a hug (which also releases other feel-good hormones); or when you perform an act of kindness. Exercise will also improve your physical and mental well-being.

I have spoken about courses I have done to improve my mental health. These radically changed my thinking. There was the cognitive behavioural therapy course and the acceptance and commitment therapy course, as well as the art for therapy course. I needed health insurance to afford to do these. I believe, with the prevalence of mental health problems in our society, these courses should be made available to the public at affordable rates through Medicare co-funding.

I have also found a sense of purpose important. It gives meaning to one's life. I always felt a sense of purpose all those years working in nursing—helping and giving to those in need. Through nursing, I enhanced the lives of thousands of people. A sense of purpose was strong when I combined nursing and beauty therapy training to bring assistance to hundreds of women in my shop. I always immensely enjoyed my work.

The voluntary work I did in 1986 for my son's school and in 1992 for the Women's Safety Unit got me back into work again and made me feel useful. I highly recommend voluntary work.

Writing this book has given me a sense of purpose. If I can inspire people and touch many lives in a positive way through this writing, then it has been worth the effort.

This brings me to almost the end of this book but not the end of my life. Writing and publishing it has been the fulfilment of a lifelong dream for me "to tell my story."

I have achieved some of my dreams. I've had a beauty therapy shop on a shop front. I've seen Paris and Europe. I've had a family / a child. I've had an art room. I completed celebrant training and almost gotten there as a celebrant. It is ever so important to have dreams and goals and to be able to distinguish between them.

What do I have planned for the future? You may well ask. I will get back into exercise and keep it up for the rest of my life. I will continue walks and take up my jazz ballet to music I love once again and will also do exercise on my bed on the days I feel I can't do jazz ballet. In September, springtime, I will commence swimming again, something that has stayed with me all my life. I will continue to look for butterflies.

I am doing another art course next year and some

holiday workshops for the rest of the year, trying to do one on portraits. This will get me back into art again. I will practise art Monday to Saturday in my art room, the sunroom.

I will get all my notes out from the ACT and the CBT courses and read them and practise the strategies they taught me in my life. I will continue to work on forgiveness of myself and others, continue to practise gratitude, and continue to purposefully connect to people and to nature.

I will continue to keep humour in my life. I will perhaps attend some book launches for this book and some promotional book signing events around Christmas and beyond. I will continue to perform random acts of kindness, good for the endorphin levels.

I will have further surgery, having the other breast removed and a double reconstruction done. For the reconstruction, surgeons take fat from the lower abdomen to form two new breasts, achieving a tummy tuck in the process. I will also have surgery for two hernias I have—an inguinal hernia in one groin and a femoral hernia in the other groin.

As I reach the close of this book, I have found an inner peace—a peace I've searched for all my life. It has been with me for about three months now. I think that comes from acceptance, forgiveness, and gratitude.

Amazingly enough, the chronic insomnia has lifted for the last month, and I've been sleeping at night after not sleeping since the assault in 1990. I did work at it, eating three meals a day at the same time and having a bedtime routine as well as not eating after 8:00 p.m., plus other things—anything to get sleep. I have practised gratitude every night and thought good things before sleep, and I've had no more nightmares.

I trust that you, my reader, have enjoyed tracing the history of the family unit. It has changed from the nuclear family unit when I was born—Mum, Dad, and the two kids—to what it is today, with a variety of new paradigms from blended families to same-sex couples. I hope you have enjoyed reading about the events from around the entire world and at home in Australia that I've included to give perspective in terms of time.

I also hope you, my reader, have found this book interesting and fascinating—for example, learning about nursing in the '70s or hearing about my experiences while living in Penang as a child. I truly hope you have found it inspiring to think about how one can overcome amazing trauma and be happy. It's all about your attitude! Choose a good one! Thank you for reading and allowing me to share my life story with you.

# Additional Reading

Gilbert, Paul. *The Compassionate Mind*. www.constablerobinson.com ISBN978-1-84901-098-6.

Hayes, Russ. *The Happiness Trap*. trumJackbooks.com ISBN978-1-59030-584-3.

Myss, Caroline. *Invisible Acts of Power*. www.simonsays.com ISBN0-7432-6425-8.

Steindl, Stan. *The Gifts of Compassion: How to Understand and Overcome Suffering*. Academic Press. ISBN-10:1925644480 www.amazon.com.

# Bibliography

*Rose-Tinted '50s: A Perfect View of the Past* (PQ Publishers Limited). ISBN073361874X.

*The Fifties in Pictures* (London: Endeavour London Ltd., A Parragon Book). ISBN978-1-4054-9522-6

*Rose-Tinted '60s: A Perfect View of the Past* (PQ Publishers Ltd.). ISBN0733618758.

*The Sixties in Pictures* (London: Endeavour London Ltd., A Parragon Book). ISBN978-1-4054-9523-3

*The Seventies in Pictures* (London: Endeavour London Ltd., A Parragon Book). ISBN978-1-4054-9524-0

*Australian Decades: The 1970's* (Jordan Johnson Trocadero Publishing). ISBN978-086427-138-9.

Harris, Carol. *Life in the 1970's* (Pitkin Guides). ISBN978-1-84165-541-3

Bongiorno, Frank. *The Eighties*. Frank www.blackincbooks.com ISBN9781863958974

Harwood, Jeremy. *Towards a New Millennium 1990's*. www.readersdigest.co.uk ISBN978-0-276-44403-6.

"The Macquarie Book of Events" produced by Bryce Fraser 10,000 events which shaped Australia published in 1983

***

I also used Google and *Wikipedia* to research information. I used my own journals and diaries to reconstruct my life.

# Afterword Acceptance

Like a thrilling book, you start at the beginning, tense.
And work your way to the end in suspense.
Now it must be read chapter by chapter by chapter.
Then you're left feeling happier.
Or could acceptance be compared to a sparkling wine?
There has to be a release of bubbles at the right time.
Oh well! Whatever it be, in acceptance, there's release.
In acceptance there's relief and an inner peace.

Anthea Louise DeVito
June 5, 2021

# About the Author

Anthea Louise DeVito lives in Brisbane, Queensland, Australia, in the suburb of Coorparoo. Anthea was born in Toowoomba, Queensland, Australia and lived in Penang as a child. She is a retired registered nurse and midwife, as well as a retired beauty therapist. Anthea was divorced many years ago and has one adult son, Steven, who has brought her two granddaughters and two great-granddaughters.

Some of her career achievements include being on the commissioning staff of Glengarry Hospital in Duncraig, Perth, Australia in 1978 and running a beauty therapy shop, Beautiful Solutions, on a shop front from 1996 to 2006. The business was nominated for Best in Beauty 2006 in the *South-East Advertiser* Business Achievers Awards. Anthea also received a Certificate of Appreciation from the Queensland Police Service, presented to her by the commissioner for police for her valuable contribution to the Women's Safety Unit in 1992.

These days, Anthea paints and draws (and colours in to be mindful). In addition, she enjoys walking near gardens and trees, as well as swimming. Anthea loves reading and writing and writes poetry, which will be her next publication. Anthea is working on her next book, an anthology of her poetry. She is a cat lover who has two cats, Lucy and Tiger. Anthea is very interested in Buddhism but is Catholic and attends the Lady of Mt. Carmel Church at Coorparoo on occasions.

You can contact Anthea at unique.beauty@bigpond.com.
For more information, go to www.antheadevito.com

# Endnotes

[1] *50's Rose-Tinted: A Perfect View of the Past* (PQ Publishers), ISBN 073361874X.

[2] *50's Rose-Tinted.*

[3] *50's Rose-Tinted.*

[4] Bryce Fraser, *The Macquarie Book of Events: 10,000 Events that Shaped Australia* (1983).

[5] Fraser, *Macquarie.*

[6] Fraser, *Macquarie.*

[7] Fraser, *Macquarie.*

[8] *50's Rose-Tinted.*

[9] Fraser, *Macquarie.*

[10] Fraser, *Macquarie.*

[11] Google.

[12] Google.

PGIL2023USA